D0781405

Reaching Audiences

A Guide to Media Writing

Katherine C. McAdams

University of Maryland

Jan Johnson Elliott

University of North Carolina, Chapel Hill

Allyn and Bacon

Boston   London   Toronto   Sydney   Tokyo   Singapore

Vice President: Joseph Opiela
Editorial Assistant: Susannah Davidson
Executive Marketing Manager: Lisa Kimball
Senior Editorial Production Administrator: Susan McIntyre
Editorial Production Service: Ruttle, Shaw & Wetherill, Inc.
Composition Buyer: Linda Cox
Manufacturing Buyer: Aloka Rathnam
Cover Administrator: Suzanne Harbison

Library of Congress Cataloging-in-Publication Data
McAdams, Katherine C.
    Reaching audiences : a guide to media writing / Katherine
C. McAdams, Jan Johnson Elliott.
        p.   cm.
    Includes bibliographical references and index.
    ISBN 0-02-378351-6
    1. Mass media—Authorship.   2. Mass media—Audiences.
1. Elliott, Jan Johnson.   II. Title.
P96.A88M38   1995
808'.06607—dc20   96-40774
                                                                        CIP

Printed in the United States of America

10   9   8   7   6   5   4   3   2   1   00   99   98   97   96   95

CONTENTS

PART TWO
Improving Writing

Chapter 6 **Editing and Polishing Writing** **164**

Chapter 7 **Recognizing Bias and Stereotypes** **184**

Chapter 8 **Testing Your Grammar** **200**

PART THREE
Gathering Information

PART FOUR
Other Media Writing Styles

PREFACE

Cable television. Video news releases. Databases. E-mail. Facsimile machines. Satellites. Cellular telephones. Internet. Information superhighway.

Technology has created a multitude of new ways to send and get information and entertainment. We are truly in an information age. While many audiences still rely on newspapers and television, they are attracted to a dazzling array of faster, electronic sources of information and entertainment. Wave after wave of invention invites attention, analysis, and adoption. Eager individuals spend hours deciphering the language to access the links that offer faster and often somewhat exotic ways to send messages. Developments seem to appear faster than they can be mastered.

Communicators are among the dazzled users. Most writers have abandoned typewriters for computers. Modems allow reporters and columnists to transmit stories to and from anywhere in the world. Writers use computer databases to research stories and to access government storerooms of information. Communicators send messages via fax machines or as videotape. They put notices on computer bulletin boards or list messages retrieved by special telephone numbers. Technology has enabled communicators to produce work more efficiently and quickly, just as it has allowed users to access information faster and in greater quantities.

Technology has also broadened the field for communicators. New writing markets have been created in publications and advertising for specialized audiences, electronic newspapers, videotext services, video news releases, graphic design, and literally hundreds of other jobs. Students in journalism and mass communications programs have many career possibilities beyond jobs on newspapers and in radio and television.

The key ingredient to success in any communications job is good writing. In today's world, good writing has suffered. Part of the decline can be attributed to technology. The proliferation of technology has diverted many communicators from their main task: good writing. In the rush to produce and send information, people often overlook the critical need for accuracy and proper spelling and grammar. Too many communicators believe that the first draft is good enough and do not spend time for editing and rewriting.

Such a philosophy has eroded informative, entertaining, well-crafted writing. Technology has enabled anyone with information, no matter how well the content is structured, to put it out for public view. As a result, much information is poorly written and irrelevant to audiences.

Students need to learn skills to become good communicators. Students seem to be less committed to the craft of writing, however. They rely on spell-checkers and grammar-checkers housed in computers. They believe they have little need to know the basics of proper sentence construction. With video a major component of new technology, students want to focus on the visual, not on the text. As children of the television age, many have little patience for writing and rewriting.

Despite student sentiment, professors in journalism and mass communication teach—or in many cases, struggle to teach—specific styles of writing. Students interested in print journalism first learn the inverted pyramid style of writing. Broadcast students follow a shorter and more casual electronic communication format. Advertising students learn copywriting. Public relations students practice writing news releases and brochures. Photojournalism students write cutlines. Each format has its prescribed guidelines.

Within each format, students must learn to make their writing clearer, more accurate, more relevant, and more appealing. They must think constantly about their audiences. They must know their audiences and their specific language uses and interests. Students need to understand the importance of good writing and to be willing to take on the task. Professors must push students harder to pay attention to their writing skills. Today's students are the communicators of tomorrow—regardless of what technology has developed and what medium they ultimately use.

The following chapters stress the basic writing skills essential to any student in any mass communications sequence: news-editorial, advertising, public relations, electronic communication, or visual communication. The essentials of good writing apply, regardless of format.

Part One starts with the basic components of the writing process and the critical role of audiences. Students will learn the fundamentals of print journalism and the value of the inverted pyramid style of writing. Informative writing must be grounded in the tenets of basic newswriting.

Part Two looks at refining writing. Specific tips are given to improve writing, from word selection to sentence length to grammar and usage. Students also will learn the stages of editing, a crucial part of the writing process, and how to avoid bias in writing. A grammar chapter includes proficiency tests on specific grammar problems.

Part Three reviews how to gather information through three principal methods: research, observation, and interviewing. Students also are introduced to computer databases as resources.

Part Four discusses other media writing: electronic communication, public relations, and advertising. Each has its particular formats and communications tools for reaching audiences.

The first three appendices focus on narrower topics: libel and privacy, a list of abused words, and spelling hurdles. The last appendix contains the answer key for the grammar chapter exercises.

Mass communication at all levels needs writing that is accurate, complete, and concise. Writers constantly must consider their audiences. Writers today can no longer write solely for their own enjoyment. They must create messages that are well written and will reach the intended audiences.

The authors clearly embrace technology. Without it, they would not have been able to produce their writing efficiently and easily. They recognize that technology will not disappear, and no one would wish it away. But technology changes and fades. The importance of good writing doesn't.

Acknowledgments

Writing a book is never the work of just the individuals whose names are under the title. So it is with this book. A number of colleagues and friends have provided invaluable contributions.

We thank Kevin Davis of Macmillan, who saw the potential in our initial concept and encouraged us to write; and our editor Joe Opiela at Allyn & Bacon and his editorial assistant, Susannah Davidson, who drove us across the finish line.

The book was written with the advice, counsel, and support of our colleagues at the School of Journalism and Mass Communication at the University of North Carolina at Chapel Hill, especially Dean Richard Cole, Professor Harry Amana, Professor Anne Johnston, Professor Cathy Packer, Professor Dulcie Straughan, Professor John Sweeney, Librarian Barbara Semonche, and student assistants Andy Johns and Antoinette Parker; and at the College of Journalism at the University of Maryland, especially Professor

James Plumb, Professor Maureen Beasley, Professor Carl Sessions Stepp, and students Erik Bucy, Andrea Hoffman, and Encarnita Pyle.

We also thank Assistant Professor Beth Haller at Pennsylvania State University at Harrisburg; Professor Thom Lieb at Towson State University; and Professor Eugenia Zerbinos at University of Dayton. We also thank the people whose spirited support helped create the Grammar Slammer: Richard Cole, Jim Shumaker, Reese Cleghorn, Bill Cloud, Phil Meyer, Greig Stewart, and Chet Rhodes.

Beyond the university, we also acknowledge the contributions of Cathy Roche, Ann Carroll, and our families, whose moral support and ability to manage without moms for a while got us through the crunch times.

1

The Writing Process

Most mornings Cathy Steele rises at 6 A.M., showers, dresses, makes coffee, turns on all-news radio, and walks down her driveway in suburban Maryland to retrieve the *Washington Post*. Today the *Post* is 78 pages, with a 24-page business insert. She eats cereal and toast while perusing the *Post*. CNN airs in the background.

Steele leaves notes and lunch money for her two teen-age sons before departing for work at 7 a.m. She tunes her car radio to the all-news AM station, hoping to catch a current traffic report. Ten minutes into her 30-minute commute, the electronic pager in her suit pocket beeps. She records a client's number from its screen as she notes construction warnings posted along the roadside.

In her office, she picks up the telephone and listens to her voice mail messages. That task completed, she pulls up more than 20 electronic mail messages from her computer. Steele sorts through the day's postal mail, which includes two brochures on upcoming seminars, four direct mail letters for public relations professionals, and copies of the *Environmental Reporter,* the *Congressional Record,* and the *Wall Street Journal.*

It is 8:30 a.m., and Steele has already processed more than 100 messages and has ignored or missed many others. By the time she returns home at 6:30 p.m., she will have processed hundreds more—before she ever sits down to check the next day's weather and to watch her alma mater play basketball on network television.

Like Cathy Steele, most people are bombarded by messages that come to them in a multitude of ways every day: via radio, television, newspapers, brochures, e-mail, voice mail, U.S. Postal Service mail, telephone, fliers, and on and on.

Some messages are saved and others are discarded. The average person, such as Steele, will quickly toss out messages that are unclear or unintelligible—that is, messages that are unfriendly. How the message is structured, its relevance, and its appeal will determine its success in reaching its audience. Thus the fate of any message lies in good writing.

This chapter discusses

- Why writing remains a critical task in communication,
- Stages in the writing process, and
- Why the writing process is important for all forms of mass communication.

Writing Is the Basic Task

No matter what the vehicle, most messages have a common basis: Each was written. Before they are printed, broadcast, aired, or distributed, messages are written. Communicators have to write first, regardless of what medium or technology they use.

For example, a school principal writes the monthly calendar of activities before announcing it at a Parent–Teacher Association meeting or printing it in the school's monthly newsletter.

A radio reporter types stories before she reads them on the 6 A.M. news show.

A working mother who wants her teen-age son to start dinner leaves instructions on the kitchen counter.

An advertising copy writer creates an insert about credit card interest rates for a bank to put in customers' statements.

Three television journalists write their scripts before the weekly Sunday morning news program.

The editor of the campus newspaper writes two editorials for each edition.

All communicators—whether they are journalism or mass communication students, newspaper reporters, or school principals—must write a message before it is sent to its intended audience. Once writers let go of the message—that is, once the message is aired or distributed—they have little control over whether the audience absorbs the message. Although the message may have arrived, it may be crowded out and ignored.

Getting through the Clutter

As we know from the Steele example, writers today have competition from other media and from busy lifestyles. Children and adults today—including you—have developed the skills to sort constantly what will and will not be read, watched, or heard in the limited time available.

The good news is that audiences have an insatiable desire to be informed and entertained. They are looking for information. They are seeking leisure activities. They are investigating new media such as specialized publications and electronic bulletin boards. They want and need information that will help them cope with or escape from everyday life.

How do writers get through the clutter of media and lifestyles to reach waiting audiences? They do it with good writing. They write messages that are simple, clear, and accurate. Audiences will not stick with messages that are confusing, incoherent, or unbelievable. Writers must craft messages that attract and hold audiences with their content and structure, and that are relevant and emotionally compelling.

Few communicators today can write messages for pleasure or for the sake of the task, unless they are writing opinion articles that they know will appeal to a large segment of the population. Writers today have a purpose in writing. They want to tell of a family's trauma during an earthquake. They want to inform voters about candidates. They want to entertain viewers of a late-night talk show. They want to highlight a product's usefulness. These writers want their messages to reach a destination, and they want audiences to pay attention.

For audiences to pay attention, writers must create messages that are accurate, appealing, organized, readable, relevant, compelling, clear, complete, and simple. Audiences today require good writing. An audience will gain no new information or entertainment if the message fails to be read or heard because it was poorly written.

The Good Writing Bonus

The hungry audience and the new technology are a boon for good writers. Traditional media such as newspapers, radio, and television continue to rely heavily on writing skills. Audiences searching competing media demand good writing because they have so many choices. Audiences will seek out the media and the communicators who provide information that is clear and relevant.

Good writers are needed in hundreds of other media outlets. Complete and readable writing is needed in manuals that teach people how to use new computer software. Accurate and relevant writing is needed to tell citizens how an expanded city park system will improve their lives. Compelling and appealing writing is needed to make elementary students read school bus safety rules. Clear, well-reasoned, and organized writing is needed in a letter asking for donations to the city's homeless shelter. The list goes on and on.

Technology itself demands more good writers. Many employees must become expert communicators as soon as they are given a terminal, a keyboard, word-processing software, and electronic mail. Never before has so much published material been produced outside the traditional editorial process by those who, professionally, are nonwriters and noneditors.

Students who can master basic writing and editing skills and who can craft appealing and compelling messages will find many ways to use their abilities. Within one career they may have half a dozen different, satisfying, and successful writing jobs. The changing environment for communication offers rewards to good writers.

Is Good Writing Inborn?

Many people believe that good, skillful writing springs not from teaching and learning but from inborn talent that eludes most ordinary people.

Nonsense.

Writing a straightforward message requires no more inherent talent than following a road map. Author Joel Saltzman compares learning to write with learning to make salad dressing:

> *This is the only way I know to make a terrific salad dressing: Mix up a batch. Taste it. Mix again.*
>
> *The secret ingredient is the patience to keep trying—to keep working at it till you get it just right.*
>
> *Do most people have the talent to make a terrific salad dressing? Absolutely. Are they willing to make the effort to develop that skill? That's a different question.*

Good writing, like good salad dressing, can make even dry material palatable and can make good subject matter great. Like ingredients in a recipe, each word, sentence, and paragraph is selected carefully with one goal in mind: pleasing the consumer. The first bite will determine whether the diner eats more; good writing will sell a piece beyond the first paragraph. Like cooking, not every writing session will produce a masterpiece, but the end product must be palatable.

The Writing Process Explained

Writers today work in the same way as writers have worked throughout time—by following a regimen we call the writing process. Seven stages of the writing process are presented here: information gathering, thinking and planning, listing, drafting, rewriting, sharing, and polishing. But before a writer begins any part of this process, he or she must have an idea or topic.

What's in a Topic?

Research shows that no matter how readable a story is, a reader will be turned off immediately if the topic is unappealing. Studies show that readers prefer interesting topics, regardless of how well the pieces are written. These studies show that audiences may be willing to plow through difficult text if it promises important information.

To be viable, a topic must pass a five-question test. The writer must be able to answer yes to each of these questions before writing begins:

1. "Is my topic of interest to my audience?" Identify several specific individuals or groups that would want to know about the topic.

2. "Is my topic of interest to me?" The topic must be interesting to the writer to stimulate energy and the motivation needed to write appealing copy.

3. "Is my topic neither too narrow nor too broad?" Readers resist biting off more than they can digest, such as a multipage article on the general topic of antiques. However, tiny topics, such as the story of one Chippendale chair, may be equally unsatisfying.

4. "Are high-quality sources of information on my topic both plentiful and available?" Writers owe their readers top-quality information. If a story topic, such as the landmark abortion case *Roe v. Wade,* requires an interview with a Supreme Court Justice who does not grant interviews, a writer might consider changing the focus of the topic rather than substituting second-rate or second-hand information.

5. "Is my topic of value?" No writer wants the audience to glance at a message and respond, "So what?" Princess Diana wears sweatpants shopping—so what? Avoid topics that are trivial or inconsequential. Writing about Diana's entire wardrobe would attract more readers.

If your topic does not pass the test—that is, if you answer "no" to any of these questions—try shifting your focus. If the topic "gymnastics" is too general, try focusing your writing on one gymnast or one gymnastics program. If getting authoritative interviews for a *Roe v. Wade* story is out of the question, write about local sentiments toward abortion rights.

Once your topic has passed the test, the writing process begins. It is important to note that three of the writing stages occur before the writer sits down to draft the actual message. In the information age, research and planning are essential to good communication. No amount of skillful writing can save a message that has been written without thorough, accurate information.

Stages in the Process

The same sequence of activities outlined here occurs in good writing of all kinds. All communicators must gather information, think about and plan the message, list key information, draft a message, rewrite the draft, share the message, and polish by checking and editing. Together these separate stages of activity form what we call the writing process: a set of behaviors common to all writers. The order of stages may vary, and some stages may be repeated, but each stage is essential to producing a good message.

Each stage in the writing process is briefly explained in the following sections; later chapters in this book will explain writing tasks in greater detail. You will be referred to relevant chapters as each stage is discussed here.

Keep in mind that following these stages will produce successful writing in business, education, advertising, public relations, the news media, and daily life. Throughout this text, you will learn what professional writers know: Writing is a skill that can be learned like other skills, one stage at a time. And the first stage is to go beyond yourself to gather information. Good writers are seekers.

Stage One: Information Gathering

Gathering information on your topic is the first stage of the writing process. To begin the search for information, you must answer questions that all people are prone to ask: Who? What? When? Where? Why? How? How much? Then what?

People of all ages ask these questions when they are curious. Figure 1.1 on page 8 shows Bert and Ernie demonstrating the art of telling, using the same basic formula for preschoolers that is described in advanced reporting texts.

Never attempt to answer all these questions without talking to other people or reading their work. Good writing requires good external information. Once you know the questions, go outside yourself to find the answers. Even if you are an expert on your own topic, you must find other reliable authorities on it.

In writing an announcement of an art exhibit at a local high school, for example, a writer might begin the questioning by talking with obvious experts—perhaps the principal and art teacher—who can provide many answers and can lead the writer to additional sources.

After answering basic questions, see what information could still be gathered to complete the announcement or add interest to it. For the exhibit announcement, we still need to know the following: What types of artwork will be shown? Will prizes be awarded? Will any special guests appear at the reception?

The new questions will guide your next steps in your information search. Generally, steps in research lead to one of three sources:

1. *Interviews.* Talk, in person or by phone, to authorities or to people your initial sources suggest. Interviewing is discussed in Chapter 10.

2. *Library work.* Any kind of writing can require library research. For example, if the art on display at Edwards High School celebrates Impressionism, the writer needs to find out about the Impressionists and their art. Basic research skills are included in Chapter 9.

3. *Other sources.* Brochures or publications can provide helpful information. Computer databases and indexes also may lead you to both old and new sources. For example, an article about last year's art exhibit could be located

FIGURE 1.1   *Ernie's Story*

through a newspaper index or online service. Chapter 9 explains how to use traditional and innovative reference sources.

It is important to gather information from a variety of sources. Ideally, a writer compiles more information than is actually needed so that he or she can be selective about which information to use.

Take notes on every source used in the information-gathering stage. A writer never knows when an important fact or statistic will emerge, or when a quotable quote will be uttered. It's best to have the notepad always ready. In addition, careful notes enable writers to attribute interesting or unusual information to sources and to answer questions about what they have written.

Some writers refer to the information-gathering stage as "immersion" in the topic. Whatever it is called, this first stage of writing turns the writer into an informal expert on his or her subject matter.

Stage Two: Thinking and Planning

Once information is gathered, the writer studies the notes taken in Stage One and ponders them. The writer scans material to see what information seems most important and feels most interesting.

A good writer always makes decisions about priorities, keeping in mind the audience that will receive the message. Successful writers actually picture the probable audience, hold that image in mind, and plan the message for that imaginary group. Some writers say they write for a specific person such as the truck driver in Toledo or Aunt Mary in Hartford; a newsroom favorite is Joe Six-Pack, the average guy. More about audiences and their needs are covered in Chapter 2.

Sometimes the thinking stage will allow the writer to see possibilities for creative approaches to writing. More often, however, this stage of the writing process helps the writer realize that more information needs to be gathered before listing and writing can begin.

Once the writer has gathered enough information, he or she will begin to evaluate and set priorities, asking "What does my audience need to know? What does it need to know first? What next?" And so on. If no further gaps in information become apparent at this stage, the writer takes pen and notepad in hand and moves on to Stage Three.

Stage Three: Listing

Before committing words to paper, writers note the facts and ideas that must be included in the message. Some writers jot key words; others write detailed outlines. Whatever form this activity takes, it yields one or more lists.

What goes in these lists? First, the writer should list elements of the message that the audience must know. Second, the writer might list audiences for the message; third, the writer could list the values and goals of each important audience. Initial lists should be made by brainstorming, jotting down each important message element, and perhaps scratching out, adding, or combining items in the lists.

Once lists are committed to paper, the writer reviews them and attempts to rank the information in each list. Imagine, for example, that the top priority item on the message list is "student art shown." One of the top audiences is "parents," and one of the top audience goals is "nurturing our young people." Isolating the items guides the writer to structure a message that will feature student art, appeal to parents, and frame the event as a constructive, positive effort for young people.

In this stage, the writer imposes order and organization on the information. Chapters 3 and 4 deal with specific ways to organize messages.

Stage Four: Drafting the Message—As You Would Tell It

For most people, even for experienced writers, writing feels somewhat unnatural. In contrast, conversational speech always seems to flow. So the efficient writer drafts a message by writing it as it might be told to a friend.

Checking the lists made in Stage Three, the writer would begin by "talking" about the first and most important element in the message—perhaps like this:

```
A student art show that displays the talents of 27 of the
city's young artists will open at 7 p.m. Wednesday at
Edwards High School.
```

Once this telling process has begun, it continues easily. The writer will move smoothly through interesting aspects of the message to a stopping point after the listed priorities have been included.

By the end of this stage, the writer has created what is called a draft, rather than a message. The term *draft* distinguishes this version from a finished product. It is different from a polished message, and purposely so. Think of the draft as a raw lump of clay, in which substance is what counts.

The stages that follow will shape the clay, giving form to the finished message. Drafting messages is discussed in Chapters 3 and 4.

Stage Five: Rewriting

In this stage, the conventions of the written language are imposed on the draft. Sentences are checked for completeness and coherence; paragraphs are formed and organized; transitions and stylistic flourishes are added.

A good portion of this book is devoted to the skills involved in rewriting. Only through rewriting—sometimes repeated rewriting—can a message be streamlined to reach its intended audience. All good writers rewrite; great writers pride themselves on painstaking reworking of their original phrases. Author E. B. White labored for three years over his slim classic *Charlotte's Web,* and he willingly revised much of his other work as many as fourteen times.

Of course, writers on deadline cannot afford the luxury of spending years, or even hours, rewriting a draft. Writers develop shortcuts to rewriting as they become familiar with print formats, as described in Chapter 4. But no good writer ever skips rewriting.

The rewriting stage is separate from polishing, in which fine points of style, such as capitalization, are debated. If a writer stops in mid-draft to debate a style point, the train of thought is interrupted, and the writing process stops. Small decisions are left for the last stage—a stage that may be conducted by someone other than the writer. Rewriting involves rearranging, adding, and subtracting information so that the clay of the draft takes a recognizable form.

Rewriting a draft is the bulk of the writing process. It is hard, time-consuming work; factors to consider in the process are discussed in Chapters 5 and 6. A rewritten draft is far from a finished work, however. Two stages remain in the writing process: sharing and polishing.

Stage Six: Sharing

The revised draft now must go to another reader—almost any other reader. By this stage, most writers have lost perspective on the message. They have become knowledgeable about the topic, and they can no longer tell how the message would be received by an average member of the audience.

Sharing your work at this stage gives you a much better idea how an audience member may react. Outside readers, after reassuring you that you have done a fine job of writing, will quickly let you know whether information is confusing or unclear, or whether any important details are missing.

It is a good idea to share your work with a naive reader—someone who knows far less about your topic than you do. Sometimes a colleague at work or a family member is an excellent choice for sharing because of that person's distance from your topic.

In large offices, outside review of your revised draft may be built in. Communication products in big companies are usually reviewed by one or more editors and often by top management. Such an editing process is helpful in many ways; certainly it saves the time and trouble of finding someone with whom to share your writing.

Regardless of who is sharing and commenting on your work, you as a writer must never forget that you did the initial research. You have expertise on your topic that even top managers may not have. Be sure to get feedback from your outside readers in a setting where you both can talk. You may need to explain why certain parts of your message are written as they are. Good editing is negotiation; no editor is an absolute dictator. You as a writer need to work with, not for, editors and outside reviewers. Together you can produce clear, correct writing.

Stage Seven: Polishing

Fear of this final stage in the writing process is what keeps many people from writing at all. Many young writers feel that all capitalization, punctuation, grammar, usage, and spelling must be perfect, even in an initial draft. Concentrating on perfection in all those areas is unimportant in the early stages of writing. You could spend ten minutes looking in the dictionary for a word that you eventually decide not to use!

Working on word-by-word perfection at the early stages of writing is wasteful and even paralyzing. Writers who worry about every comma will find it difficult to get through the stages of drafting and revising. Writing becomes a much more comfortable and speedy task when polishing is put off until its proper place at the end of the process. Once the important substance and form of the message have been established, it's fine to spend time with style books, dictionaries, and thesauruses.

In truth, this final stage of editing may well be performed by another person. An editor or editorial assistant may make the final checks for correctness and consistency and put a message in final form. The polishing process comes last also because it may come after the writer passes the message along. Confident writers welcome assistance with this final, cosmetic touch, knowing that letter-perfect writing will add to the credibility and clarity of their message.

Chapters 5, 7, and 8 discuss the work of polishing your own or another person's writing. Chapter 6 outlines the editing process.

Consider the Audience

E. B. White, in the introduction to *The Elements of Style,* explains that good writing is a writer's responsibility to the audience. He tells how his professor and coauthor, William "Will" Strunk, taught rules to writers out of sympathy for readers.

> *All through* The Elements of Style *one finds evidences of the author's deep sympathy for the reader. Will felt that the reader was in serious trouble most of the time, a man floundering in a swamp, and that it was the duty of anyone attempting to write English to drain this swamp quickly and get his man up on dry ground or at least throw him a rope . . . I have tried to hold steadily in mind this belief of his, this concern for the bewildered reader.*

Today it is time to return to Strunk's wisdom. As a teacher in the early twentieth century, Strunk knew that audiences were hindered by poor type quality and low levels of literacy. Today writers contend with new distractions Strunk could never have imagined. But the remedy in either era is the same: clear messages that show consideration for audiences.

The principles of effective communication are more important now than ever, regardless of the medium, as will be discussed in Chapters 11 through 13. Even essential messages are in danger of being crowded out in an increasingly competitive media marketplace. This is the age of instant, constant communication. Challenges for writers have never been greater; but at the same time, communication opportunities have never been so great. The potential power of media messages is unlimited in our society, where people are confounded by change and unlikely to have traditional networks of family, church, and community. Chapter 2 discusses the complexity of today's media audiences.

Today's complex communication environment calls for simple, direct messages. The chapters that follow provide a guide to writing messages that audiences will search for and understand in the information age.

EXERCISES

1. Try to remember the times during the day today, so far, when you have been exposed to media messages. List the exposures you can remember. For each exposure, also record where it occurred and how—by what medium—each message came to you.

2. Look at your list of incoming media messages. Circle those that you would have missed if we were to substitute the technology of 1895 for the technology of today.

3. List three topics that you think pass the test for viable topics.

4. Select one of your topics from above and explain how you would gather information on this topic. Be sure to include research in each of the following: interviews, libraries, and other publications and sources.

5. Write a few paragraphs describing the characteristics of the audience for your student newspaper. Then explain how you could follow Strunk and White's advice to help the audience use and understand the student paper better.

REFERENCES

Joel Saltzman, *If You Can Talk, You Can Write.* New York: Ballantine Books, 1993.
William Strunk, Jr., and E. B. White, *The Elements of Style.* New York: Macmillan Publishing Co., 1979.

2

Audience, Audience, Audience

When writers complete the writing process described in Chapter 1, they have a message to send: a news brief, a television advertisement, a brochure, a feature story, or a novel. But all the steps in the process are wasted if the message is ignored.

You learned from the Cathy Steele example in Chapter 1 that audiences do not accept or assimilate every message that comes their way. They sift through messages and choose which ones they will hear and read. Successful writers know that about their audiences. Writers must understand an audience's lifestyles, media preferences, interests, and language. That knowledge will aid them in selecting topics, writing a draft, and polishing the message so that it fits an audience's needs and interests.

Writers must find out who makes up their audiences. Audiences have changed just as dramatically as society has changed. During the last four decades, audiences—and writers—have been affected by changing lifestyles, an increasingly diverse population, and new technologies. Good writers take into account the impact of these forces on their audiences.

In this chapter, you will learn

- How audiences and the world they live in today have changed,
- How writers can analyze audiences,
- How to be successful with audiences, and
- Roadblocks to messages reaching audiences.

How Audiences Have Changed

The 1990 census showed that most people in the United States live in family households but that less than half of those household groups are stereotypical families: a mother, father, and several children. Multigenerational households, single-parent families, and blended families are more common than the so-called typical family. Neighborhoods and communities, increasingly diverse, are home to many racial and ethnic groups.

The information revolution has also directly affected society and audiences. New technology has given audiences greater access to information and entertainment. Consumers have welcomed new technology and its gadgets. The dramatic drop in the price of personal computers since 1990 has brought them within the price range of more and more people and given them, via telephone, quick access to hundreds of information databases. Millions of homes have videocassette recorders (VCRs), which have created in-home movie libraries.

As forms of technology, media themselves continue to evolve and change, taking their audiences on a roller-coaster ride into an unimagined future of interactive video and virtual reality. More specialized media, more electronic media—in fact, more media of all kinds—are on the market. And all these media, old and new, compete fiercely for audience share and attention.

Today's media audience is filled with people who have become accustomed to fast food, fast travel, and fast information. A 1994 Times-Mirror study reveals "an American public that uses more media outlets more frequently than at any time in recent history." More and more people are accessing the information highway, for example. By the year 2000, more than 180 million people worldwide will be hooked into the Internet. While much information is being dumped into the system now, audiences increasingly will insist that the new information providers offer accurate information of high quality.

But while some audience members are out searching for information and are using new media, other audiences may be more resistant to messages. Caught in the demands of daily living, they may be less ready, willing, and able to listen. Writers cannot assume that all audiences are waiting for their messages. They must stretch to reach less cooperative audiences, who also need information for daily living.

Changing Lifestyles

The family that fifteen years ago may have started the day together at the breakfast table may now find itself scattered at sunrise. Adults and kids depart early and separately for demanding days in jobs and classes—sometimes both.

Lifestyles have become hectic. Lives are filled with distractions: children, media, sports, work, overtime, fatigue, more media, too much information at work, too much junk mail, housework, commuting, and family commitments, just to name a few.

Families increasingly resemble Cathy Steele's: More than 70 percent of American women are in the work force, and 55 percent of women in the work force have children under the age of six. Women have less time, as they work outside the home and still tend to be responsible for the majority of household and child-related chores.

Men too have found their lives to be changing. Many men have less time because of their increased work hours and because they have additional home duties as their wives have joined the work force. What used to be leisure time may now be spent picking up dry cleaning or children. A 1989 Scripps-Howard study estimated that by the year 2000, four out of five women will be working and managing households, and men's and children's lives again will change accordingly.

The trend toward less leisure time and more time at work was well underway by the late 1980s. The Scripps-Howard study showed that "discretionary" or leisure time—the hours in which people do what they want—had decreased by one-third since 1973. What had risen was the average amount of time spent at work each week: forty-seven hours per week in 1987, compared with forty-one hours in a 1973 work week.

The trend is continuing. In 1994 the average white-collar work week was almost forty-four hours a week; for manufacturing, it was forty-one—the highest average since World War II. Executives averaged between forty-six and forty-seven hours a week.

An Increasingly Diverse Society

At the same time people's lifestyles are changing in the United States, the country is witnessing another trend that affects media use: diversity.

What used to be a primarily white, male-dominated society has altered significantly in the last twenty years. Women account for 55 percent of the

United States population. Racial and ethnic groups, such as Hispanics, are increasing. The latest United States census data show that minorities make up almost 25 percent of the population. African Americans constitute 12.1 percent of the population, Asian Americans 2.9 percent, Hispanics 3.9 percent, and Native Americans 0.79 percent.

Demographic experts predict an increasing shift. By the year 2000, 30 percent of the country's residents will be of a racial or ethnic minority. By 2025, Hispanics will constitute the largest ethnic group. And by 2056, Caucasians not of Hispanic descent may constitute slightly less than half, or 49 percent, of the United States population.

While ethnic- and gender-specific media have long had a role in this country, the changing complexion of the United States has meant an increase in media that addresses specific groups and individuals. The changes have meant new topics, new discussions, and new themes. Many groups are no longer invisible, and writing about certain groups has become less negative. Media, particularly general-interest newspapers, have begun to write about issues that for many years were carried only in specialized media, such as the black or Hispanic press.

Changing diversity has meant that media are also working to hire employees who represent differing groups. Opportunities have increased for good writers interested in topics on minority groups.

Arthur O. Sulzberger, Jr., publisher of the *New York Times,* has been emphasizing the need for diversity since he was associate publisher. He sees diversity as the big challenge facing newspapers through the end of the century and beyond. Addressing audiences' needs means employing a staff that reflects the city's or country's population.

"I need that Asian American reporter if I am to reach that segment of the population," Sulzberger says. "In a society that is witnessing increased numbers of women and ethnic groups, that means catering to those audiences' needs. We're no longer writing for the white male. The audience looks less and less like me."

Information and Media Glut

Writers must remember that today's increasingly diverse society offers more to read, watch, and listen to than anyone could possibly consume, even with unlimited leisure time. Marshall McLuhan, more than twenty-five years ago, predicted today's trends, suggesting that new media would alter our society in dramatic, unanticipated ways.

> *. . . electronic technology is reshaping and restructuring social patterns of interdependence and every aspect of our personal life. It is forcing us to reconsider and re-evaluate practically every thought, every action and every institution formerly taken for granted. Everything is changing—you, your family, your neighborhood, your education, your government, your relation to "the others."*

He was right. Society has changed. McLuhan could hardly have envisioned the information explosion today. In the United States, the three commercial networks and scores of publications of thirty years ago have grown into a media system that numbers 1,590 daily newspapers, 8,313 weekly newspapers, 8,843 magazines, 1,004 commercial television stations, 406 cable systems, and 10,238 radio stations.

No one person can possibly read or see the tiniest fraction of what is available today. Media pervade daily life. To the traditional media have been added new forms of communication, such as direct mail and telephone marketing, that can reach anyone who has a zip code and a telephone number. Technology has so overcome such barriers as geography and cost that almost anyone can buy the equipment to be in touch with anyone anywhere in the world. People in remote areas can tune into events via satellite dishes; a sailboat captain in the Caribbean can receive a fax on board.

Audience Impact on Traditional Media

The changes in lifestyle, emerging ethnic groups, and competing media have had a major impact on traditional media. Studies have shown that consumers spend about 4 to 5 percent of the country's gross national product on media. Even during good and bad economic times, the percentage has remained constant. That means that in times of prosperity, more dollars are spent on media, and media flourish.

But in a nongrowth economy, fewer actual dollars are spent on buying publications and subscribing to cable channels. Consumers are spending their money in other ways—but in ways that relate to their hunger for information. They have opted to spend on new media, investing in computers, digital color monitors, modems, and accompanying technology. Consumers buy the equipment that gives them access to information. Such spending is not factored into the dollars spent on media but rather is hidden in the cost of electric bills and the amortization of equipment.

The need for information and entertainment is constant, therefore, but the preferred sources change—perhaps for the good. But the change has not been so good for traditional media, such as newspapers. Research has shown that fickle audiences may not return to a medium once they have abandoned it for another means of getting information and entertainment.

Impact on Newspapers

Newspapers have been hardest hit by change as audiences have moved to television and other technology to get information and entertainment faster. Research has shown that newspaper circulation and use have declined steadily over the past decade, partly because people have less free time. A 1989 Scripps-Howard study warned, "when newspaper reading feels like 'work,' it gets short shrift."

In describing the "vanishing newspaper reader," Professor Robert L. Stevenson noted in 1990 that 73 percent of people in a national sample reported in 1967 that they read a newspaper "every day." Twenty years later, in a 1988 survey, only 51 percent answered that they were daily newspaper readers.

Another 1990 study indicated an even further reduction in the number of Americans pursuing what was once thought to be a national habit: reading a daily newspaper. Only 43 percent of nearly 5,000 people interviewed by the Times-Mirror Center for People and the Press said they had read a newspaper the day before—a conventional measure of daily readership—indicating that 57 percent do not read a paper on any given day. By contrast, a Gallup poll in 1965 had reported that 67 percent of adults under age 35 said they had read a newspaper the day before.

Effect on Television Viewing

Newspapers aren't alone in the decline. A 1994 Times-Mirror study also found low rates of news magazine readership: 18 percent reported regular readership of a news magazine such as *Time* or *Newsweek,* and only 5 percent regularly read financial magazines such as *Forbes* or *Business Week.*

Watching television news, however, still is a daily activity for most Americans. Eight out of ten survey respondents in the 1994 Times-Mirror study said they watched television news regularly. Although television appears to be the main source of news, it too has dealt with declining ratings and increased competition. Television use dropped slightly in the past decade: The average American in 1987 watched about 20 hours of television each week, down from 22.5 hours in 1980.

While predictions are that media use will continue to decline, some kinds of media, such as weeklies, have gained in popularity. And more than half of Americans—61 percent—responded that they read at least six books a year, according to the Times-Mirror Center study in 1994.

To attract and retain attention, media executives have had to stop and consider audiences more carefully so they can reach them successfully with advertising and editorial content. And to retain and attract audiences, they have had to consider content in relation to convenience, habit, interest, and other factors.

Media leaders are more aware of the constraints that keep audiences away, such as money, lifestyles, increasing demands on time, and the lure of other media. The smart ones have realized that they must adjust and be flexible to reach specific audiences. They have recognized that often they need to create a profile of their audience, by research and other means, to find out exactly who they are and what they need. Armed with knowledge about audiences, media leaders—and writers—can do more to aim messages more specifically to their targeted destinations.

Analyzing Audiences

People who write tend to read more than the average person does. They are likely to be more educated, have a larger vocabulary, and a greater interest in various topics. Often they write to please themselves or to satisfy what they think audiences want to know. As writers they may be out of touch with their audiences and not know truly who their audiences are.

Such ignorance is dangerous. Writers are at risk if they assume that audiences are masses of uneducated folks—or if they assume that audiences can grasp complicated, technical messages. Successful writers take several prewriting steps in an effort to know and to get in touch with their audience.

Steps to Audience Success

First, writers must accept that they have to work hard to win readers; second, they must consider and analyze their audience and needs; and third, they have to invest time and energy in caring about their audience. Good writing requires that writers understand and practice these steps.

Step One: Acceptance

First, and perhaps most importantly, writers need to accept what has been laid out earlier in this chapter: Writers compete for audiences. They cannot change the ways in which lifestyles or diversity constantly change, nor can they reduce the proliferation of media and new technologies that compete for audiences and distract them.

Before writing, writers must accept that they will have to work hard to craft a message that will catch and hold an audience. They must also accept that audiences have a desire for information and entertainment and search both traditional and new media to satisfy that desire. To be successful, writers must know their audience and know what they want.

Step Two: Audience Defined

For many writers, defining specific audiences is a new experience. Through-out our school years, most of us think of "the teacher" as our audience, unless perhaps the teacher instructs us to "write a children's story" or "write a letter to grandmother." In such cases, few writers stop to describe and ana-lyze that audience. Hardly anyone who is told to write a children's story ever stops to think, "Now which children do I want to reach? All children? Pre-schoolers?"

Asking such questions is the most basic kind of audience analysis—whereby writers put their wants and needs aside and think about those of the audience. Such analysis is essential for today's writer and is obvious in the work of master writers.

Children's author Roald Dahl, an older writer at the peak of his career, thought constantly about children and what their lives were like. Dahl de-scribed his audience in *Meet the Authors and Illustrators*:

> *They [children] love being spooked. They love suspense. They love action. They love ghosts. They love the finding of treasure. They love chocolates and toys and money. They love magic. They love being made to giggle.*

In Dahl's *Charlie and the Great Glass Elevator,* the characters travel through time and space in a large glass elevator, along with Mr. Willy Wonka, a character made famous in Dahl's well-known book *Charlie and the Chocolate Factory*. Dahl made the most of children's past experiences with elevators, with glass, with silly adults, and with his previous book. Rather than featuring a starship with alien creatures, Dahl used familiar thrills to build a great adventure for everyday kids—and it sold more than a million copies.

Here are a few questions that may guide a writer in defining audiences:

Who will read this?
Who needs to read it?
Whom would I choose as an ideal listener or reader?

Step Three: Audience Care and Feeding

The name "audience care and feeding" truly sums up priorities for writers in the information age. Good writers care about audiences and take time to learn about them, to think about them, and to please them rather than themselves. Good writers also feed audiences by giving them information in a palatable form—one that they can use and understand.

Dahl cared about his audience: children. "Unless you hold them from the first page, they're going to wander away and watch the telly or do something else," he noted. Dahl took the time to discover what elements appeal to children. Then he constructed his storybook in a format that children could use and understand. He created a fanciful world that captured children's imaginations and that was related to their interests. He cared so much about his audience that he precisely crafted an appealing writing style and story. And his writing proved successful.

Writers must think long and hard about the audiences for their messages, just as Dahl did. Writers must care so much that if readers reject their work, the writers have also lost. They need to undertake careful thinking before a first draft is attempted.

Identifying Audiences

Few writers have a single audience, although many mistakenly write for what they call a "mass audience." In today's world, *mass audience* is only a rough term used to describe a conglomeration of many smaller, specific audiences. The members of the small audiences share much in common. Some typical smaller audiences are veterans, working mothers, union members, and power company customers. Your audience may be tiny (members of St. John's Parish) or it may be huge (Americans interested in better health care).

Regardless of size, every audience may be subdivided into smaller component audiences. For example, members of a church parish will include smaller audiences of children, teens, young adults, singles, marrieds, new parents, empty nesters, choir members, grounds workers, and so on. Even a smaller audience, such as veterans, could be further divided into veterans of specific wars, such as World War II or the Vietnam War.

Breaking an audience into its composite groups is an important activity for people who need to communicate essential messages. Each subgroup may have specific needs for information and a specific way of getting it. A university, for example, has many publics, including students, faculty, staff, alumni, potential students, governing bodies, the press, and potential donors. No one message will effectively reach all of these publics. Most universities spend a great deal of time and money developing specific messages that are targeted to their many audiences, such as the alumni newsletter for alumni, direct mail for potential donors, and news conferences for the media.

Writers need to identify their audiences. A shortcut is to state the topic, then to ask the question "who cares?" The answer will be a list of groups or audiences who are potential consumers of the message.

Let's try the "who cares?" method for listing audiences for a message. You are writing an article for your company newsletter on a new policy that provides preventive health care benefits to employees who have children. "Who cares?" yields this list:

- Married employees with children,
- Single employees with children,
- Employees thinking about having or adopting children, and
- Employees who have no children but who wish they had preventive health care benefits.

Why is listing audiences important? Because even if writers go no further in getting to know their audiences, once they have at least listed them, they may change their writing approach. For the employee newsletter, your initial attempt at an introduction might have read

`A new company policy will provide health care benefits for preventive medicine.`

But after you list audiences, your introduction becomes more personal:

As a single parent, staff geologist John Payne has worried about the extra expense of annual medical exams for his three children and a doctor's visit if children were only mildly ill.

But Mega Oil's new health benefits program will ease those worries. The plan will reimburse employees with children for preventive health expenses, such as office visits and well-child checkups.

As audiences are subdivided and defined, so are writing tasks. When writers take time to identify specific audiences, such as single parents, messages can be targeted for those audiences, the approach, structure, and language can be chosen to suit the audience, and communication becomes possible—and even likely.

Researching Audiences

To be more successful at reaching audiences, writers should go beyond just listing them. Once writers have listed their audiences, they often need to do research, both formal and informal. Writers do research to become familiar with audiences. Research gives writers information such as audiences' likes and dislikes, the media they use, their values, and their goals.

Audiences will not turn away from a message that is consistent with their values, needs, and goals. An audience interested in women's health will be attracted to a message that begins with "Free mammograms . . ." rather than with the name of the sponsoring agency or the name of the government official who announces the program.

Realtors frequently cite the three most important words in their business: location, location, location. They must know where house hunters want to live. Any good realtor knows what matchups to avoid: Don't show the townhouse on a busy avenue to the couple with four young children, or the retiree's garden apartment to the aggressive young professionals.

Much as realtors select a location or a sample of homes to show to potential buyers, writers can tailor messages once they know their audience.

Just as realtors need to find out immediately where clients want and need to live, so must writers find out what the intended audience wants and needs to know. A writer can't begin to write an effective message until the characteristics of the audience have been assessed.

To gather information about audiences, four techniques are commonly used by researchers. No single technique can provide complete information about any audience; most writers should use some combination of these methods.

COGITATION. Yes, that's right. Writers can just think about their audience. For example, when writing a letter to Grandma, gifted grandchild-writers stop to think, "What in my life is of greatest interest to Grandma? What kinds of things make her laugh? What will she want to know more about?" Asking these questions about Grandma is a form of audience research. Such analysis is also essential for today's writers, who must ask, "What do I think my audience is interested in?"

LIBRARY RESEARCH. Sometimes a writer needs to go to the library or to an online reference service. Consulting with a reference librarian can also help build a better understanding of most audiences. For example, when developing family management tips for working mothers, a writer may need to know how many working mothers are in the United States and in the potential audience. What kinds of jobs they have? How old they are, and how old their children are? What is their average income? Answers to these questions are available in census data and in articles about the census. The answers can tell a writer what kinds of information will appeal most readily to the working mother audience. For example, cost-effective management tips will be best received.

INFORMAL AND FORMAL SURVEYS. Surveying is a scientific way of asking questions, usually from a wide variety of people. Informal surveys are part of a writer's daily life. Interviewing various people, both on and off the record, is a staple of daily journalism that works well for all writers as a way of learning more about audiences.

Spending time observing the way people live or conduct business can add to a writer's knowledge. The novelist who writes about life in Appalachia may spend months gathering oral histories, which will serve as the basis for her next book. Novice reporters learn the value of "hanging out" at the police station or at city hall, where they can talk to many people who are interested in their news beats.

More formal survey techniques are sometimes used for understanding audiences. Suppose that the circulation of a community sports newspaper has been dropping steadily. Before abandoning or changing the paper, the editor conducts a readership survey, asking people what they would change about the publication. Students who are thinking of starting a new on-campus publication may distribute surveys to determine audience interests and needs.

No formal survey is worthwhile unless careful methods are followed. Before attempting to conduct a formal survey, a writer should consult a professional or professor in public opinion research, or consult a book about survey research.

Both formal and informal surveys protect writers from making dangerous assumptions about their audiences. Perhaps the most common assumption is that everybody in the audience is alike—and is even like the writer! Audiences are diverse and ever-changing, and surveys can help today's writer monitor their varying needs.

FOCUS GROUPS. Focus groups are gatherings, usually of seven to ten audience members or potential audience members, to discuss audience needs and preferences. In selecting focus group members, researchers strive to represent all components of the audience or audiences. One of a series of focus groups for a state-wide religious publication, for example, included nine people: two mothers of school-age children, a young father, a newly-wed, an older woman, two retired men, and two active church women. The group was considered to be nearly an ideal representation of the church membership statewide. The nine-member group talked for seventy minutes and produced a variety of suggestions for improving the publication, as well as many ideas about topics that should be covered. The church implemented their suggestions for change.

All types of media use focus groups to determine what their audiences like and don't like. Focus groups can be helpful for a public relations practitioner in evaluating a new service, such as a telephone call-waiting feature. Advertisers use focus groups to test packaging and assess the perceived quality of a product.

Some publications bring together focus groups solely for the purpose of generating new story and service ideas. Readers have a unique and private perspective on what they read, and the focus group is one of a very few methods that allows writers and editors to share their responses and ideas. Many focus groups were held prior to the design of *USA Today Weekend,* the weekend magazine of *USA Today.* Discussion in the early focus groups led to a design of the new magazine based on what readers said they liked and didn't like.

Professional users of focus group research advise caution in generalizing too broadly from the results. Researchers hear only from a select few people who are willing to take time from their lives to come and talk about a topic—perhaps an obscure topic. Writers or marketers should never base a decision on a single focus group and its conclusions.

All kinds of research on readers should proceed carefully and with the understanding that no study is perfect—and that audiences may not always be trusted to know what they like. In the late 1970s, research indicated that television news audiences wanted more smiles and informality on evening news shows. Once such "happy talk" journalism was implemented, people found it unappealing; the juxtaposition of jokes with traffic death tolls made for an unsettled audience. We must consider the audience in all that we do, but we also must remember that professional judgment is also needed to put audience comments in perspective.

Success with Audiences

Some general rules apply that may give a message an immediate winning edge. These rules will be reiterated in subsequent chapters in the book, but it is worthwhile to set them out here.

• *Give accurate information; check and recheck facts.* An announcement of freshman orientation must send new students to the right building at the right time on the right day. An error can result in a big mixup for hundreds of students and their families. Writing that misinforms or misleads an audience discredits the message, the writer, and the medium. Research has shown that accurate writing preserves a writer's reputation and the goodwill audiences have for the media.

• *Give complete information.* Every bit as frustrating as inaccurate information is incomplete information. And incomplete messages may inadvertently be inaccurate. Coverage of the arrest of football star O. J. Simpson would have been incomplete—and wrong—if it had failed to include the history of his domestic disputes with his wife.

• *Don't make assumptions about your audience.* Writers often assume a certain background and lifestyle among their readers and listeners. If you write a lead that says

```
Remember the good old days when you were sick, and your
mother fed you baby aspirin and chicken soup,
```

the lead assumes that the audience is a uniform age, old enough to have had a childhood in the days before acetaminophen. It also assumes that all audience members had a mother and that they grew up in a society where mothers stayed home with sick children.

• *Deal caringly and ethically with people you are writing about.* Avoid libel or information that may damage a subject's reputation or put that person in an unfair light. Appendix A explains the danger of libel that can occur in any writing. Make sure any descriptive words accurately define the person or people in your message.

• *Avoid offensive words or topics, except when they are crucial to the message.* Daily newspapers traditionally have cautioned writers to observe a breakfast-table standard: Don't publish information, language, or pictures that will make readers lose their appetite for breakfast. In reality, many media have moved quite far away from that advice. Television brings horror into living rooms and kitchens every day, and media have been roundly criticized for insensitivity. Writers need to be circumspect about the value of offensive, crude, or gory material and weigh it against audience needs and interests. The choice is often difficult. Look at the following example that appeared in a newspaper. The writer might argue that the description shows good reporting, but audiences have little need to know all the details.

NEW YORK—A runaway elevator decapitated welfare clerk James Chenault, 54, as he straddled the doorway in an attempt to help his frightened fellow passengers to safety.

One made it out before the elevator, with the doors still open, shot up to the next floor, cutting off Chenault's head, police said.

The head, with stereo headphones still on, landed in the elevator with the three remaining passengers, police said. The body fell down the shaft.

Reaching Audiences

So where are we? In this chapter we have tried to show that writing is critical to communication, despite increased use of electronic media and other transmission devices such as facsimile machines. Most communication is written first.

We have considered the changes in society, both in lifestyle and in diversity. We recognize that every day, people are bombarded with dozens of messages from television, newspapers, mail, flyers, magazines, billboards, other people, and on and on and on. In today's information age, many messages cruise from writer to audiences. Many reach their destination—audiences—but are immediately discarded before they have a chance to be assimilated.

Why? Because many factors must be considered as roadblocks between writers and audiences. Even when writers know their audiences, they have to overcome roadblocks.

To summarize and review, here are the major kinds of obstacles that exist between writers and their audiences:

• *Taxing lifestyles.* Audiences today, despite labor-saving devices, are busier than ever with multiple commitments to work and family. People are spending more of their leisure time on family activities and household chores and less on media consumption.

• *Media and information glut.* More kinds of media become available almost daily. Each memo, letter, article, or news brief has infinitely more competition for an individual's attention than could have been imagined a decade ago. An overwhelming smorgasbord of media offers information. People use online services, direct mail, and an array of cable and satellite channels in addition to the traditional media. They are hungry for information, and they are able to choose media that are most relevant to their lifestyle.

• *Diversity of audiences.* Audiences no longer resemble most writers. An increasingly diverse society has changed audience needs and interests from those of even ten years ago.

- *Unfriendly messages.* Poor writing interferes with messages getting through, just as do commuting, working, children, and too many media choices. A message that bores or taxes an audience or that takes too long to understand can be the greatest roadblock to complete communication.

The Writing Challenge

Writers and communicators must accept that getting messages to people in today's society is an unparalleled challenge. Writers have to accept that they cannot do much to change individual consumer's lifestyles. They cannot reduce the number of media. They cannot alter society's diversity. They cannot alter the fact that only a few messages get through the daily clutter.

But they can control one aspect: the structure of the message. Trained writers know techniques for ensuring that messages reach their destination and are consumed. For some audiences, the succinct three-paragraph news story will suffice. Others will seek the longer, more detailed, narrative account. Good writers know which techniques and which structures best fit their audiences.

Today's technology dramatically increases the need for good writing. Although information is packaged differently in the technological revolution, audiences are still seeking information that is accurate and relevant, and they will ultimately abandon sources that don't provide that information clearly and concisely.

EXERCISES

1. Keep a media log for a twenty-four-hour period between today and the next class. Make a chart showing which media you used, how long you viewed or read, a summary of messages, and what else you were doing while using each medium. Indicate whether you had interference or distractions that prevented you from understanding the message. Be prepared to compare your media use patterns with those of others in the class.

2. Get a written example of one of the messages recorded in your media log. Study it for clarity. Did you understand the message? How did the writer make it clear? What kept the message from being clear? If the mes-

sage was not clear, rewrite it to make it clearer. List any missing information that would help the message be better understood.

3. Interview a relative about his or her media use, formulating questions based on your log. Explore how his or her media use has changed during the last five years, ten years. Where does the person get most news? Entertainment? Information that is dependable? In-depth information?

4. Get together with a friend or classmate. Identify his or her roles. For example, your friend may be a cheerleader, daughter, church member, sister, or Girl Scout, or have several other identities. Select one. Through an informal interview, find out what interests your friend when she is in one of those roles, such as church member. How does she get information pertinent to that role? Then switch to another role, say cheerleader. Compare the media she uses to get information in that role.

5. Pick a major national event that was reported in the media two weeks ago. Go to the library and select several sources that reported the event. Examples would be community newspaper, national newspaper, local daily newspaper, national news magazine, or political party publication. Compare the way each introduced and developed the story. Look at writing style, language, length of story, anecdotes, and quotations. Does the format for presenting the news fit the medium's audiences? How?

REFERENCES

Bacon's Newspaper Directory. Chicago, IL: Bacon's Information Inc., 1994.

Bacon's TV/Cable Directory. Chicago, IL: Bacon's Information Inc., 1994.

Deborah Kovacs and James Preller, *Meet the Authors and Illustrators.* New York: Scholastic Inc., 1991.

Marshall McLuhan and Q. Fiore, *The Medium is the Message: An Inventory of Effects.* New York: Bantam Books, 1967.

"News and Newspaper Reading Habits." New York: Newspaper Advertising Bureau, May 1988.

Clarice N. Olien., Phillip J. Tichenor, and George A. Donohue, "A Changing Media Environment in the U.S." Paper presented at the annual meeting of the Association for Education in Journalism and Mass Communication, Boston, MA, August 1991.

"Reading Newspapers: The Practices of America's Young Adults." Paper prepared for the Education Writers Association by Irwin Kirsch, Ann Jungeblut, and Donald Rock, April 1988.

Donald L. Shaw, *The Rise and Fall of American Mass Media: Roles of Technology and Leadership,* The Roy W. Howard Project, School of Journalism, Indiana University, Bloomington, IN, 1991.

Times-Mirror Center for People and the Press, *The American Media: Who Reads, Who Watches, Who Listens, Who Cares?* Washington, DC, 1990.

Times-Mirror Center for People and the Press, *The People, the Press and Politics: The New Political Landscape.* Washington, DC, 1994.

"Women's Lifestyles: A Special Report." *Scripps-Howard Editors Newsletter.* Cincinnati, OH: Scripps-Howard Newspapers, Spring 1989.

Paula Span, "Quality Time on Cable: In Queens, Experimenting with 150 Channels," *Washington Post,* February 12, 1992.

1990 Census of Population. U.S. Department of Commerce, Economics and Statistics Administration, Bureau of the Census, Washington, DC, November 1993.

3

Getting to the Point

When reporters covered President Clinton's State of the Union address in January 1995, they had to sift through the president's lengthy remarks to uncover the most relevant points for their audiences. A writer for a lobbyists' newsletter would focus on Clinton's call for legislators to turn back perquisites from lobbyists. A reporter for a broad, general-interest audience would lead with the president's call for a new convenant that focuses on opportunity and responsibility to repair what Clinton called "the frayed bonds of our communities." The publisher of a veterans' magazine would consider Clinton's reminder of the debt the country owes veterans.

Writers who are familiar with their audiences know what information will be relevant and appealing. They know what will attract the individual who juggles time for job, home, spouse, children, hobbies, and friends. Writers must alert audiences to messages that are important.

Messages must therefore hook the audience. The hook must be set in the first few sentences or paragraphs. That's when writers must show the relevance of the message and attract, entertain, and inform. That's when readers or listeners will decide whether the message is compelling, entertaining, or informative enough to warrant attention. Why toil over constructing messages that don't hook or reach audiences?

This chapter will discuss lead writing, specifically

- The role of audiences,
- Elements in lead writing,

- News values, and
- Types of leads.

What's the Point?

To hook a particular audience, writers must know why they are writing. It sounds simple enough. But many people regard writing as an endeavor, not as a craft. They avoid thinking about the substance of what they are going to say. These writers sit down to write with a broad purpose or goal in mind, such as informing an audience about government waste. They haven't figured out the main point of the specific message, however. Getting to that point without delay is essential in hooking the audience.

Determining the point requires critical thinking. Writers must look at the components of the message and weigh each vis-à-vis their audiences. They must lay out the facts and evaluate their importance and relevance to their audiences. As they consider information, they get closer to the point of the message. Writers establish where they want to start and where they will go.

Getting to the point is like eating an artichoke: As you peel off the outer leaves and examine them, you get closer to the real heart of your search. You may toss out heavy, less interesting leaves. Closer to the center, you will find more succulent, flavorful leaves worthy of attention. And finally, you unveil the heart.

Finding the heart, or kernel of your story, is essential to writing. Along the way, writers will discover facts and pieces that relate to the main point, surrounding and supporting like the artichoke's tasty leaves. But the examining process must be completed first.

Consider the advertising copywriter who says, "I want to write an ad that will get more business for my client." He is still handling the whole artichoke—a big and unworkable problem. Thinking and planning will help him work from the broad idea of producing an ad to the more specific task of communicating his client's specific benefit.

If the client makes hand lotion, the advertiser's point may be beautiful hands or healthier skin or convenient packaging. If the client owns a tax service, the point may be customer peace of mind and the accountant's knowledge of tax laws. Once that benefit—the point—has been identified, the writer's job is to select precise words that will emphasize that point and grab a consumer's attention.

In the Beginning Comes the Lead

In journalism the first sentences or paragraphs of a story are called a lead. The lead has a heavy responsibility. It is the bait to hook the reader. By educating, entertaining, or enlightening, it stimulates the reader to pay attention. The lead shows relevance and is relevant to the audience. It also entraps. A publisher once wrote that a lead must be provocative, vigorous, and even at times startling to the reader.

Every piece of writing has a beginning or opening statement; every piece of writing has a lead. Long-time syndicated columnist James J. Kilpatrick once wrote

The lead is vital to any writing, whether one is writing a novel, a short story, a book review, a term paper, a newspaper editorial, or a homily to be read in church on Sunday morning.

Erma Bombeck led with this opening sentence in her book *A Marriage Made in Heaven, or Too Tired for an Affair:*

It would have been a wonderful wedding—had it not been mine.

The most important information was sketched out: A successful wedding has occurred with some anguish on the part of the bride, who is about to tell the tale of her marriage. Instead of being bored by what could be a ho-hum account, the reader is amused and curious after only twelve words from Bombeck.

The lead, therefore, sets out the message's relevance. Bombeck's lead is relevant to anyone who has been through a wedding. As it sets out the relevance, the lead gets to the point quickly. In the Bombeck example, the point is the anguish of weddings. The lead whets the reader's appetite to stay with the message.

A church newsletter used this short lead to establish relevance for parishioners:

Hymnals continue to disappear from the church. They need to be brought back so they are here for use at Sunday services.

The lead contains the stimulus for reading, sets out the message's relevance, and gives the reader the most important information first. As the stimulus, the lead entertains, enlightens, and educates; as it sets out the relevance, it whets the reader's appetite to stay with the message; and in giving the most important information first, the lead ensures that the reader gets the point quickly.

By digesting the most important information first, audiences know the essential details after the first few paragraphs. They are informed. They have the information they need because the writer hooked them and got to the point right away. They can be informed and can move to other messages.

The lead must also set up the story. After reading or hearing the lead, audiences should know the main points of the message that follows. If not, the lead has misled them, and the writer's credibility is damaged. How does a writer know whether the lead sets up the story? When the story is complete, a writer must consider the main points in the body of the message and ensure that they are noted in the lead. The lead sets up the story; the story backs up the lead. For example, a story reporting a robbery at the campus dining hall includes details about the robber locking the dining hall manager in a closet. That fact should be in the lead, along with the information that the robbery occurred and how much money was taken.

Journalists, primarily print journalists, have recognized for decades that getting to the point is essential to attract and retain readers. They have adopted a format—the inverted pyramid style of writing—that ranks information in descending order of importance. Other media writers, competing for audience attention, have found that they too must set out immediately the critical aspects of the message for their readers, listeners, consumers, or other audience members. Writing a lead has become a crucial assignment for any information-age writer.

How to Get Started

To construct a lead, writers must know their information thoroughly. They must evaluate the information, using their judgment and experience to determine what is most relevant to their audience.

As a prewriting activity, some writers go through their notes and add priority numbers next to information. Before writing the lead asking for hymnals to be returned, the newsletter writer listed information such as this: The budget for hymnals is $300 this year; 42 books are missing; we need them back; 10 percent of hymnals have been taken since January 1; we don't have money to replace them; if you want a home copy, we can order one for you for $15; replacement cost is $15 per book. Next to each fact, she put a number corresponding to its importance to the audience.

In writing the lead, the writer determined that the audience did not need to know about book counts or budget information. Priority No. 1 is that hymnals are missing and the church needs them to be returned. The writer sets out the main purpose of the story—to tell the audience that hymnals are missing—and the relevance—without hymnals parishioners can't sing during services.

Writers can avoid the actual numbering of facts through another approach. They can simply ask "What must my audience know?" and then list three to five things. In the case of the hymnals, the list would be something like this:

1. Hymnals are missing and must be returned.
2. If people want home copies, we can order them.
3. Cost is $15.

The main point would become the lead. Other main points would be fashioned into the rest of the copy.

Writers who struggle with relevance should remember that most people want to know the personal angle first. It all comes down to the audience's automatic question, "How does this message affect me?" The audience immediately looks for the explanation. In the hymnal story, the lead states simply how parishioners will be affected: no hymnals.

Sometimes stories or messages don't have that simple, personal component. Then writers must look beyond the "what about me?" or relevance rule to other factors that make some pieces of information more important than others. Such factors are also guides to the selection of information for the lead.

News Elements

Certain elements are of interest in all writing. Journalists over the years have spelled out the elements that must appear in news stories every day: *who, what, when, where, how,* and *why.* That list is a basic starting point for any writer in determining what will go first.

These news components can form a question: "Who did what to whom, how, when, where, and why?" Every letter, news article, news release, or advertisement will answer this question.

Why are these elements important? Because people are most interested in other people, who they are, what they say and do, where they live and work, what happens to them, why they make certain choices, and how they deal with those choices. They are interested in conflict, competition, and achievements. People want to know about other people who overcome adversity, who are defeated, and who do the unusual.

—A Hollywood, Fla., man and woman exchanged wedding vows at 1,300 feet as they plummeted to earth hand-in-hand under silver parachutes 5 miles west of here Wednesday afternoon.

Grace Mason and John Kempner met while skydiving at a local club and decided it would be the most significant way to start their married life together.

The elements are there:

Who: Grace and John.

What: Got married.

When: Wednesday.

Where: Near Hollywood, Fla.

How: By parachutes.

Why: Because they wanted to start married life in a manner meaningful to their courtship and to them.

The two-paragraph lead summarizes what happened. Readers can decide whether they want to read further to learn more about Grace and John. The author has also set it up so that after reading two paragraphs, the reader knows the most important information and can turn to another story.

Where to Put Who and What

Putting all the elements in the first sentence can result in long, convoluted sentences. Consider the following lead and how it was rewritten more clearly.

—Sam Atwood, an associate professor of political science at the University, told students in a speech Thursday in MacPherson Hall as part of the University's Bicentennial observance that they should be more concerned about world events that more and more directly affect their lives and their future.

Rewritten:

—Students should be concerned about world events that more and more directly affect their lives and their future, an associate professor of political science at the University said Thursday.

Rather than the professor's complete name, a descriptive phrase or identifying label can be used to describe him. The location of the speech and why he was giving it can be included in a subsequent paragraph.

Writers must decide which elements deserve emphasis and are most relevant before they write a lead. All elements will be included somewhere in the story. As a general rule, *who* and *what* will be in the first sentence. So will *where* and *when* because they take up little space. *Who, what, when,* and *where* also follow the natural order of the English language: subject, verb, object. *Who, what, when,* and *where* set up an active structure: A masked man robbed the University dining hall of $3,000 Wednesday night and locked the dining hall manager in a closet. *How* and *why* can be included in the first sentence if they are unusual. A full explanation will require several sentences or paragraphs.

Consider this lead, which focuses on *who, what, when,* and *where.*

HO CHI MINH CITY, Vietnam—Fifty-five U.S. cyclists arrived here Wednesday after a grueling 22-day tour through the country's mountains and plains.

Who: 55 U.S. cyclists.
What: Arrived after 22 days of cycling through Vietnam.
When: Wednesday.
Where: Ho Chi Minh City is where the tour ended.

A Closer Look at the Elements

Let's define the lead elements and what role they play in the copy.

Who defines the person carrying out the action or affected by the story. *Who* may not be a specific name, such as Grace or John, but rather an identification or label. For example, a news release may say in the first sentence that two marketing employees have been promoted and in the second sentence give their names and titles. But if the president is retiring, his name will be given first because it has recognition among company employees and in the community.

—Charles Southwick, chief executive officer of Englewood Mills who began his career as a bookkeeper, will retire April 1 after 42 years with the company.

The *who* is Charles Southwick, who is prominent because of the role he plays in the local business community.

What represents the action. It can be simply stated in a verb. Consider this news lead:

—A Richmond, Va., man died Wednesday when he lost control of his car and it crashed into a bridge railing on I-95 South.

The verb "died" tells *what.*
Or in a letter to a high school's alumni:

—Southeast High School's PTA is asking alumni to donate money to put at least two computers in every classroom by the end of the year.

What in the example is asking alumni for money.
When tells the audience the timeliness of the event being reported or the time frame of specific actions. Often it is one word. In most writing, *when* will go after the verb. Few leads begin with *when.* In the car accident example, "Wednesday" tells when the accident occurred. In the lead on the alumni letter, the time frame is less specific. But an alumnus reading the letter will know that the goal for installing the computers is December 31 of that year, so contributions should be made between receipt of the letter and well before December 31.

—The Wee Tots Day Care Center Board of Directors will meet March 31 to decide whether to offer a summer camp program for older children.

March 31 tells interested parents when a decision will be made.
Where gives the reader the geographic context of the story. In many cases that will pique audience interest because readers want to know about events

that affect them. The closer the story is to the reader's backyard, the greater the interest will be.

Wire service and other stories in newspapers often start with *where* by using a dateline, the name of the city in capital letters, to let readers know immediately where the event occurred.

WASHINGTON—President Clinton decried terrorism Wednesday after two U.S. officials were killed in Pakistan.

In non-newspaper writing, the exact location would be the first word or words in the lead only when it offers some unusual aspect to the story. Usually the *where* is tucked into the end of a lead.

—A slice of history awaits you at the Tastee Diner in Silver Spring.

How expands on the *what* aspect. Look at the following lead from the *Washington Post*.

—A man was killed and his body crushed yesterday when a dumpster he and a woman companion were sleeping in was emptied into a trash compactor in the Hampshire Knolls section of Northeast Washington. The woman was seriously injured.

The lead tells *who, what, when,* and *where* but also talks about *how:* how the man died.

Why gives the audience the reason a decision or a change was made or is pending or the cause of an event. In the Richmond accident example, the audience knows why the man died: because he lost control of the car. In the alumni letter, alumni are asked to give money. Why? So the school can buy computers.

To reiterate: *how* and *why* will go in the first sentence or lead if there is some unusual aspect or if they are essential to the heart of the message.

—Yelling to police that he would never be taken alive, a Washington fugitive raced his motorcycle through a police roadblock and was shot to death by law enforcement officers Thursday.

Why the man drove through the roadblock is immediately clear to the reader.

Watch Out for Too Much

Sometimes all elements will fit concisely into a lead, as in the example about the Washington fugitive. But since all elements do not have to be in every first sentence, a writer can set up the point of the story using a few elements in the first sentence and explain the other elements in later paragraphs.

Consider this lead:

—A major housing development that preservationists believed had died last year has been resurrected by developers who say local planning officials are much more receptive to the revised version.

Are *who, what, when, where, how,* and *why* all answered in this first sentence? No.

Who: Developers.
What: Are resurrecting a housing development plan.
When: Implied now, but not stated.
Where   Implied in the county, but not stated.
How: Not stated.
Why: Because planning officials seem more receptive.

The second paragraph of the story gives more explanation of *what* has happened, *when,* and *how.*

—Jonathan Gardner, one of the developers of the project, said a revised plan was submitted to the county planning board earlier this week. Developers resubmitted the plan after conversations last month indicated certain revisions could erase planning officials' objections.

The third paragraph answers *where* and gives more information, and the fourth paragraph moves into the controversy.

—The revised plan uses the same 300-acre site in southeast Granger County but has 46 fewer houses and relocates the swim and tennis club. Developers expect a public hearing to be set next month.

Preservationists have vowed to fight the renewed development efforts. They say the issues haven't changed despite what they call minor modifications in the original plan.

The first sentence, or the first paragraph, stands as the lead to the story. The other elements, particularly how developers decided to resubmit the plan and what changes were made, are later components of the article. The lead would have been quite complex if the writer had tried to include all the elements there.

A lead attracts readers to the story because it has other elements—beyond *who, what, when, where, how,* and *why*—that must be considered when the writer is structuring the first sentence. The other elements are called news values.

News Values

In structuring leads, writers are also guided by what journalists traditionally have called news values, or aspects of an event that make it worth knowing about. These values or qualities carry over into any writing. Because people are interested in other people and their lives, we can also define news values as qualities that are of interest to people or are satisfying in some way.

The traditional news values that journalism professors teach and that become second nature to reporters are prominence, timeliness, proximity, impact, magnitude, conflict, oddity, and emotional impact. Let's look at each of the news values and how they affect lead writing. Several of them are closely allied to the elements *who, what, when, where, how,* and *why* discussed earlier in this chapter.

Prominence

When the main character or characters in your story are well known, that is a signal to put those names in the lead. When President Reagan was in office, the Associated Press wire service sent out a story about a cricket in the first couple's bedroom. Because the president is a prominent figure, the bug in the bedroom was a news item.

> WASHINGTON (UPI)—Crickets are regarded as good luck in some households, but to the family in residence at 1600 Pennsylvania Ave., the noisy little insect in the bedroom was akin to a plague of locusts.
>
> After two nights of lost sleep, the man of the house took charge of the great cricket hunt at the White House, and first lady Nancy Reagan reported to her staff Wednesday that the cricket was chirping no more. (Reprinted with the permission of United Press International Inc.)

People who are related to famous people also are lead-worthy. For example, people are still curious about the children of the late Princess Grace of Monaco, the American socialite who became a movie star and then a princess. Prominence extends to people who surround famous people and even to their pets. Millie, the White House dog of George and Barbara Bush, made front page news nationwide when she had puppies.

Timeliness

One adage in journalism is that old news ain't news. People want to know what is happening as soon as it happens. They want newness in the news. They want to know information they didn't know yesterday. They want timely, up-to-date news, as is evidenced by the increased dependence on television and even radio as initial sources of people's news information. Therefore, *when* an event happened is almost always in the first sentence of a story so that people will have a context for that event.

—The governor will honor five National Merit Scholarship winners from the state in a special ceremony at the Governor's Mansion Friday afternoon.

Proximity

People are most interested about news that happens close to them. Audiences easily identify with stories with a geographic proximity, that is, those that occur in their own neighborhood, town, county, or state. They like to read stories about friends' successes and even defeats.

Audiences are also interested in what happens to people from their communities in other locations. For example, people in Cleveland would want to know about an airplane crash in Washington state that kills residents from their city. A Cleveland newspaper might run this lead:

SEATTLE, Wash.—Two Cleveland businessmen were among 19 people killed early this morning when a jet struck a radio tower just outside Seattle.

The lead emphasizes Cleveland's loss while telling that the plane crash occurred. Writers call this localizing a message, or putting the local angle on a story that originated miles away, so that audiences can see how the message relates to them and their community.

News reports may also have an emotional or nonspatial proximity, whereby readers identify with a certain group of people. People who have suffered heart attacks are interested in articles about how other heart-attack victims have coped. People who live in a college town may be more inclined to read about stories originating from other cities with campuses, even if the cities are far away.

Residents of a college community that has sports fever may relate empathetically to this story from the *Washington Post:*

> —The NCAA yesterday placed the Syracuse University athletic program on two years' probation and banned its men's basketball team from post-season competition this season for rule violations in 18 categories, including recruiting and extra benefits.

Impact

Audiences always want to know how they will be affected, whether by a road closing while a sewer line is being laid or by a sale on ground beef at the local supermarket. Reporters often hear people ask, "But how does this affect me? What does this have to do with me?" High in any message should be an explanation of how an event affects individuals' daily lives or why they should be concerned.

When possible, the impact should be translated into tangible terms. A water and sewer rate increase approved by the Town Council Tuesday night will mean that the average Little Rock resident will pay $3.52 a month more for service, bringing the average monthly bill to $31.96. Congress passes legislation to reduce Social Security benefits, leaving most recipients with $20 less a month. The impact of an earthquake is on the hundreds of people affected.

> LOS ANGELES—Searchers pulled body after body from a crumpled apartment complex Monday after an earthquake that snapped freeways like matchsticks, left hundreds of thousands without power and water, and turned the nation's busiest highway network into a commuter's nightmare.

The impact of the earthquake that rocked Los Angeles in January 1994 was noted in the above Associated Press lead: Hundreds of thousands had no power, and thousands of commuters had no roads to travel on.

Magnitude

Some folks like to distinguish between impact and magnitude in defining news values. Magnitude is defined as the size of the event. Death, injury, or loss of property are all elements of magnitude that attract audience attention. Large amounts of money, such as lottery winnings, and disasters, such as hurricanes, carry magnitude and are always big news. When a typhoon rips through the Philippines, the amount of damage inflicted and the speed of the winds are the magnitude of the storm. In an earthquake, the magnitude is the reading on the Richter scale.

Consider this lead, which has magnitude and an understood impact:

—Tuesday morning 54 school buses will drive more than 1,000 miles as they pick up 2,500 school children for the first day of classes this year.

The understood magnitude is represented in part by the 2,500 students, the 1,000 miles traveled, and 54 school buses. The impact of the first day of school is much broader, affecting any household in the county that has school-age children, or an employee of the school system, or an early morning commuter.

Conflict

Most news events reported contain some kind of conflict: contract disputes such as the one with the Detroit teachers, continuing struggles in the Middle East or in the emerging countries of the former Soviet Union, the battles between neighbors in rezoning issues, or a grievance filed by an employee against a supervisor. People like to read about conflict.

The extent of the conflict, either its size or its duration, will determine whether conflict is included in the lead of the message. The conflict between Gregory Kingsley, the twelve-year-old Florida youth who sued his natural mother for divorce so he could be adopted by his foster parents, made media headlines for days in September 1992. The trial of Lorena Bobbitt, who cut off her husband's penis after he allegedly raped her, attracted the international media.

Conflict permeates the news, as is shown in this Reuters news service lead:

LONDON—Prospects for an end to violence in Northern Ireland faded further Monday as Britain brusquely turned down a new IRA demand for clarification of an Anglo-Irish peace plan.

Oddity

Editors often encourage writers to look for oddity or some unusual twist to a story, such as the police officer who responds to the accident call and discovers that one of the injured people is his son. The Bobbitt story also carries human interest because of the unusualness of the case.

Look at this Reuters lead:

MARATHON, Fla.—A Cuban windsurfer caught a favorable breeze and sailed his board to Florida, where he asked for asylum, sheriff's deputies said Thursday.

Eugenio Maderal Roman, 21, made the 110-mile trip from Cuba's Varadero Beach resort to Marathon in the upper Florida Keys in about nine hours.

Reprinted with Reuter permission.

Whenever a writer is working on a message that has an element of oddity about it, care must be taken to ensure that people are not portrayed as freakish or unnatural. For example, a story on the largest baby born in the county in thirty years may not need to be written at all.

Emotional Impact

Writers are recognizing more and more that people like stories that affect them emotionally. The value also is called human interest and universal appeal. It's the quality that draws audiences to children, young people, and pets.

Think about your own interests. In looking at a page of a company newsletter, the photo of children and balloons at the company picnic will probably have more appeal than the picture of the president presenting a $5,000 check to the local PTA president.

Consider a story, with accompanying photographs, of children at a petting zoo:

—The animals came by twosy, twosy, twosy—goats, sheep, ducks and a wallaroo.

And there were Jim and Angie, the monkeys; Goldie and Scarlett, the macaws; and Ralph, the chimpanzee.

People also like stories tied to love and romance. The article about a couple who both are line workers for a local utility company has great appeal. Including that aspect in the lead will attract readers.

Remember the Audience

In applying news values, writers must think about what is important to their audience. Knowing the audience determines the lead and also affects how the writer will rank information.

For example, a college community audience hears the former mayor speak in a lecture series. What he says looks like this in the college newspaper's lead:

—Students play a vital role in boosting the town's economy when they shop at downtown businesses, Mayor Leo Ryan said Wednesday.

The primary audience for the college newspaper is students.

What he said has a different focus for the lead in the town's general-circulation newspaper:

—Town and college administrators need to develop a joint long-range plan that will address growth, particularly along the campus perimeter, during the next 20 years, Mayor Leo Ryan said Wednesday night.

A general-interest audience, primarily made up of town residents, would be more interested in what the mayor said that affected them directly.

Sorting It Out

At this point you are educated about the elements of a lead, but you still are unclear about what goes first. That sorting process is learned best through practice.

Let's walk through the process.

You are a writer in a bank's corporate communications department. In three months, the company will open a fitness center for employees. The center will be in the old YMCA building next door to corporate headquarters.

You are to write a news release for the local newspaper. Make your list of elements, and do the necessary research to gather any needed information. When you have finished, your list looks like this.

Who: Amana Savings and Loan.
What: Will open a fitness center.
Where: Next door to corporate headquarters in the old YMCA.
When: In three months.
Why: To improve employee health. To provide a benefit to employees.
How: By renovating the old YMCA.

Now look at the news values. Ask whether each applies and if so, how.

Prominence: No.

Timeliness: Yes. Within three months.

Proximity: Yes. In downtown.

Impact: Yes. The renovation will mean local jobs and other economic benefits to the town. It will affect the lives of the company's 450 employees and the townspeople who have been wondering what will happen to the old YMCA.

Magnitude: Yes. The acquisition and renovation will cost the company almost $1 million.

Conflict: No. Shareholders approved the expenditure at the annual meeting.

Audience: Townspeople.

*Emotional
impact:*   Could be for people who remember using the old YMCA.

In writing the lead for the news release, you as the writer must consider the audience—the townspeople—and ask, "What will they want to know first?" The answer is the timeliness of the renovation. The renovation is new news.

A first draft of the lead might read like this:

—Amana Savings and Loan will spend $1 million to renovate the vacant YMCA downtown on Sycamore Street to create an employee fitness center that will open within three months.

Here you have answered *who, what, when,* and *where.* You also have addressed the magnitude of the project.

The second paragraph will answer *why* and *how,* and the third paragraph will explain impact.

—The bank will renovate the old YMCA building to provide a convenient way for employees to remain physically fit, said employee manager Kay Barnes. The bank will use the existing layout and install new equipment and furnishings.

The project will mean additional jobs during the renovation and later when the center opens, Barnes noted.

General Rules for Leads

No matter what type of lead you choose to write, all leads have common features.

Leads should be short. As a guide, some writers use no more than thirty words. Many wire service stories have leads no longer than twenty words in the first sentence or paragraph. If one word or phrase works, use it.

—Native American.

Matthew Moore checked that box on his admission application to the University of Michigan two years ago, and got four years of free tuition worth $15,000 and a coveted student research job in a computer lab.

Leads should be concise and to the point. Writers must eliminate unnecessary words. Look at the following lead and see what has been eliminated in the rewrite and how the focus has changed:

—Two 14-year-old boys have been arrested and charged with breaking and entering and cruelty to animals after a local day care center was broken into last night and property vandalized, toys overturned and a pet rabbit, named Ray, killed with a nearby broom.

Rewritten:

—Vandals who broke into a local day care center Wednesday night, killed the center's pet rabbit with a broom, overturned toys and damaged property.

Two 14-year-old boys have been charged with breaking into Hillside Day Care Center and with cruelty to animals in the death of the center's pet rabbit, Ray.

Words should be precise and in the general vocabulary. Examples in the Native American lead are "box," "free," "job," and "lab." The words in the following Associated Press lead are precise and show the impact:

LAND O'LAKES, Fla.—When 3-year-old Mikey Spoul took his father's car for a joyride last month and explained "I go zoom," the act grabbed national attention and even became fodder for late-night show monologue jokes.

But nobody's laughing now. Mikey torched his bedroom curtains with a cigarette lighter and burned down his family's home, authorities said.

Leads should use active verbs. Consider the verbs in the lead example above: "grabbed," "torched," and "burned down," or the verbs in this lead:

—A Forest City man smashed the glass door on a Laundromat washing machine and yanked a 3-year-old child from the swirling waters Saturday morning.

Leads should be simple sentences, not rambling, convoluted sentences. No one wants to work too hard at understanding most communication. The writer has lost if the "huh?" factor enters in. That's when a person has to stop and reread a lead to understand what the writer is saying.

Compare the simple lead about the Forest City man with this more convoluted lead:

—Under a handgun-control plan, announced by state and county grass-roots organizations Monday, a person who sells a handgun to an unlicensed customer would be liable to a victim for three times his losses if that handgun is used to commit a crime.

Apply what you have learned about leads so far to untangle this report on controlling handguns. What's the point? Some grassroots organizations have come up with an idea for making handgun salespeople more responsible for crime.

What does the audience have to know? How about this lead:

—If a local citizens group gets its way, people who sell guns will help pay for the lives and property lost in handgun crimes.

Summary Leads

Writers base the structure of their leads on the type of story and the audience. Some information, such as police reports, lend themselves to summary leads. Other material works better in a descriptive or anecdotal lead.

The most common lead format is a summary lead that tells or summarizes the most important information:

—Four Northern High School students have received National Merit Scholarships.

—To reduce attrition, Telstar Corp. will build an on-site day care center that will enroll 125 children of its employees in May.

The summary lead serves the audience who skims newspaper stories, company newsletters, or handouts from school; who listens with one ear to radio news reports and one ear to the kids in the backseat of the car; or who casually tunes into the morning television news while getting dressed. Because of the crowded field of communication today, summary leads are used often to give people information quickly.

Summary leads are useful. They can be the introduction of a letter, the hook of a news story, the beginning of a news release, or the headline of a broadcast story.

Beyond One Paragraph

Although most summary leads consist of one sentence or one paragraph, they may be longer. Leads can be longer if they are clear and easy to understand.

Look at this lead from the *News & Observer* in Raleigh, North Carolina.

—On the big Monopoly board of radioactive waste disposal, Chem-Nuclear Systems Inc. seemed to have passed "go" last month.

That's when the company submitted a license application for its proposed radioactive waste repository in southwest Wake County and was expecting to receive a $2 million bonus from a state authority.

But the company might have skipped a few spaces. After thumbing through Chem-Nuclear's license application, the N.C. Division of Radiation Protection has determined that the 6,000-page document doesn't include at least 13 key pieces of information.

The writer sets up a complicated subject through a clever use of the familiar Monopoly game. Readers know in the third paragraph that there is a problem, a potential conflict. They are hit with an "oh, my" thought: How could a 6,000-page document leave out anything?

Also note the use of the verb "thumbed." The verb gives the sense of scanning the hefty document, and it makes readers curious to know whether a closer look would reveal more missing pieces.

A writer in a company's corporate communications department needs to tell employees about changes in the benefits package. She must do so in a way that is informative, pertinent, and clear.

—Long Branch Entertainment employees will see in their paychecks Feb. 1 some changes that represent good news and bad news.

The good news is the company's health insurance company has reduced the annual deductible from $500 to $250 per person per year.

The bad news is each employee with a family plan will pay $10.16 more a month in insurance premiums and employees with individual plans $6.32 more a month.

The three-paragraph summary lead contains information essential to employees: reduced pay if they use the company's health insurance plan. The writer wanted employees to know right away that they were about to be hit in the pocketbook and why. Employees who want to know more about how and why the changes occurred will continue to read the message.

Multiple-Elements Leads

The Long Branch lead also illustrates how a writer presents more than one aspect to a message. Often a lead has multiple elements or more than one point it must convey to readers. A multiple-elements lead summarizes information for readers and sets up what will be covered in the rest of the copy. It presents a challenge to the writer, who must be wary of complex or convoluted sentences. The best approach is to rank the elements, put the most important in the first sentence, and then create a second or third paragraph to present the other points.

> —A group of University students has presented a list of concerns to Chancellor Paula Walls, asking foremost that the University allow 24-hour visitation in women's dormitories.
>
> The letter, hand delivered to Walls Wednesday, also asks the administration to name more minority students to campus-wide committees, to recruit minority faculty members, and to put a ceiling on student fees.

From this lead, readers have the most important information first: the list of demands and the high-priority demand. And they know the content and structure of the message.

Delayed-Identification Leads

Another type of summary lead is the delayed-identification, or sometimes called blind, lead. When an individual or individuals in a news story carry no prominence, their proper names are not given in the first paragraph. Rather, they are identified by a generic label: "An Orange County woman died when . . ." or "A Lockwood High School student has been named a National Merit Scholarship winner. . . ." Immediately, in the next paragraph, the individual is named. If more than one person is in the lead or first paragraph, the individuals are renamed in that order in the next paragraph.

Consider this:

> —An Orange County woman died Tuesday night when she lost control of her car and it overturned on Highway 125 near here.
>
> Sarah Louise McFee, 29, of Rt. 6, Box 34, Lewisville, was dead on arrival at University Hospitals.

Or this:

—One of two local fishermen who spent two days floating in life preservers in the Atlantic Ocean was released from the hospital Sunday, while his companion remained in good condition.

George Livermore, 37, of Cedar Grove left University Hospital after being under observation for two days. Colin West, 35, also of Cedar Grove, is expected to be released by the end of the week.

Other Lead Formats

Although the summary lead is the most useful, writers sometimes find other lead formats better suited to the kind of message they need to send. Some types of leads, such as anecdotal or descriptive, are popular in newspapers and magazines today. They can be risky because they don't hook readers soon enough. They must therefore be well written to entice readers to stay long enough to find out what the message is about.

In general, when using other lead formats, make sure you get to the point by the fourth paragraph. Otherwise, you may lose your reader. If you are writing for a newspaper, the story may have jumped or the end moved to another page before the reader ever gets to the point.

Let's evaluate some types of alternative leads.

Anecdotal Leads

Writers use anecdotal leads to put a human element into their messages. These leads can be particularly effective because they tell a story and have a plot themselves. Although they delay the point of the message, they set up complex problems and their effects on individuals.

Consider this lead in the *Philadelphia Inquirer* by Pulitzer Prize-winning writer David Zucchino:

—Someone is knocking, quite gently, at the door.

"Who?" asks the gatekeeper of a shooting gallery near Cambria Street, where a man with a syringe tucked behind his ear is mixing heroin with water in a bottle cap.

A woman's voice answers, "Angela!"

The gatekeeper lifts a wooden barricade and the door swings open. A slender woman named Angela and her wild-haired friend Maureen bound through the breezeway, smiling and waving, intent on getting high. They have just spent $10 each at Fourth and Cambria Streets for two blue glassine bags of "Mercedes" heroin.

Soon needles are in the women's arms and heroin is coursing through their veins. Their heads droop and their eyes glaze and they are at peace. A few hours will pass before they must again shoplift to raise the cash to buy the drugs that lure them back to Cambria Street.

The daily journey of this pair of heroin addicts from their homes in New Jersey to a shooting gallery in North Philadelphia is a shopping trip. It is an expedition made thousands of times a year by thousands of drug customers, whose cash lubricates the economy of a place some narcotics officers call the Badlands.

The illegal drug trade pumps at least $250 million in cash a year into a three-square-mile swath of North Philadelphia anchored by the Badlands, the Drug Enforcement Administration estimates.

Reprinted with permission of *The Philadelphia Inquirer.*

Zucchino takes seven paragraphs before he specifically tells us that his story is about illegal drugs, though most readers have a good idea by the second paragraph. The lead uses two women and how their lives are affected by drugs. The simple writing and description are compelling and pull the reader further into the story.

Descriptive Leads

Like an anecdotal lead, a descriptive lead puts emotion or a human element into a message. It sets the scene for the reader. Consider the *Herald-Sun* lead into this story:

DURHAM—A crowd of curious children and adults gathered on the lawn and street in front of an apartment complex at 1108 Drew St. as homicide investigators began their work once again Saturday afternoon.

At the top of the stairs, the body of a man in his late 20s lay half inside an apartment, blood pooling beneath his head, a baseball cap still clenched tightly in his hand. Blood streaks ran down the glass of the open door.

But before officers could finish snapping photos and questioning witnesses, shots rang out from across the road on North Hyde Park Street.

Toddlers screamed and the crowd ducked for cover behind patrol cars as several men ran out of an apartment, guns blazing as they fired at random. Someone yelled, "Get the kids out of the street!" as people fled inside, slamming doors.

The gun-wielding men jumped in a car and sped toward Alston Avenue, scattering people caught in the street as they left.

Question Leads

Question leads should be avoided. They are rarely successful. In most cases, they are the lazy writer's way out, and they turn off audiences. In almost every case, they give the audience the option to turn elsewhere.

Look at this *Fort Worth Star-Telegram* lead:

WASHINGTON—Want to see a pained expression on Lloyd Bentsen's face?

Before reading the second paragraph, a reader might say, "No," and go to another message. Or the reader might ask, "Who's Lloyd Bentsen?" In either case, the writer has lost his reader.

```
Did you ever wonder how a church steeple is painted?
```

The reader's answer could be "No, and I don't care to know."

If you find yourself leaning toward a question lead, think of another angle. The easiest alternative is to turn your question into a short statement and use that as the lead:

```
It takes a rare kind of courage to paint a church steeple.
```

Quotation Leads

Such leads should be used sparingly because rarely does someone sum an entire speech or premise for a decision in one simple quotation. A quotation can be used if it is short, is relevant to the rest of the message, and does not need any explanation. It must be clear within itself. Look at this lead by a *New York Times* reporter:

LEVITTOWN, N.Y.—"These houses may be small, but they're solid and well-built," said Michael Hale, hauling yet another load of old wood and insulation to the dumpster at the curb.

Hale, a printer by day, has been spending his nights and weekends stripping the interior of the house at 20 Farm Lane so he can remodel it.

The house was built nearly half a century ago by William Levitt, the Long Island developer regarded by many historians as the man who made suburbia affordable to the middle class.

Copyright © 1994 by The New York Times Company. Reprinted by permission.

The quotation lead here leaves the reader hanging. Readers may not identify the Levittown dateline with William Levitt, the revolutionary homebuilder who died in January 1994. And they may not know that Levitt was credited with making home ownership available to many middle-class families after World War II. A reader may wonder why Hale is hauling wood if the houses are so well built. The quotation would have been more meaningful if Hale had been examining beams rather than dumping trash.

A partial quotation could be used effectively, as in this example from the Associated Press:

—Smoking and drug use among U.S. teenagers are increasing after a decade of decline, a study showed Monday, and its author warned that "the stage is set for a potential resurgence of cocaine and crack use."

Affective Leads

Many newspapers have developed a lead style that focuses on people. A story about a big social or economic problem can lead with one person to illustrate how individuals are affected. The lead makes readers feel the abstract on an interpersonal and even emotional level. The abstract then becomes real.

Look at these two examples.

Associated Press reporter Tina Susman wrote the following lead:

KEMPTON PARK, South Africa—Faith Nkosi falls into probably the most oppressed group of South Africans: She is black, female and a domestic worker.

But when she stands on a stage in her apron and aims her piercing voice at a crowd, the cheers prove she is more than a maid.

Nkosi, head of the Domestic Workers' Union, is among a growing number of women who are entering the political limelight to make sure they are not forgotten after the April elections.

The larger issue here is women who are domestic workers.

Patrice Gaines wrote in *The Washington Post:*

—Keith Ricardo Walker Jr. is an invisible man.

His life is not described by crime statistics. He does not use or deal drugs. He has never fired a gun or been fired at. He is not a high school dropout. He has never been to jail.

Walker, 20, is like the millions of young black men who do not distinguish themselves as either geniuses or felons but live ordinary lives—often against the same odds that have beaten their friends. In a city where so much is said about delinquent youth, the Keith Walkers go unnoticed.

Gaines' story is about young black men. Walker is just one of them.

The key to using the affective lead is to keep it short and get to the point right away. Writers must quickly reveal the social or economic issue the message is about.

Direct Address Leads

The direct address lead talks straight to the reader or consumer. It usually gives advice or has a "hey, you" aspect to it.

—If you haven't had your car inspected this month, you need to do it soon. The fee for state-required inspections will double July 1.

Staccato Leads

A series of single words identifies a staccato lead. It can be used for news, feature stories, or almost any kind of message.

—Popcorn. Peanuts. Candy.

All those good things you buy at the movies will cost you more in local theaters starting Sunday.

Choosing a Lead Type

In many cases the information will dictate the type of lead. A crime story, for example, generally will use a summary lead. A story on a city council meeting will need a multiple-elements lead to cover the council's different actions. Lack of prominence will dictate a delayed-identification lead. But sometimes a writer must ponder and decide which lead will set up the story best.

Look at this Associated Press lead about a 911 operator:

NEW YORK—"You want the police to your house because your mother didn't come home?"

It's nearly 7 p.m. on a Wednesday in the weeks before Christmas and somewhere in New York City, two scared young girls watch the clock more frightened by the minute. They call 911 and reach Ivey Bruce.

Her voice is soothing and steady. "OK, what apartment are you in? And what's the telephone number? And how old are you and your sister?"

As she speaks Bruce types on a battered gray computer. The figures 10 and 11 appear on her screen, then "HOME ALONE." Another tap of a key speeds the girls' telephonic SOS to a police dispatcher in a nearby room.

Bruce, a 45-year-old mother of two sons, nods as if to reassure the unseen child and then tells her police will be there soon.

Like a novel half read, a mystery never solved, this story has no end for Bruce. After 14 years on the job, she knows that's as it must be.

It's only suppertime in New York, and by the end of her 3:30 P.M. to 11:30 P.M. shift, this 911 operator will have heard accounts of panic and terror by the score.

Systems vary widely, from the hectic and gargantuan New York operation that will field an estimated 10.1 million calls in 1994 to rural systems where response time is measured in hours, not seconds.

But everywhere, this nearly ubiquitous lifeline—a 1993 Federal Communications Commission report found 911 service available in 89 percent of the country—rests on individuals like Ivey Bruce, police operator 1784.

The writer chose a long, anecdotal lead to set up a story about 911 operators. The story specifically follows one operator, Ivey Bruce, before it gives information about 911 services. By focusing on one typical call, the writer lets readers know how a 911 operator reacts to a call and interacts with the caller. The writer could have written a lead that said

> NEW YORK—The hectic and gargantuan New York City 911 service will field an estimated 10.1 million calls in 1994.
>
> The system represents a lifeline found in 89 percent of the country, according to a 1993 Federal Communications Commission report. The success of the operator rests largely with the 911 operators, who answer scores of accounts of panic and terror during their shifts.

Which lead works? The one with the human element will draw more people into the story than one that tosses out numbers. The faces behind the digits set up the story, and readers know by the end of the second paragraph that the key elements are 911, operators, Ivey Bruce, and calls.

Does It Work?

Once you have written a lead, scrutinize it, keeping in mind the guidelines in the leads checklist at the end of the chapter. Consider this lead from an athletic department newsletter:

> —Anyone with a pulse has thought about it.
>
> Hitting the winning shot. Driving in the go-ahead run. Sinking the clinching putt. Serving up an ace on match point.
>
> It's your own personal canonization as the country's newest sports deity. There you stand, a ball of sweat, embracing the crowd as it madly descends upon you . . .

As the reader, what do you think the story is about? The lead says that the story will cover those moments in sports when an individual's actions clinch the win. That's what the "it" in the lead implies: the shining thrill of athletic prowess.

Wrong. The story is about media training for athletes. Here's the full lead into the story. See how far the reader must go to find out what the story is really about.

> —Anyone with a pulse has thought about it.

Hitting the winning shot. Driving in the go-ahead run. Sinking the clinching putt. Serving up an ace on match point.

It's your own personal canonization as the country's newest sports deity. There you stand, a ball of sweat, embracing the crowd as it madly descends upon you. But your celebration is immediately interrupted by a grinning face with immovable hair that shoves a microphone in your face and asks that all too deep and penetrating question.

"So, uh, how do you feel?"

Then you wake up. Your celebration was cut short but, hey, at least your psyche was smart enough to dodge that interrogation. The real athletes aren't as fortunate.

"That [question] comes up a lot, though it's usually a less experienced reporter," Dr. Celia Hooper says. "For instance, Charlotte Smith still gets that question about the shot she made. If I were her I'd get sick of that."

Hundreds of athletes enter UNC each year, most unaccustomed to the media crunch that follows what is currently the most successful athletic program in the nation. Some embrace their newfound attention; some abhor it. But since the Charlotte Smiths on campus really can't escape the media microscope, Hooper, a professor at Carolina's Division of Speech and Hearing Sciences, has started a Communications Skills Group for UNC athletes.

The reader learns at the end of paragraph 7—a long paragraph—what the story is about: a communications skills group for athletes.

The first two paragraphs are a good lead—if the story were about those glory moments set up in paragraph 2. The writer has a good topic, but the lead is misleading. The writer has no need to create an imaginary scenario when he has Smith and her team as examples. A rewrite would begin this way:

```
When the UNC-Chapel Hill women's basketball team won the
national title last year, Charlotte Smith was unprepared
for the avalanche of media attention...
```

In the first sentence, the revised lead, poses the problem of media attention for those who are unaccustomed to the limelight. Readers will continue to read and to look for a solution, and at the same time they will know more about Charlotte Smith.

Leads Should Do the Job

Remember to read through your stories carefully and ensure that your leads are honest: that they have set up for the reader what the story covers. Review the checklist below. Readers will be disappointed if they believe that a story is about one topic and discover that it is about another. Writers will lose credibility if they make false promises in their leads.

You can become a good lead writer, whatever the copy, by focusing on what is important to your audience, learning the guidelines of good writing, and reading good leads that are specific and present information accurately, clearly, and concisely. Look for such leads in everything you read.

The lead is the first step in writing your message. Completing the job will be discussed in Chapter 4.

Leads Checklist

Essential Lead Elements
1. I have looked at the facts and decided which are the most important.
2. My initial sentence is simple and complete.
3. My lead is accurate.
4. My lead is relevant to my audience.
5. My lead comes to the point, is well edited, and makes sense.
6. I have used understandable, fresh words and strong, active verbs.
7. My lead sets up the story.

Desirable Elements
1. I have emphasized the latest information.
2. I have included unusual aspects of the message.
3. If possible, I have put a local angle to show how the information relates to readers.
4. I have kept my lead short and readable: no longer than 30 words.
5. My lead attracts the audience's attention.
6. My lead summarizes the message.

EXERCISES

1. Read the following lead. Identify the elements and the news values present.

   —A Forest City man smashed the glass door on a Laundromat washing machine and yanked a 3-year-old child from the swirling waters yesterday morning.

   Sammy Smithers, 27, rescued Tammy Childers after she climbed into a washing machine and the machine started running. The child had some cuts and bruises and was listed in good condition at Mayview Hospital.

   Elements:

   Who:

   What:

   When:

   Where:

   Why:

   How:

   News Values (identify only those present; not all will be):

   Conflict:

   Timeliness:

   Proximity:

   Prominence:

   Magnitude:

   Impact:

   Audience:

   Oddity:

   Emotion:

2. Read the following lead. Identify the elements and the news values present.

The American Heart Association now offers a cookbook specifically designed to encourage children to discover the wonderful world of cooking and to develop healthy eating habits early in life.

The kid-tested and -approved *American Heart Association Kids' Cookbook* is geared to healthy children ages 8–12. The cost is $15.95.

Elements:

Who:

What:

When:

Where:

Why:

How:

News Values (identify only those present; not all will be):

Conflict:

Timeliness:

Proximity:

Prominence:

Magnitude:

Impact:

Audience:

Oddity:

Emotion:

3. Read the following lead. Identify the elements and the news values present.

WASHINGTON—The Federal Reserve, concerned that the economic recovery may fuel inflation, took action that raised interest rates Friday for the first time in five years, signaling an end to an era of declining loan costs and sending a shiver through Wall Street.

Elements:

Who:

What:

When:

Where:

Why:

How:

News Values (identify only those present; not all will be):

Conflict:

Timeliness:

Proximity:

Prominence:

Magnitude:

Impact:

Audience:

Oddity:

Emotion:

4. Read the following lead. Identify the elements and the news values present.

   RENNES, France—Thousands of fishermen battled riot police Friday during a visit by premier Edouard Balladur, prompting government promises to protect the ailing fishing industry from foreign competition.

   Authorities said 61 people—25 police officers and 36 protesters and bystanders—were treated for injuries they suffered in day-long clashes in Rennes.

Elements:

Who:

What:

When:

Where:

Why:

How:

News Values (identify only those present; not all will be):

Conflict:

Timeliness:

Proximity:

Prominence:

Magnitude:

Impact:

Audience:

Oddity:

Emotion:

5. Read the following lead.

> —Raymond Lineberger looked as if he were asleep. He was curled up on the sofa, his back to the television set tuned to a local game show. A red and green plaid blanket covered the lower part of his legs and his feet. He wore khaki pants and a red knit shirt.
>
> A bullet had pierced the side of his head. Lineberger was dead.
>
> Emma Jean Lineberger has been charged with first-degree murder in her husband's death.

What is the point of the story?

Has the writer considered the audience?

Rewrite the lead to focus on the point and what the audience needs to know.

6. Look at the information for the following two stories. List for each exercise *who, what, when, where, how* and *why*. Identify the news values and where they apply, then rank them in order of importance. Then write the lead. You are to write only the lead, not the entire story, for each.

> A Super Bowl party was held yesterday in your town. In a fight during half-time, a guest pulled out a gun and fired shots. A mother of 3 children and her niece were shot and killed. They were in a house at 143 Elm St. with about 20 other guests and party-goers in attendance. They died instantly from the wounds. Police have a suspect but have made no arrests and have no motive.

Elements:

Who:

What:

When:

Where:

Why:

How:

News Values (number them 1–9 in order of importance, 1 being most important):

Conflict:

Timeliness:

Proximity:

Prominence:

Magnitude:

Impact:

Audience:

Oddity:

Emotion:

Lead for Shooting:

> The Armored Car Co. has a plant in your town. It employs
> 350 people. It has been operating in the town for 12
> years. It has been hit by recessionary times and has
> announced it will lay off half its work force during the
> next six months. The company has plans to relocate or
> secure jobs for all displaced workers. A special
> committee has been established to work with fired
> employees. The company wouldn't say whether more
> employees eventually will be fired.

Elements:

Who:

What:

When:

Where:

Why:

How:

News Values (number them 1–9 in order of importance, 1 being most important):

Conflict:

Timeliness:

Proximity:

Prominence:

Magnitude:

Impact:

Audience:

Oddity:

Emotion:

Lead for Armored Car Co.:

4

Organization for Print

Once writers have fashioned the lead, they face the task of organizing the rest of the message. They must decide what will come after the first sentences or paragraphs that hook the audience. The ranking decisions discussed in Chapter 3 that help them write the lead are invaluable in helping them develop the body of the message. Again, with audience needs and interests in mind, the writer outlines how the message will evolve.

As mentioned in Chapter 3, journalists have traditionally used the inverted pyramid form of writing to get to the point quickly and to set priorities for basic news stories. The principle behind the inverted pyramid style—to order information according to its value to the audience—is valuable in much writing today, whether it is for church newsletters, e-mail messages, news releases, or magazine articles. The process of ordering information for the inverted pyramid involves critical thinking, an important skill for writers.

Different styles of writing may be more suitable for other audiences or for a particular medium. Students will find various styles as they read print publications: newspapers, magazines, company newsletters. If you find yourself reading a story from start to end, clip it, and study it to identify the elements that pulled you into and through the message, then save it. Some day you may want to adopt the style for a written piece of your own.

This chapter discusses

- The inverted pyramid form of writing,
- News peg and nut graph,
- Other organizational styles, and
- How to unify writing.

The Inverted Pyramid

Leads must get to the point quickly, and messages must provide important information right behind the lead. Newspaper editors have recognized that need for decades. Henry A. Stokes, assistant managing editor for projects at the *Commercial Appeal* in Memphis, Tennessee, wrote in a staff memo in 1989 that because newspapers were competing against other media, primarily radio and television, they had to ensure that stories attracted reader attention.

Stokes told staff writers that they were to "tell the news in an identifiable, functional format that guarantees the reader will receive the best information we can provide, written in a way that the reader can quickly and easily understand."

As a result, the newspaper adopted the four-paragraph rule: Tell the essential message in four paragraphs of reasonable length: the first four paragraphs of the story. Details—that could be cut—would follow.

The format that Stokes advocated was the inverted pyramid style of writing, long a standard in journalism. With the inverted pyramid, information in a message is organized in descending order of importance. The most important and compelling information comes first and is followed by information of lesser value. To be successful at using the inverted pyramid, writers must be able to evaluate and rank information, and they must know what is most important to their audiences.

This model shows how the inverted pyramid works:

Lead summarizes information. Next few paragraphs back up lead.

    Next section provides background and additional important information.

        Next section has information of lesser importance about the topics introduced in the lead.

            Final section contains least important information that could be cut.

In the inverted pyramid, the lead paragraph or paragraphs summarize the most important news values and elements and set up the message. The next paragraph or paragraphs usually give additional crucial information that won't fit into the first paragraph. Background information comes next. From there, subsequent paragraphs develop the topics presented in the lead, introduce other important information, expand the significance of the information, and give details.

Each section will vary in length, depending on what the writer has introduced in the lead and whether he or she is building the message with quotations. A writer may devote four or five paragraphs to dialogue from a meeting before moving on to support other actions set forth in the lead paragraph.

The inverted pyramid format helps a writer organize information logically, whether the topic is a single subject or has multiple subjects or elements. If the writer plans to develop several issues in the message, the summary multiple-elements lead would set up the organization in the following way:

—The Rockland City Council voted unanimously Tuesday night to renew the city manager's contract for three years and to annex 325 acres south of Lewisville and Maxton roads.

Through the inverted pyramid, the writer sets up the order of importance in the lead and how the message will be organized. The most important item is the city manager's contract, which includes a pay raise. Because no one objected to the annexation of acreage, it carries less importance because it is not controversial. It can be discussed second. The important point, the action of annexation, is contained in the lead. The rest of the story follows the lead like this:

—In discussing City Manager Larry Morgan's new contract, council members agreed that Morgan had done an exemplary job in his six years as manager.

"We couldn't find anyone better," said council member Dick Haynes, who made the motion to give Morgan a 10 percent pay raise in the first year of the contract and 5 percent in the second and third years.

"We have maintained quality town services with only modest tax increases while Larry has been here," added council member Loretta Manson.

The council voted to annex the Heather Hills subdivision following a public hearing in which no one objected to the annexation plan. Residents who spoke said they wanted to come under the town's water and sewer services and to gain improved fire and police protection.

The inverted pyramid is more than just an organizational tool. It has been identified traditionally as a writing style that uses simple words, short sentences, and one idea to a paragraph. It also represents critical thinking: it forces writers to evaluate information and rank it in order of importance. Some critics have said that the inverted pyramid puts pressure on reporters to craft an attention-getting, information-packed lead, leaving them little time to follow through with a well-organized message. To be successful, writers must do both: write a compelling lead and organize a story logically. In reality, time constraints or deadline pressure may interfere with both functions.

Why the Inverted Pyramid for Media Writing?

Newspapers traditionally have used the inverted pyramid format for two primary reasons: to give readers the most critical material quickly so they can move to other stories if they wish, and to allow a story to be cut easily from the bottom, leaving important information intact at the top of the story.

Many beginning writers question why they should follow the inverted pyramid style of writing when they plan careers in public relations, advertising, or marketing. They object to what they see as a rigid way of writing or formula writing—a basic format devoid of creativity.

At first glance, the objections seem true. But as students use the inverted pyramid they will discover plenty of opportunity for description and for their own style to develop. As they will learn, the critical thinking that goes along with the inverted pyramid style fits the writing process outlined in Chapter 1. For the inverted pyramid, writers must gather information, list or rank information, write a draft, and rewrite.

John Sweeney, an associate professor in the School of Journalism and Mass Communication at the University of North Carolina at Chapel Hill, teaches advertising courses. He advises all students, no matter what their major, on the value of learning the inverted pyramid structure.

In demonstrating the value, he shows copies of painter Pablo Picasso's readily identifiable abstract artworks. He then exhibits Picasso's earlier works, in which Picasso used traditional craftsmanship in form, color, and style, pointing out that Picasso didn't develop his trademark style until after he had mastered basic art techniques. Writing requires the same discipline, Sweeney contends.

"Before you can develop your own style, you have to master the basics," he says. "You have to be taught to be meticulous. To say it succinctly, concisely, precisely. You have to be able to distill information, whether it's a 30-second spot or a piece of newswriting or an ad distilled from a 100-page document on product data.

"Writing also has to have access: Anyone can read it and understand it," Sweeney advises. "You have to focus on what's key, get to the heart of the matter, and put the issue in perspective."

The inverted pyramid thus aids writers in conveying information quickly and succinctly. Stokes recognized the logic of using the inverted pyramid in the dawning information age when busy consumers were—and still are—bombarded with messages. For his paper, the four-paragraph byte had to do the job.

The Inverted Pyramid for Other Formats

Assistant professor Jacqueline Farnan and newspaper copy editor David Hedley noted in their research that the inverted pyramid remains the basic format for breaking news and that many newspapers have found it difficult to abandon the style. Their research supports the belief that the inverted pyramid retains value today, when the majority of messages are becoming shorter—many being no longer than a dozen paragraphs. The shorter length is tied to economics; it is costly to send a lot of words.

Consider broadcast messages, which usually begin with a short, catchy headline to grab the viewer's attention and then summarize the main points. Because broadcast news stories are short, it is imperative for TV and radio reporters to fit in as many compelling facts as possible in the few seconds allotted. The inverted pyramid allows for the speedy, information-rich writing that broadcast demands.

Corporate communications and nonprofit agencies, whether staffed by professionals or volunteers, more and more follow the traditional inverted pyramid style. It puts their agenda where readers and editors can see it. Even advertising depends on the inverted pyramid style, communicating to consumers in an abbreviated way a product's qualities and the reasons for buying it. Brevity is essential: Every word and second costs the client money.

The inverted pyramid can fit most kinds of media writing and other kinds of writing in the real world—even the garden club's minutes. While it works best in shorter pieces, it can be adapted for longer, more complex pieces, many of which use the inverted pyramid format early and then other organizational patterns later. For example, nondeadline pieces, such as feature stories and documentaries, attract readers best by getting to the point and summarizing first. Simple pyramiding in nondeadline writing can attract readers by creating a mood, setting the stage for more detailed information or providing a memorable image.

Feature writer Greta Tilley, reporting on a lengthy press luncheon with President Ronald Reagan, opened with a six-word lead: "The president doesn't dye his hair." Her pyramid continued with details of luncheon conversation. Tilley's article follows:

Do You Ask the President to Pass the Salt?

BY GRETA TILLEY
Staff Writer

WASHINGTON—The president doesn't dye his hair.

It is not blue black or sunrise red or shoe polish brown or any other color that the people who describe presidents talk about it being, and it doesn't flounce about in flamboyant pompadour waves like you see in the cartoons.

Ronald Reagan's hair is a subdued black at its darkest, and his cut is on the short side.

There are too many gray hairs to count during a one-hour lunch in the White House; too many to count even if there wasn't anything better to do. Mention this to the president and he thanks you the way he might if you had surprised him with a prize Arabian stallion to ride in the hills above Santa Barbara.

"All these references to dyeing my hair go all the way back to when I was governor," he says. "I not only never dyed my hair, I never even wore makeup in any of my pictures. Cary Grant never wore makeup, either. If your beard doesn't show, you don't need it. I don't need TV makeup."

The president puts the proof on the table. He bends down, lowers his head and volunteers to have it examined.

"You know what dyed hair looks like," he says, holding still as a Marine at morning muster. "Now, take a good look at the roots and tell me what you think."

An impulsive move to touch the president's hair freezes a few inches above his head. The instructions from the press assistant were not to grab the president's hand, not to solicit an autograph for Aunt Hilda and not to beg for a private audience. Surely his hair would be off-limits, too. Mothers don't enjoy watching their daughters being dragged off handcuffed to the Secret Service on the six o'clock news.

By the time it would take to get back in, lunch would be over.

Eating consommé Celestine next to the president of the United States in the State Dining Room isn't the same as gulping clam chowder and a frankfurter delight with the girls at the Irving Park Delicatessen.

The noodles are hard to capture gracefully and harder to swallow. A lipstick mark on the water glass stands out like the Scarlet Letter. No one else leaves a grape tottering on the edge of the sterling silver serving platter after taking a helping of wild rice amandine.

Maybe White House dining is what makes the president's cheeks rosy without makeup. He says it is getting fit early in life and sticking with it later.

"Nothing is better for the inside of a man," he says, "than the outside of a horse."

You want to know how he's going to ride the range since the doctor ordered no more sun after two skin cancers on the nose, but these kinds of questions are considered trivial by the five other reporters at the table.

They have been invited from all over the place for something bureaucratically known as a budget briefing, which means they are supposed to find out more than what they have read in the newspaper about the administration's newest tact to rein in the national deficit.

They have come so they can tell everyone back home that they have eaten mango mousse with raspberry sauce and the president, and that the only person whose dessert kept sliding away from the spoon was the woman on his left who asked inconsequential questions and took notes on everything from the centerpiece to the chandelier.

("Chandelier huge, ornate and gold, fills center of room, glass enclosed bulbs, too many tiers to count without pointing. Draperies yellow gold brocade, high big windows with lots of space between panels, magnolia outside, snow falling, looks like in movies.

(Centerpiece—flowers look real, are real—tulips, red and what look like pinkish red lilies, cigarettes, filter tips up, and nuts and gold wrapped mints in little silver containers, salem, winston, barclay, rich lights.

("Tablecloth, color of the green crayon you never used in box, and matching napkins folded in pyramid in middle of plate—different wildflowers—10—along inside edge and gold around border, flowered carpet kind of go with plate colors, soft greens and beiges and yellows and blues and grays, chairs covered with little twirled gold bars along back and covered whitish cushion, president should have a bigger chair.")

Actually the president seems smaller than he does on television. When he walks into the room, he looks more like a caricature of himself than a real person, except for the hair. This is probably because the experience of being in the White House with the president still feels unreal.

Variation on Pinstripes

He is wearing hearing aids in both ears and a brown suit with dominant lapels and large stripes. In between the big stripes are smaller stripes in rust and navy blue. Nancy has been quoted as saying she would like to weed out his closet. This suit may be one reason why.

His tie is a solid burgundy, his shirt white, his Italian loafers cordovan-colored. He must have had them awhile because the leather beneath the presidential shine is cracked enough to look comfortable.

The caricature image disappears two or three minutes after the president starts talking. Ronald Reagan is comfortable being Ronald Reagan. He is real.

Yes, he saw his son Ron in his underwear on "Saturday Night Live."

"We were amazed at his good sense of comedy."

No, he doesn't know when he's going to Nevada, home state of the television newswoman on his right.

"I don't even know what I'm doing next week. I learned when I was governor just to wait until they hand you the schedule. Every night I get handed the schedule for the next day and that's when I find out what I'm going to do."

No, he doesn't know who came up with the idea of rolling this year's budget out on a litter and calling it dead on arrival, but he liked it.

"We need more humor in government."

The president says "gov'ment" the way he does on TV. The voice that has been imitated by every impersonator in the business is hoarse but not as strained as it sounds sometimes in news conferences and speeches. It is soothing, almost hypnotic.

His dark blue eyes are his best physical asset. They listen to you talk and respond quickly. The whites are clear except for a spot around the left pupil, perhaps a broken blood vessel. President Reagan's teeth are white and a little bit uneven on the bottom row. His smile doesn't have the look of being manufactured in an assembly line for political parts, then used too much.

President Can Take a Joke

In the ratings game, the president may have two strikes against him as an actor and a politician, but there's no getting around it. He's a decent guy. He doesn't patronize or build security moats with affectation. He doesn't go to war against people who say he is not smart enough or young enough, he has fun talking about his movie acting days, and he can tell or take a joke on himself about as well as anyone.

Lunch tastes good and moves quickly. Everyone is pleasant. The president eats much of the time with his arms on the table, and saves his broccoli until last. The meat dish is Chicken Breast Veronique. The waiter fills the president's glass with Parson's Creek Chardonnay 1981, California, and serves a little less to the ladies on either side. The president sips every now and then but doesn't go overboard. He does most of the talking. He manages to clean his plate, he says later, by talking with his mouth full.

President Reagan likes to tell stories, and weaves them in while answering questions about the Philippines and Haiti and trade deficits and Japanese cars and mandatory retirement and other serious matters that have been reported that morning in *The Washington Post.*

The first few replies make it clear that he isn't going to tell any national secrets.

While on the subject of humor in government, he announces he has a better joke than the one he told on his 75th birthday the week before.

"At my age," he says, "if I ever had to have a transplant, I'd have a real problem. I've got parts they don't make anymore."

"Mr. President, do you get weary of people talking so much about your age?"

He smiles and nods. "That's why I try to beat 'em to it and talk about it myself."

Third Term Should Be Allowed
What if it were legal for a president to run for a third term? Would you try for four more years?

"Not in my case. But if it ever changes, and it should, it would have to be done with the idea that it would start beyond the incumbent. It's counter to our democratic principles to limit a presidential term. We have congressmen and senators who have been here 40 years. Why should people be denied the right to vote for who they want for president?"

So what does a president do after being president?

"Well, there's this ranch I haven't seen in a long time," he says. "And there's a mashed potato circuit I've spent a lot of time on. I expect I'll have opinions that I'll want to pass along. I expect I'll stay busy."

The president said "when I was governor" more than "well." He may have said "well" only once. He referred more than once to the hard times of the Depression. He hadn't heard Clint Eastwood was running for mayor of Carmel, Calif., and was amused when someone suggested the country's favorite tough guy would be appealing to him for federal money.

He put down a medium-sized bite of chicken to tell the joke he had tried on Soviet leader Gorbachev at the summit:

An American and a Russian are arguing about freedom and who has the most of it. The American says to the Russian, "I can go in the Oval Office whenever I want to and pound the president's desk and say, 'I don't like the way you are running the country' and nothing would even happen to me. The Russian turns to the American and says, 'That's nothing. I can do the same thing. I can go in Gorbachev's office whenever I want to and I can pound on his desk and I can say to him, 'I don't like the way Mr. Reagan is running the country,' and nothing will happen to me, either."

The joke sounds better with the right adjectives and phrasing and the president's sense of timing.

Gorbachev laughed. President Reagan was encouraged.

Joking with Gorbachev

He told Gorbachev this true story:

Winston Churchill drank a little too much during an evening meeting with Stalin and couldn't remember the next morning what they had discussed the night before. So when they met later that morning, Churchill turned to Stalin and said, "I wonder if we could review what we were talking about last night."

"Mr. Churchill," Stalin replied, "You don't have anything to worry about. We were all in the same condition last night and I've had the interpreter shot."

Gorbachev liked that one, too.

"I left out the last line," President Reagan says. "Churchill said later, 'You know, to this day I didn't know if Stalin was joking or not.'"

This is the most interesting conversation during the meal. The president says he and Gorbachev got along well. There was good chemistry. He says he told Gorbachev that they represented the two nations in the world that could bring about World War III, and that they also represented the two nations that could prevent it, and that they shared the responsibility to do so.

"This won't work just because we're nice fellows," the president says. "We have to be realistic. He wants to improve his economy for his people. If we can convince him that the way to do this is by reduction of arms so there will be more money for consumer products, we can have peace. But we have to be convinced that they are doing the same things that we are. There can't be deception."

The waiter brings out a towering cream-colored castle of mango mousse crowned with a blossoming white flower. Around the outside of the castle is raspberry sauce circled with slices of kiwi fruit.

Cutting into the mousse is tricky. It shimmies. The kiwi looks good but forboding with memories of the tottering grape from the wild rice amandine. What the heck, it's dessert.

The president begins eating as the men across the table serve themselves. He enjoys dessert, and doesn't always get it.

He is talking about how easy it was to set up the summit meetings for the next two years. It happened after he and Gorbachev spent an hour and a half meeting by the fireplace the first day. The president, through the interpreter, told Gorbachev there were things he wanted to show him in America in 1986.

"I accept," Gorbachev said.

"And there are more things I want to show you in Russia in 1987," Gorbachev said.

"I accept," the president said.

His staff was amazed it happened so simply.

There is one more crisis to face before the meal ends. A finger bowl filled with clear water and a fingery green leaf unidentified on the menu is before each of our plates. If the president used his, he set a record dipping and drying. Still, what to do?

"Let me tell you another joke," the president says, and he does.

Sorry. He made us promise not to tell.

Reprinted with permission from the *News & Record*, Greensboro, North Carolina.

Organizing a Story

The basic work of organizing a message in inverted pyramid style is done when you use the steps outlined in Chapter 3 for writing leads. The writer first identifies news values and the elements to structure a lead. News values and elements introduced in the lead will be developed in greater detail within the message. The writer will use the remaining news values and elements in subsequent paragraphs based on ranking information that is important to audiences.

For example, a news value, such as oddity, may be referred to in a lead but must be developed fully later in the message. Remember the lead in Chapter 3 on the couple who got married as they were skydiving? While readers have the basics from the lead about how the wedding happened, they may want more information about why skydiving was important to that particular couple. The body of the message answers that question.

—A Hollywood, Fla., man and woman exchanged wedding vows at 1,300 feet as they plummeted to earth hand-in-hand under silver parachutes 5 miles west of here Wednesday afternoon.

Grace Mason and John Kempner met while skydiving at a local club and decided it would be the most significant way to start their married life together.

"Skydiving brought us together," said Grace Mason Kempner after the ceremony. "It seemed to be the appropriate way to tie the knot."

She learned to skydive while a student at Dade Community College. Her husband was a paratrooper in the Army. They have known each other two years and have been jumping partners for the last six months.

Each wore a silver jumpsuit, but the bride carried a nosegay of white satin roses.

Applying News Elements and News Values

You can do the process yourself. But first it's important to note a difference between paragraphs in an essay for an English composition or literature class and paragraphs in media writing. In an essay or composition, a paragraph is a whole presentation or argument on a topic. But in mass communication, a paragraph is identified as a single unit of information. It is a solitary fact, thought, or "sound bite" out of the larger message. When a writer is concerned with transmitting information quickly, his or her ideas about paragraphing change.

Journalists rarely use the word "paragraph." Their way of thinking about paragraphing is reflected in their language: short. In the newsroom, a paragraph is a "graph." This abbreviated word symbolizes the abbreviated form that paragraphs take in news stories. A graph (or graf) generally will still have several sentences, but on occasion it may be just one sentence long.

So now let's consider a message about the community theater in a town called Rockland. You are to write a news story about auditions for an upcoming production. The elements *who, what, when, where, how,* and *why* can be easily listed:

Who: Rockland Theater.

What: Will have auditions for the play "Gypsy."

When: 7–9 p.m. Monday and Tuesday.

Where: The Theater at 211 W. Sycamore St.

How: People will read a piece of their own choosing, then one impromptu piece from the director.

Why: So the play can be produced.

Look at the news values we discussed in Chapter 3 and determine which ones apply here. The magnitude of the production and the timeliness of the pending auditions are relevant; news values such as conflict, oddity, and impact may not exist. Prominence is a factor if the lead role will be held by a well-known stage actress and local residents will have the chance to act with her.

You might write this lead:

—Local residents can audition 7 to 9 p.m. Monday and
Tuesday for parts in the Rockland Community Theater's
September production of "Gypsy," which will star stage
actress Rosie O'Donnell.

The lead identifies the elements *who, what,* and *when* as well as the news value of prominence. To handle the overflow from the lead, you must add a second paragraph to answer *where* and to show impact:

—Auditions will be at the theater at 211 W. Sycamore St.
and led by Director Neal Folger. He is looking for 16 local
actors and actresses.

Anyone interested in auditioning has the basic information from the first two paragraphs. In subsequent paragraphs you will expand on the lead, noting that the production also will require a 30-member chorus and explaining what people will have to do during the audition.

You would continue the story:

—Local residents wishing to audition must prepare a song and a part to read, said Folger. Each audition is not to exceed 5 minutes.

People interested in being in a 30-member chorus need prepare only a song not to exceed 3 minutes. They will audition with the music director, Carole Banner.

You have determined that the audience would be most interested in the requirements for auditioning and how to audition. If aspiring actors could not meet the requirements, they would have no need to read further.

Those who are potential actors would want to know more about the selection process and when rehearsals would start. In the final paragraphs, you would state:

—"We will let people know by Friday if they are selected," Folger said. "Rehearsals will start the next week."
—The community theater produces six shows each year. One in the fall and one in the spring have professional actors or actresses.

"Having professional talent promotes the theater and makes the acting experience much more exciting for our local talent," Folger said. "We have had wonderful success in the past, and we expect the same for 'Gypsy.'"

In the last paragraph, you would use the director's quote to wrap up the message and look to the future.

Breaking It Up

Let's look at the story and see how the information was ordered and why.

```
Local residents can audition
7 to 9 p.m. Monday and Tuesday
for parts in the Rockland
Community Theater's Septem-
ber production of "Gypsy,"
which will star stage
actress Rosie O'Donnell.
```

The lead tells *who* can do *what when* and *why*. It also includes the news value prominence of Rosie O'Donnell, which might attract some people to audition.

```
Auditions will be at the the-
ater and led be Director Neal
Folger. He is looking for 16
local actors and actresses.
Local residents wishing to
audition must prepare a song
and a part to read, said
Folger. Each audition is not
to exceed 5 minutes.
```

Graph 2 expands the first graph by telling where folks can audition and what is required during the auditions for the major roles.

People interested in being in a 30-member chorus need prepare a song not to exceed 3 minutes. They will audition with the music director, Carole Banner.

Graph 3 continues to expand the information, giving details about auditions for lesser roles.

"We will let people know by Friday if they are selected," Folger said. "Rehearsals will start the next week."

Graph 4 moves to the next step after auditions: when people will be notified and when rehearsal begins.

The community theater produces six shows each year. Two, one in the fall and one in the spring, have professional actors or actresses.

Graph 5 provides background on the theater and its productions.

"Having professional talent promotes the theater and makes the acting experience much more exciting for our local talent," Folger said. "We have had wonderful success in the past, and we expect the same for 'Gypsy.'"

Graph 6 is a follow-up quote to graph 5. A quote also makes a good ending.

Another Approach: The Second-Day Story

In the story just given, you have followed a traditional inverted pyramid format to announce the auditions. The story represents what could be called a first-day story. In looking at newspaper clips about the Little Theater, you believe another story is warranted. So you decide to do what is called a second-day story that gives new information and also includes background from the first-day story.

The lead and message might go something like this:

—When Director Neal Folger starts auditions for the season opener of the Rockland Community Theater in early August, most board of directors members will be crossing their fingers for a smooth year.

The board hired Folger, the former director of the River Road Theater in Danville, a year ago, and soon the theater was embroiled in controversy. Last year's season opener of "Grease" showed nudity when three performers dropped their pants as part of a song on mooning. This year's season opens Oct. 15.

"We felt we went through a wringer right off the bat last year," board member Mary Tyson said today. "While some people like Neal's productions, most people in our community prefer more traditional entertainment. Nudity just has no place on our stage."

Board member Justin Fellows said the board hoped for a successful season with less turmoil than the previous year.

"We think Neal is quite talented, but we are just a community theater, and we want fun, not indignation," he said.

Folger said he was surprised at the reaction to "Grease."

"I certainly learned what this community will accept on stage," he said. "This year we intend to produce shows that keep people fairly well covered."

Fellows added the board hoped Folger's appealing season lineup will attract a substantial audience to the Rockland Theater.

The director will have auditions for "Gypsy" from 7 to 9 p.m. Monday and Tuesday at the theater at 211 W. Sycamore St. Folger is looking for 16 actors and actresses who will play opposite actress Rosie O'Donnell in the season's opener.

Local residents wishing to audition for the major roles must prepare a song and a part to read, said Folger. Each audition is not to exceed 5 minutes.

People interested in being in a 30-member chorus need prepare only a song not to exceed 3 minutes. They will audition with the music director, Carole Banner.

People will be notified by Friday if they have been chosen, Folger said, and rehearsals will begin next week.

For the second-day story, you opted to put controversy in the lead. The second graph gives readers background on how the controversy occurred. The lead notes conflict, so readers expect to read comments from both sides, which you include. In paragraphs 3 through 8 come the quotes from Tyson, Fellows, and even Folger that balance the story. Readers interested in auditioning will continue to read the message to find out information about the auditions, which are mentioned in the lead. The specific times are included in graph 9, and audition information in graphs 10 and 11.

Again as the writer, you followed the inverted pyramid style of writing, ranking the material in a way that is important to your audience. You set up the lead about auditions and controversy. The need for answers to the controversy will come first, followed by information on the auditions—information that has been reported.

Getting There

As Sweeney noted in the comparison between the young Picasso and the older Picasso, all artists and communicators must first be able to master the traditional before they can be avant-garde. Mastering the inverted pyramid style of writing gives any student journalist or communicator the basic plan for writing messages that focus on what is important and emotionally compelling for the audience. The style organizes information so that it is accessible, appealing, simply stated, and easy to understand.

On the practical level, mastering the inverted pyramid style also means throwing out the clutter that plagues most beginning writers. It means writing and rewriting and cutting unnecessary words to make the message cleaner and clearer.

Many writers abhor such admonitions. They wonder how their writing will have any style or be differentiated from anyone else's. For routine assignments, it won't. But the personal style, such as that in the article about the Little Theater's upcoming season, can be added to make messages more appealing—as long as the message still remains uncluttered.

Look again at the Greta Tilley story. It's simple and direct, but it has clear hallmarks of her style, such as varied sentence length and description. The topic is one she likes to write about. Also look at Tilley's story and how her organizational style helps the reader move through the article.

News Peg and Nut Graph

Newspaper reporters talk about the "news" peg when developing stories. The peg, just like a peg on the wall where you hang a coat, is what a writer hangs the story on. It is the reason for writing the message. In our Rockland theater examples, the news peg in the first-day story is the auditions; in the second-day story, it is the residents' concern and hope for a smooth season.

Every piece of writing—whether it appears in print, is aired, or is shared—has a news peg. Writers, no matter what their skill or medium, have a reason for composing a message. That reason is spelled out in the "nut graph:" the paragraph that defines the point the writer is making. The rest of the message expands and clarifies the singular idea in the nut graph.

The nut graph should be in the first four to five paragraphs, and sometimes it is more than one paragraph. Writers who put the nut graph any lower risk losing audiences who want to know the point of the message quickly. In some cases, the lead serves as the nut graph, particularly if it is a summary lead. Audiences who hear a summary up front know why the story was written. When writers use anecdotal or descriptive leads, as described in Chapter 3, they must summarize and focus the message for audiences after drawing them in. In longer pieces, such as those described in the following section on other organizational styles, the nut graph becomes more crucial. A story may have an anecdotal lead, such as the example in Chapter 3 about the media training class for athletes. The nut graph eventually tells what the story is about:

—In more visible sports, such as football and basketball, players are accustomed to reporters and their questions. But hundreds of athletes enter UNC each year, most unaccustomed to the media crunch that follows what is the most successful athletic program in the nation.

To help them, a professor has started a communication skills group for UNC athletes.

Look at the stories that follow. Identify the nut graph or nut graphs, and see how quickly each occurs.

O. J. Tragedy Unfolds as Real-Life Drama on Live TV

BY FRED BAYLES

Associated Press

LOS ANGELES—A slow-speed chase along freeways lined with cheering spectators. Two fugitives talking to police by cellular phone. A standoff outside a mansion surrounded by fans.

Los Angeles in its unique way sustained the strange, live-on-television drama of O. J. Simpson, as he went from grieving husband to murder defendant to fugitive on the run.

"I don't think anyone in town could have written this script," said KABC-TV anchorman Harold Greene.

Crowds flocked to freeway overpasses and roadsides to watch a white Bronco pass. It was carrying Simpson, holding a blue-steel revolver to his head to keep police at bay.

The Bronco led a parade of 20 police squad cars. A dozen helicopters swarmed overhead.

People waved. "Go, Juice, Go!" they yelled.

"When the president came through there were not this many people that came to see him," said Mike Gurgus, a service station owner near Interstate 405.

In the city's restaurants, stores and health clubs, people were transfixed by the televised image of Simpson wandering Los Angeles' roads. They became part of the electronic loop, calling in to news and talk shows offering support and advice to Simpson, who faces murder charges in the deaths of his ex-wife Nicole Brown Simpson and her friend Ronald Goldman. They were killed Sunday.

"Stand up. Be a man. Face the situation," Jim Hill, a television sportscaster and friend of Simpson, pleaded in hopes that Simpson was listening and would surrender.

John McKay, who coached Simpson at the University of Southern California, and football greats Walter Payton, and Jim Brown also called.

Hundreds more converged on Simpson's Tudor-style mansion in Brentwood where Simpson surrendered after the Bronco driven by a friend finally stopped in his driveway.

The gathering seemed a cross between a revival meeting and a public hanging.

"Hallelujah, hallelujah," one woman prayed from under a jacaranda tree down the street from Simpson's gated estate.

"God deliver him," she said.

The drama began Friday morning, when Simpson's attorney Robert Shapiro received confirmation Simpson would be arrested. Shapiro agreed to turn over his client by 11 a.m., then he went to the San Fernando Valley home where Simpson was staying.

A retinue of doctors and lawyers slowed the process. A psychiatrist consoled the distraught Simpson; a doctor checked an enlarged lymph node. Forensic specialists hired to prepare a defense examined the football legend and media celebrity.

Simpson called his mother, children and personal attorney to change his will. Police grew angry at the delays and threatened to consider him a fugitive. They were given directions to the home. But when they showed up, Simpson had vanished with former teammate Al Cowlings.

Speculation began on Simpson's whereabouts. An emotional letter from him read by his friend Robert Kardashian and an impassioned plea by Shapiro raised fears Simpson might kill himself.

A crowd gathered at Nicole Simpson's townhouse, where she and Goldman were murdered, after reports of a 911 call by her parents. As helicopters hovered overhead, television reporters speculated that Simpson's body might be found inside.

It turned out to be a false alarm.

Then at 6:25 p.m., Cowling's car was spotted in Orange County. What followed was a 60-mile odyssey viewed live on television.

The chase meandered over Los Angeles' maze of roads at a sedate 45 mph: north on the Santa Ana Freeway past Disneyland, west on the Riverside Freeway, then north again on the San Diego Freeway and onto Sunset Boulevard to his home. Police used cellular phones to keep in contact with both Cowlings and Simpson.

Highway pursuits are nothing new to Los Angeles. Regular television coverage of cops chasing crooks has bloomed into a spectator sport; people have become skilled at charting on which overpass they can see the chase race by.

But there has been nothing like the crowds that witnessed the Simpson parade. Traffic jammed on both sides of the road as a wave of cheers followed Simpson down the road.

"I want to see him. This is history I guess," said Martin Griego, parked near a San Diego Freeway exit.

The route ended where it had begun days earlier, at Simpson's mansion. Many of those who followed behind the chase gathered at police lines.

People came carrying babies and folding chairs. They exchanged opinions. Was he guilty? Innocent? Framed? Part of a conspiracy?

"No way one man could have done it alone," said one woman from Hawthorne, 15 miles south. "Somebody else did it or he's not guilty by himself."

Dusk became dark, illuminated by a half moon. An hour later, those monitoring police calls shouted: "They got him. He's not hurt."

Cheers went up from the crowd. "O. J.! O. J.!" they chanted and then, with reluctance, slowly drifted off to their homes.

The exclusive neighborhood remained a gathering place on Saturday. Some came to put signs on Simpson's gate. "We love you O. J. May God be with you," read one. "Be strong my brother," said another.

L.A. Police Fear O. J. Suicide Try

Attorney Reports Simpson Crying, Deeply Depressed; Cowlings Charged with Aiding Flight

BY SETH MYDANS

N.Y. Times

LOS ANGELES—O. J. Simpson, whose thrilling play on the football field seemed to symbolize freedom, sat locked Saturday in a 9-foot-by-7-foot jail cell on a double murder charge; with only a toilet, a seat and a bunk for furnishings.

The authorities said that all sharp objects had been removed and a deputy was peering through a window every few minutes to make sure he did not kill himself.

He was admitted to Men's Central Jail at 10:20 on Friday night, said Sheriff's Deputy Angie McLaughlin, ending an extraordinary day in which he was charged with the murder in the slayings of his former wife and her friend, disappeared, and then led police on a bizarre 90-minute tour of

the freeways, broadcast live on television nationwide, before surrendering meekly at his house.

Police said he could be arraigned as early as Monday, beginning what could be a long legal journey that will explore the brutal double killings, which Simpson on Friday denied committing in a desperate open letter his lawyer described as a suicide note.

Saturday, the lawyer, Robert Shapiro, talked to Simpson by telephone, and said his jailed client was deeply depressed and crying.

Al Cowlings, a football teammate from the University of Southern California and the Buffalo Bills who drove the white Ford Bronco in which Simpson fled police, also was arrested and booked for aiding and abetting a fugitive. He was freed early Saturday on $250,000 bail, police said.

The police's handling of the case was being scrutinized Saturday, with politicians and former police officials criticizing what they saw as lax treatment that allowed Simpson to escape and elude capture for nearly nine hours.

At a late-night news conference, Comdr. David Gascon of the Los Angeles police, defended his department, saying: "We always evaluate what we do. We are not too proud to admit that. But at this point we are not prepared to say we did anything wrong in our handling of this case."

He voiced anger at both Simpson and Cowlings, who he said absolutely interfered, obstructed and caused a problem in our efforts to take Mr. Simpson into custody."

Fans Divided by Actions

While police were pursuing Simpson on the freeways Friday, crowds were cheering him on as they once had on the football fields, waving and sometimes chanting, "Juice, Juice, Juice!"

Saturday morning, fans gathered at his home in the Brentwood section of Los Angeles to construct a makeshift shrine and wish him well.

Marlan Washington, 27, who was standing at police headquarters waiting for Simpson to be brought in Friday, said "I grew up on O. J. He was someone I thought of and looked up to. But not today."

Simpson is being held without bail on charges of first-degree murder that could carry the death penalty in the stabbing deaths late Sunday night of his former wife, Nicole Brown Simpson, 35, and her friend Ronald Goldman, 25, a waiter.

Fitting in the Pieces

For four days, police gathered evidence from the crime scene outside Mrs. Simpson's condominium and from Simpson's own Bronco and nearby house as well as from a hotel room in Chicago, where he flew to immediately after the killings.

They compared blood samples, studied the wounds of the victims and interviewed witnesses until, District Attorney Gil Garcetti said, they were prepared to take their case to him on Friday morning.

"It's a giant jigsaw puzzle," Gascon said on Friday night in defending the department's slow and methodical approach. "You are picking up pieces one at a time. A major mistake in any investigation is to jump to conclusions. You lose objectivity, overlook evidence and go off in wrong directions."

At a news conference Saturday morning, Chief Willie L. Williams angrily rejected a suggestion that Simpson might have escaped because he was given preferential treatment as a celebrity, with officials allowing Shapiro to bring his client in rather than going out to arrest Simpson.

He said the procedure was common practice and that "the difference was the world wasn't watching."

Celebrity prison wing

Even in the isolation of his prison cell, Simpson retains his high profile.

Deputy McLaughlin of the Sheriff's Department said he is in a special wing for celebrities and people who are considered security risks.

Among those who are also in the wing are Lyle and Erik Menendez, who are awaiting a new trial in the slayings of their parents in their Beverly Hills home.

This is the wing that has housed Charles Manson and the two officers convicted in the beating of Rodney King, and where Lyle Menendez became friends with Damian Williams, who was convicted of assaulting Reginald O. Denny during the 1992 riots.

When Simpson was admitted, she said, like other inmates he exchanged his street clothes for a pullover shirt and elastic banded pants. Any shoelaces were removed and he was given rubber slippers. He was not allowed to keep any sharp objects such as a pen or a comb.

Simpson will be allowed one visitor a day, in addition to his lawyers and doctors.

Meet Fudge

TV's New Too-Cute Tyke Can't Help it if He's Funny

BY MARK SCHWED

Television's newest hotshot needs to cool down. He flails his hands, stomps his feet, rampages right in front of the whole cast and crew. He's fed up. He's furious. He's outta here.

"I wish I was never discovered," the star screams, "I don't want to be famous."

Move over Macaulay Culkin and make room for little Luke Tarsitano, a not-yet-5-year-old tyke whose tiny toes are in TV's fast lane. He's starring in "Fudge-A-Mania," the *ABC Family Movie* installment that introduces his *Fudge* series.

Fudge bears the stamp of Steven Spielberg's Amblin Television, and was inspired by the works of Judy Blume, whose books have sold more than 60 million copies. "Fudge-A-Mania" tells the tale of a New York City family with two boys: Peter (Jake Richardson) and his pesky younger brother, Fudge (Tarsitano). And even though Tarsitano has been working with veterans like Florence Henderson and Darren McGavin (who play grandparents in the film), plus a host of equally adorable child actors, he's emerged as a natural born scene-stealer.

"It's those eyes," says Blume. "He doesn't even have to say anything. In fact, I don't always understand everything he says. But it doesn't matter."

"He is amazing," adds *Happy Days* vet Anson Williams, who's directing seven of the 13 planned *Fudge* episodes. "I can change a line or change a shot, and he's got it down on the first take."

Well, maybe not today. "Boy do I hate coming here," he says with a frown, bounding out of his parents' Lincoln at 8:17 a.m. "I hate working." Of course, he's lying. And he tears across the parking lot like an eager pup, headed for the set.

Tarsitano's favorite part of making a show? "The breaks." The worst part? "The work." But the truth is he turns the whole set into a playground. "I love the people I work with," he says. "My dad says sometimes I don't want to be Fudge. But I do want to be Fudge. But I'm different than Fudge. He's a troublemaker and I'm not."

Troublemaker, no. Trouble, yes. Give him a break from filming and he's history. He scampers off to the nearest computer for a quick game of *Rodent's Revenge,* only to be corralled by production assistant Louis Tocchet, whose job description now includes tracking down Tarsitano. "Ten minutes is up."

"Your watch is wrong," says Taristano, toeing the line between dissent and tantrum. But as soon as he's back on the set, Luke is all business. He whips through rehearsal and then nails his scene for the cameras. "Print," yells the director, but Luke

has already scooted off to his secret hiding place in his TV bedroom.

"There are more important things than the movie business," says Tarsitano's dad, Ralph.

"Yes," replies Williams. "But not right now."

You've got to feel for the director. Not only must he sweet-talk Taristano through his scenes, but he's now working with a St. Bernard puppy named Trucker who is completely uncooperative. And then Jake, who plays brother Peter, has a terrible stomachache and retreats to a bunk bed to recover.

"Days like this one make me wish I were back selling shoes," says Williams. In spite of the frustrations, however, the adults are mindful of the fact that they're working with young kids who need special attention.

As for Tarsitano, his future appears paved in gold—that is, if he isn't warped by the fame and fortune. "I was afraid at first," say Tamara Tarsitano, Luke's mom. "You hear so many rotten things about kids in show biz. But this is such a nurturing environment."

Yeah, but 15 years from now?

"I worry about that," says Amblin TV's Carol Monroe, who says she and Spielberg may make a movie with Tarsitano after the series wraps. "Are we creating a monster?"

But Tarsitano's dad thinks everything is under control as long as parents keep a close watch. "I see no downside. If the parents screw up, the kid is in trouble. But show business has nothing to do with that. Anyway," the proud father reasons, "Luke can act until he's old enough to play baseball. He's *really* good at that."

Reprinted with permission from *TV Guide,* © 1995, News America Publications, Inc.

Other Organization Styles

Although the inverted pyramid works for much writing, you may find other formats that are better for a particular message to recap an event. Some formats use the inverted pyramid format to introduce material, then move into another organizational pattern.

Chronological Format

In some cases, making the decision how to organize a message is easy. Chronology—telling events in the same order in which they occurred—often can meet audience needs. A news story about a bank robbery, for example, would have a summary lead telling that the robbery occurred, where, and when. Then events would be revealed chronologically. The writer would organize the rest of the story by using time elements, as in the following article:

—A masked woman robbed the First Guaranty Savings and Loan on Main Street shortly after 9 a.m. today and escaped into a thickly wooded area nearby. Police have made no arrests.

The robbery occurred when the woman entered the bank and approached a teller. She handed her a note asking for money and saying she had a gun in the sleeve of her sweatshirt.

Although the teller did not actually see a gun, she gave the woman an undisclosed amount of cash. The woman put the money into a purple sack, ran from the Savings and Loan, and disappeared in the woods behind the bank's parking lot.

At 6 p.m., police were still looking for the suspect, who was described as a white woman in her mid 20's with shoulder-length blonde hair. She wore a purple sweatsuit and had pulled a stocking as a

mask over her face. Bank employees could not describe her facial features.

Here the lead, or first paragraph, states *who* did *what where* and *when* and
the latest information. Graph 2 shows how events unfolded. The last time
element tells readers the status of the investigation at the newspaper's deadline.

While some messages can be developed chronologically, organization
generally is not that simple. Not all messages involve characters and action;
for example, a high school principal cannot use chronology to inform teachers about changes in ordering classroom supplies. Teachers aren't interested
in the events that led up to the changes; they want to know the specific
changes immediately. That's when another format is needed.

Hourglass Format

Some writers have adapted chronological development to longer stories in
what they call the hourglass format of writing. A summary lead followed by
the inverted pyramid style gives readers the most important information in
four to six paragraphs, allowing them to stop at the end of the inverted pyramid segment. But the writer sets up more information with a simple statement by a source: "Maynard described the events this way."

Beyond the transition statement, the message unfolds chronologically.
Writers can use the style for many kinds of stories, such as telling of the
search for a lost child, recounting a day in the life of a popular singer, or
bringing out the details of a baseball game. Many arrest stories on football
hero O. J. Simpson appeared in 1994. In the first example given, the writer
used the inverted pyramid format up front, then developed the message
chronologically using the hourglass format.

Electronic media writers often use the hourglass format. For example, a
local television station aired a story about a crime that police had been
unable to solve. After noting the latest information, the reporter said:
"Here's how police have recreated the sequence of events." The details that
followed were a chronological account of the crime. The story ended with
the reporter showing the local telephone number for Crimestoppers.

Mapped Format

Assistant professor Jacqueline Farnan and newspaper copy editor David Hedley have discussed another variation on the inverted pyramid style called the

mapped format. They note that the inverted pyramid becomes confusing for longer pieces, but they believe it serves as a way to introduce the most important elements of the message.

The name "mapped format" describes the technique of indicating points of interest within the message, just as a map includes highlights for its readers. The mapped format benefits topics that are of mild interest to readers, such as business and government. It also aids readers in finding information that is of particular interest to them in longer stories.

A mapped message is organized into sections. The first is the inverted pyramid lead. Subheads in a subject-verb-object sentence help readers, especially those who just scan stories, define categories of information. Farnan and Hedley say the mapped format "conveys news in a form that is easy to grasp for disinterested scan readers and easy to follow for interested readers." Readers can quickly find the segments of information that most benefit or appeal to them.

The mapped format can also help the writer organize. Let's assume you are writing a story on the cost of funerals and the alternatives to traditional burial. Your research finds categories of information: reasons why funerals are expensive, caskets and their costs, funeral home expenses, cost of burial plots, cost of cremation versus burial, memorial services, how to cut costs, and alternatives. After drafting the lead, you can group categories of information under subheads, which help organize the story and readily identify parts of the story for readers.

An example of mapped format is in the second story on O. J. Simpson, which uses subheads to clue readers where to find information.

Numerical Format

A writer could organize a message numerically or by points. For example, a city council votes on three issues: water and sewer rates, a rezoning application, and the town manager's contract. The writer would list in the lead the actions taken and the votes, thereby setting up the three points to be expanded in the body of the story.

Writers covering a speech will often use a numeral or point-by-point format that follows the organizational structure of the speech after summarizing the speaker's remarks. For example, a speaker discusses three major risk factors in heart disease. The writer notes the three risk factors in the lead: risk factor one, smoking; risk factor two, lack of exercise; risk factor three, lack of a well-balanced diet. The points serve as transitions between sections of the message.

The reporter's story might read:

—Cardiovascular disease is the No. 1 cause of death in the United States, but it can be reduced with lifestyle changes such as no smoking, regular exercise, and a well-balanced diet, the chairman of the American Heart Association's Wayne County chapter said Tuesday.

Gus Rivas said Americans should pay attention to the risk factors at an early age and get children to be aware of healthy lifestyles.

More than 3,000 children smoke their first cigarette every day. This number will translate into more adults who are at risk for cardiovascular disease.

"Children consume more than 947 million packs of cigarettes in this country," Rivas said. "More than 25 percent of high school students who smoke tried their first cigarette while in the sixth grade."

Youngsters need to exercise, he noted. Studies show that today's youth do not get enough regular exercise.

"Riding a bike, walking, even doing household chores can establish fitness patterns," Rivas said.

A well-balanced diet low in fat is essential to reduce the risk of heart disease, Rivas said. About one out of four children is obese, and obese children are at a risk for obesity as adults.

The writer followed the lead, using the three points or risk factors as a way to organize and unify her story.

Unifying Writing

Any story, memo, news release, or broadcast message needs unity to be a coherent and complete piece. Each paragraph in a written piece must follow the preceding paragraph logically. Each paragraph must build on previous information. Each section of the piece must fit the subject or theme. Unifying writing takes careful thought and planning, and it often requires rewriting or reorganizing once a draft is done.

Transitions and repetition of certain words are ways to unify writing and to get readers from the beginning to the end. The first two or three paragraphs set up many of the unifying elements, for example, people, places, things, controversy, or chronology.

Repetition of Words

Some writers are uncomfortable repeating words in their writing. They pore over the thesaurus or dictionary, looking for synonyms that may not be as good as the word itself repeated. Repetition is okay. Repetition offers unity in a message and gives readers familiarity. Repetition is also clearer: Readers aren't stopping to match synonyms and words.

The topic will determine the words repeated. A memo that covers changes in employee benefits should use the word "employee" throughout rather than switching from "worker" to "staff" to "professional" to "craftsman." The same applies in writing about an organization; "organization" or the organization's name can be used throughout rather than "group," "agency," or "company."

Transitions

Transitions are cues for readers. Transitions set up changes in location, time, and mood. They keep readers from getting lost or confused.

A simple sentence or word may be needed as a logical bridge from one section of the message to the next. Any transition should wrap up the previous thought and introduce the next one.

"We must continue our efforts to reduce teen-age pregnancy, and our programs are aimed to do that," the governor said.

While the governor defended his policies, others in state government cited lack of action on welfare issues for his dwindling popularity.

The second sentence indicates a shift from the governor's words to those of state government officials.

Most writers are accustomed to simple words or phrases as transitions. Look at some words and phrases that give readers certain information about where a story is going.

A change in opinion: "but," "on the other hand," and "however."

Clarification: "in other words," "for example," "that is," "to illustrate," "to demonstrate," "specifically," and "to clarify."

Comparison: "also," "in comparison," "like," "similarly," "on the same note," and "a related point."

Contrast: "but," "in contrast," "despite," "on the contrary," "unlike," "yet," "however," and "instead of."

Expanded information: "in addition," "an additional," "moreover," "in other action," "another," "further," "furthermore," "too," "as well as," and "also."

A change in place: "above," "higher," "beneath," "beside," "between," "across," "after," "around," and "below."

Time: "while," "meanwhile," "past," "afterward," "during," "soon," "next," "subsequently," "until then," "future," "before," and "at the same time."

Look at how a few transitions work. In developing a story chronologically, time serves as a transition. Look at the First Guaranty bank robbery story earlier in this chapter. The time elements pull the reader from shortly after 9 a.m., when the robbery occurred, until 6 p.m. when the woman still had not been caught. In other stories, time-oriented words and phrases could be "at the same time," "later that day," "Tuesday," and "last week."

A message about voter reaction on election day uses polling sites around town as geographic transitions: "Voters at Precinct 35 (Town Hall) said...," "Those voting at Precinct 15 (Main Street Presbyterian Church) said...," "Precinct 2 voters (Blackwell Elementary School) said...." Other geographical phrases would be "on the other side of town," "at his father's 25-acre farm," "next door," and "at the White House."

Tone to Unify a Message

Knowing audiences will help the writer determine what tone to set in organizing and writing a message. The tone or mood of a story can act as a unifying device. A PTA newsletter editor knows that her audience is busy, fast-moving, and distracted by children, work, day-to-day routine, and a deluge of media bits. She knows her audience is in need of quick information about kids and school. She must write lively copy with short, pithy sentences and paragraphs. Active parents need newsletter copy that looks like this:

```
Spring cleaning may leave you with trash and treasures.
Please donate them to Southview School's Trash and Treasure
sale! This year's sale is planned for May 9.
     Doris Tucker will begin receiving donations April 26
at her home, 322 Dale Drive. For more information, call
499-2342.
```

In contrast, a newsletter for a group of World War II veterans requires a more serious, thoughtful tone and should include some nostalgia and humor as well as careful, complete news updates and obituaries for members. Its readers have time to pore over news and recollect their memories of a heartfelt topic. An article might begin this way:

```
When members of Company B gather this year in France, we
will take time to honor our 22 buddies who died on the
beaches there in 1944, giving their lives so that we and
our families might enjoy the freedom we often take for
granted today.
     A two-day schedule of interfaith memorial services, as
well as fellowship activities on June 5-6, will provide
much opportunity for veterans to come together, share
memories, and get reacquainted.
```

A writer's knowledge of audiences will determine the mood or tone that will best maintain interest and retain it throughout the message.

Quotations to Unify Stories

Quotations can be effective transitions throughout writing. They add liveliness and an emotional element, allow people to speak directly to readers and listeners, and help them feel more connected to personalities and events. They can supplement facts and add detail. News stories and news releases should have a good balance between direct and indirect quotes. Information on direct and indirect quotes, attribution, and punctuation of quotes is given in Chapter 10.

Look at the *TV Guide* example. Writer Mark Schwed uses quotes as transitions from one speaker to another and from one Luke Tarsitano mood to another. The quotations answer questions and reveal the feelings of child, parents, and directors about the show specifically and the film business in general. The quotations also add a fast pace and liveliness to the story, moving the reader from Tarsitano as television's new hotshot to his father's view of kid stars.

As you can see from the Schwed piece, quotations are good endings for stories. They can refer to the lead and wrap up a piece, they can leave a piece looking to the future, or they can add a touch of humor. You also will see other organizational devices in Schwed's story, such as tone and repetition of key words.

Near the end of a story on North Carolina tobacco markets, a *Durham Morning Herald* reporter wrote:

> —One man said he came to the opening just to watch and "to get out of picking butter beans at the house."
>
> Similar sentiments were expressed by a retired Imperial Tobacco Co. employee who said that although he's seen hundreds of tobacco sales, he'd rather be at the market than do the "honeydew " work of retirement.
>
> "You know how it is at home," he said. "It's honeydew this, and honeydew that."

Even though the quote is not essential to this story about how tobacco markets operate, it adds a chuckle. In most cases writers know how long a story will be and know that a quotation won't be cut from the end. But sometimes writers have to be careful in using a quote at the end; if the story is cut from the bottom, readers should miss only a chuckle, not important information.

Unifying Devices in Practice

Let's go back and look at the second-day newspaper story on the Rockland Community Theater. What are the unifying devices? First, see what the lead set up.

> —When Director Neal Folger starts auditions for the season opener of The Rockland Community Theater in early August, most board of directors members will be crossing their fingers for a smooth year.

Broadly, the lead hints at a controversy and lets readers know that board members will be quoted. Words that are established for repetition are "theater," "board," "directors," "year," "Folger," "audition," "director," and "season."

—The board hired Folger, the former director of the River Road Theater in Danville, a year ago, and soon the theater was embroiled in controversy. Last year's season opener of "Grease" showed nudity when three performers dropped their pants as part of a song on mooning. This year's season opens Oct. 15.

The second paragraph spells out a controversy and describes what occurred. Words repeated for unity are "board," "Folger," "director," "theater," and "season." We are also given a time element: last year and this year.

—"We felt we went through a wringer right off the bat last year," board member Mary Tyson said today. "While some people like Neal's productions, most people in our community prefer more traditional entertainment. Nudity just has no place on our stage."

Graph 3 uses a quotation from a board member. Readers expect to hear from at least one. The quote gives board members' feelings and why the nudity was a problem. Repeated are the themes of last year's controversy, nudity, and the director.

—Board member Justin Fellows said the board hoped for a successful season with less turmoil than the previous year.

Graph 4 introduces another speaker and reiterates last year's controversy and the upcoming season.

—"We think Neal is quite talented, but we are just a community theater, and we want fun, not indignation," he said.

Graph 5 gives readers more information about the director and repeats the idea of a community that disapproves of nudity on stage.

—Folger said he was surprised at the reaction to "Grease."

Graph 6 is a complete sentence, which lets readers know that a change in speakers and a defense are coming. It continues the unity through the words "Folger" and "Grease."

—"I certainly learned what this community will accept on stage," he said. "We intend to produce shows that keep people fairly well covered."

Graph 7 repeats "community" and begins the transition from last season to the current season's offerings.

—Fellows added the board hoped Folger's appealing season lineup will attract a substantial audience to the Rockland Theater.

The Fellows quote in graph 8 completes the transition from last year to the current year. It also repeats the words "Fellows," "board," "Folger," "season," and "theater."

—The director will have auditions for "Gypsy" from 7 to 9 p.m. Monday and Tuesday at the theater at 211 W. Sycamore St. Folger is looking for 16 actors and actresses who will play opposite actress Rosie O'Donnell in the season's opener.

Graph 9 introduces the new information about the auditions. Again, the familiar words are there: "director," "audition," "theater," "Folger," and "season."

—Local residents wishing to audition for the major roles must prepare a song and a part to read, said Folger. Each audition is not to exceed 5 minutes.

People interested in being in a 30-member chorus need prepare only a song not to exceed three minutes. They will audition with the music director, Carole Banner.

People will be notified by Friday if they have been chosen, Folger said, and rehearsals will begin next week.

Graphs 10, 11, and 12 are complete ideas about different aspects of the auditions. Graph 10 begins with information about the major roles, while graph 11 is about the lesser parts. Each uses words such as "audition,"

"Folger," "director," and "song" as unity. The last graph wraps up the story with an indirect quote and looks to the future.

News vs. Feature

Students may wonder where the feature story fits in the discussion of print formats. Most articles printed today are news-features or features. Traditionally, writers have used one value to distinguish news from features: timeliness. Features have a timeless quality: They can be published any time and remain useful and entertaining. News, however, must be printed immediately. A story about fashions and body shapes is a feature; a nationally known fashion designer jumping off a 15-story building is news.

Because electronic media have assumed the role of breaking news, newspapers and magazines have taken on an explanatory role. Their job is to flesh out the headline on television or radio and to provide the substance and follow-up. To make the story different, writers have adopted more feature formats, using anecdotal and descriptive leads before getting to the nut graph or the actual news. The example of the 911 operator in Chapter 3 shows how a feature approach can be adopted for a news story.

Writers call the news-feature approach soft news. It doesn't carry the hard-hitting lead: City Council voted 5 to 3 Wednesday night to raise property taxes 3 cents per $100 valuation. The lead instead focuses on someone affected:

> —Darcy Little has lived on Southbend Street for 35 years. Each year she fears what increased property taxes on her two-bedroom home will do to her fixed income.
>
> Her fears were realized Wednesday night when city council voted to raise property taxes. It means Little will pay $235 a year more and raises doubts that she will be able to remain in her home.

Students will find that they use news and feature formats in whatever career they choose in print journalism. Newspaper reporters, magazine writers, freelance writers, newsletter editors, novelists, columnists, and others rely on the organizational styles discussed here to produce messages.

Writing formats change. Newspaper reporters, for example, have adopted more narrative styles of writing, using anecdotal and descriptive approaches. Some editors believe that style will attract more readers; others say the style will pass. Time will be the test of whether new formats attract and retain audiences.

But no matter what style or format they use, and whatever medium they work for, print journalists follow the same writing process outlined in Chapter 1. Some, such as magazine writers, have time to put their work aside before editing. Newspaper reporters who work under deadline pressure, however, find that they compress the stages. They may have little time for rewriting and editing, and those tasks may fall to others in the newsroom, such as metro editors and copy editors. In any case, the written piece proceeds through those stages before it is published for audiences.

The Professional Writer

The examples in Chapters 3 and 4 give you as a student journalist a peek at the kinds of careers you can pursue as a writer in the print field: newspaper reporter, magazine writer, novelist, columnist, or even a church bulletin editor. Other chapters will pose additional opportunities, such as wordsmithing as a copy editor or analyzing information as a database journalist.

Throughout the text, the need for good writing skills in any of those professions will be stressed over and over. But basic skills aren't enough. Students who want to be successful must be scrupulously honest and adhere by a personal code of ethics. All writers, regardless of which medium will publish their work, must be accurate in gathering and printing information. Editors at all levels can improve their copy, but no editor will know whether the information is correct. The reporter must accept the burden of accuracy. Failure to check and doublecheck facts can result in libel suits for newspapers and destroyed credibility for writers. Once a writer has ruined his or her reputation, it may be impossible to regain believability.

The writer also must bear responsibility for gathering information ethically. Sources must know when they will be quoted, and writers should not accept gifts for information. Unlike doctors and lawyers writers cannot be barred from practice for performing their jobs in an unethical manner. Again, what suffers is their reputation—and that could cost them jobs and income.

Organizations such as the Society of Professional Journalists (SPJ) have developed codes of ethics for journalists as guidelines for behavior. News outlets generally have ethics statements for their reporters and writers to follow. For example, a publication may not buy a travel story if the writer received a free trip from the resort featured in the piece. Newspaper reporters may be banned from accepting anything from a source, even a cup of coffee.

Students starting out in the profession may find it helpful to join professional organizations such as SPJ. Groups exist for different types of writers. Organizations hold workshops to keep writers up to date on trends in the field and can even provide writers a sense of belonging, particularly freelance writers, who are on their own. Professional contacts help individuals who want to make career moves. Students should become aware of groups and people who can guide them in attaining a rewarding and satisfying professional life.

Code of Ethics

The Society of Professional Journalists,
Sigma Delta Chi

The SOCIETY of Professional Journalists, Sigma Delta Chi believes the duty of journalists is to serve the truth.

We BELIEVE the agencies of mass communication are carriers of public discussion and information, acting on their Constitutional mandate and freedom to learn and report the facts.

We BELIEVE in public enlightenment as the forerunner of justice, and in our Constitutional role to seek the truth as part of the public's right to know the truth.

We BELIEVE those responsibilities carry obligations that require journalists to perform with intelligence, objectivity, accuracy, and fairness.

To these ends, we declare acceptance of the standards of practice here set forth:

I. Responsibility:

The public's right to know of events of public importance and interest is the overriding mission of the mass media. The purpose of distributing news and enlightened opinion is to serve the general welfare. Journalists who use their professional status as representatives of the public for selfish or other unworthy motives violate a high trust.

II. Freedom of the Press:

Freedom of the press is to be guarded as an inalienable right of people in a free society. It carries with it the freedom and the responsibility to discuss, question, and challenge actions and utterances of our government and of our public and private institutions. Journalists uphold the right to speak unpopular opinions and the privilege to agree with the majority.

III. Ethics:

Journalists must be free of obligation to any interest other than the public's right to know the truth.

1. Gifts, favors, free travel, special treatment or privileges can compromise the integrity of journalists and their employers. Nothing of value should be accepted.

2. Secondary employment, political involvement, holding public office, and service in community organizations should be avoided if it compromises the integrity of journalists and their employers. Journalists and their employers should conduct their personal lives in a manner that protects them from conflict of interest, real or apparent. Their responsibilities to the public are paramount. That is the nature of their profession.

3. So-called news communications from private sources should not be published or broadcast without substantiation of their claims to news values.

4. Journalists will seek news that serves the public interest, despite the obstacles. They will make constant efforts to assure that the public's business is conducted in public and that public records are open to public inspection.

5. Journalists acknowledge the newsman's ethic of protecting confidential sources of information.

6. Plagiarism is dishonest and unacceptable.

IV. Accuracy and Objectivity:

Good faith with the public is the foundation of all worthy journalism.

1. Truth is our ultimate goal.

2. Objectivity in reporting the news is another goal that serves as the mark of an experienced professional. It is a standard of performance toward which we strive. We honor those who achieve it.

3. There is no excuse for inaccuracies or lack of thoroughness.

4. Newspaper headlines should be fully warranted by the contents of the articles they accompany. Photographs and telecasts should give an accurate picture of an event and not highlight an incident out of context.

5. Sound practice makes clear distinction between news reports and expressions of opinion. News reports should be free of opinion or bias and represent all sides of an issue.

6. Partisanship in editorial comment that knowingly departs from the truth violates the spirit of American journalism.

7. Journalists recognize their responsibility for offering informed analysis, comment, and editorial opinion

on public events and issues. They accept the obligation to present such material by individuals whose competence, experience, and judgment qualify them for it.

8. Special articles or presentations devoted to advocacy or the writer's own conclusions and interpretations should be labeled as such.

V. Fair Play:
Journalists at all times will show respect for the dignity, privacy, rights, and well-being of people encountered in the course of gathering and presenting the news.

1. The news media should not communicate unofficial charges affecting reputation or moral character without giving the accused a chance to reply.

2. The news media must guard against invading a person's right to privacy.

3. The media should not pander to morbid curiosity about details of vice and crime.

4. It is the duty of news media to make prompt and complete correction of their errors.

5. Journalists should be accountable to the public for their reports and the public should be encouraged to voice its grievances against the media. Open dialogue with our readers, viewers, and listeners should be fostered.

VI. Pledge:
Adherence to this code is intended to preserve and strengthen the bond of mutual trust and respect between American journalists and the American people.

The Society shall—by programs of education and other means—encourage individual journalists to adhere to these tenets, and shall encourage journalistic publications and broadcasters to recognize their responsibility to frame codes of ethics in concert with their employees to serve as guidelines in furthering these goals.

Reprinted with permission from the Society of Professional Journalists, copyright 1987.

Moving on with Writing

Writing is a series of choices—choice of language, pertinent facts, introductions, organizational pattern, tone, quotes, and topics—and all need to be made in an informed way, based on what writers know about their audiences.

Books and other writers can give you tips on how to organize your writing. The best way to learn is to apply the techniques through your own efforts. Don't let organization just happen. Make an outline. Consciously apply a certain organizational style to your writing. Let someone else read your piece to see whether it makes sense.

Good organization helps you reach your audience. Look at the Associated Press story. The reporter uses all the strengths of simple writing, repetition for unity, and quotations as transitions to pull readers through an emotionally compelling story that could have been just another routine drug bust story. The following chapters will guide you further in knowing your audience and writing for it.

Crime, Fear, Poverty All Part of Life in America

Young Woman's Eyes Reflect Despair of Violent Nation

BY JULIA PRODIS

Associated Press

DALLAS—Her eyes are the color of earth, and as vacant as the lot next door.

She's sitting on a concrete step holding a baby that's not hers. Her 16-year-old friend is lying face down on the sizzling sidewalk beside her, his arms arched awkwardly behind him, his hands cuffed in plastic police ties. A girlfriend is similarly contorted at her feet.

"What's your name?" a policewoman asks this hot August day in Dallas.

In a low, slow whisper, she answers, "Latasha."

"La-what?"

"La-Tasha," the thin, moonfaced 19-year-old says with slightly more effort, her blank gaze never looking higher than the holster holding the officer's 9 mm semiautomatic.

Minutes ago, eight muscular members of the Dallas drug enforcement squad, wearing black boots and bulletproof vests, had stormed the faded yellow bungalow behind her. It took two heaves of "the slammer" to break down the door, blocked only by an empty bookcase.

Shrieks from inside, then blurs of motion as the young man bolted out the rear and the woman ran toward the back fence. Latasha Smith never said a word, and the baby didn't cry.

She has the dull look of someone who had seen this rerun too many times. Her look of despair, so deep it turns everything gray, is the same look that flattens the faces of the young and hopeless in poor, violent American neighborhoods everywhere.

Neighborhoods where crack heads fear friends and neighbors more than the cops. Where homes are so filthy detectives can't pick up evidence without something crawling on it. Where neighbors scatter when someone screams for help.

For Americans who say crime is their gravest concern, these calloused Latashas and their criminal friends stir angry fear. But for Latasha, it's just another day.

The baby with cocoa skin and heavy brown hair spits up on Latasha's chest as she rocks negligibly back and forth. Indifferently, she wipes his face with her droopy white tank top.

"Who's payin' for that baby?" the policewoman asks.

"It ain't MY baby," she retorts.

"It's my baby," says the 16-year-old boy, squirming awkwardly on the sidewalk. As he strains to lift his head to speak, the pebbles clinging to his cheek dribble to the ground.

Latasha tells the officer she has three children of her own and she's on welfare. She quit the last job she had washing dishes because she didn't like it. Her children are scattered with relatives and friends today.

"Did you grow up like this baby is growing up?" the reporter asks.

"My daddy shot my momma dead when I was 2." She speaks flatly, like a kid bored with homework. She was raised by her grandfather.

She doesn't explain why she is at this house that isn't hers holding somebody else's baby.

An undercover officer recently bought drugs at this house. The police had come back to clean it up and close it down—one of nearly 400 Dallas dope houses stormed this year.

After running background checks on the three, the sergeant in charge decides to arrest the handcuffed youths on drug charges and ticket Latasha for failing to appear in court after being cited for driving without insurance.

"Do you ever dream of a better life?" the reporter asks.

She shrugs.

She doesn't watch the van carry her two friends away. She just sits in front of the house with the For Rent sign and the broken door, holding someone else's baby, and stares blankly at the vacant lot next door.

Brights

Not all short articles are news. Some news stories can be written so that they become a bright, that is, a short news-feature no more than five paragraphs long and with a twist at the end.

Consider the following bright that resulted from a routine police report of a missing man:

PHOENIX—Tammy Plumb called police when her husband didn't return from a one-day hunting trip. Four days later, Jesse Plumb was found by an army of searchers—unharmed, but feeling sheepish about a tryst with another woman.

Plumb might be billed $13,000 for the mountain search, which involved a helicopter, dogs, and more than 40 deputies, sheriff's Sgt. John Kleinheinz said.

Tammy Plumb has moved out.

EXERCISES

1. You are a reporter for the *Rockland Chronicle*. You have picked up the following police report—written last night—from the Town Police Department. Write a message with a summary lead, then develop the message in chronological order.

```
Report: Tony's Restaurant Robbery
Investigating Officer: Sgt. Rodney Carter

   At 10:00 p.m. a robbery at Tony's Restaurant was
reported. Owner, Tony Hardy said that he was working late
preparing the payroll when a man wearing a stocking mask
entered the back door of the kitchen at about 8:40.
   Hardy said that the man told him to go into the office
and open up the safe. Hardy took almost $3,000 out of the
safe and put it into a blue, waterproof sack.
   The restaurant closes at 9 p.m. Hardy said he thought
the robber knew he was there alone, but that he didn't
think the robber was a Rockland resident.
   Hardy said he got a good look at the man: a stocky white
man, about 5'6" and round-faced. He estimated the man's age
to be 24. Hardy said the man's shoulders were so broad that
```

he might have been a weight lifter. Hardy suggested that if the thief wanted to lock him up somewhere, the storage closet off the kitchen was as good a place as any. The thief agreed and locked him up there. The thief wrapped a clothes hanger around the door. He told Hardy he had a partner, and that Hardy wouldn't live to see his family and relatives if he came out of the closet before 15 minutes had passed.

Hardy said he waited the 15 minutes even though he didn't believe the story about the partner, or at least a partner who would be stupid enough to hang around for 15 minutes. He had no trouble getting out and then called the Rockland Police.

We have some leads on the suspect and the investigation is continuing.

2. From the following information, write a summary lead for the *Rockland Chronicle* that focuses on *who*, *what*, *when*, and *where* plus human interest. Then develop the message chronologically.

From the Rockland police chief, Ralph Robinson, you learn the following:

Two sisters were playing at a Laundromat about 5 p.m. yesterday. The girls are the daughters of Nancy and Phillip Childs of Rockland. The girls were with their aunt, Janice Childs. The 3-year-old, Jennifer, climbed into one of the washing machines. Her sister, Elizabeth, 7, closed the door. The machine started filling up with water. When she realized the washer was running, Elizabeth ran to get her aunt. Ms. Childs tried to open the washer door but could not, because the washers are equipped with automatic locks on the doors.

Robinson said the girl was trapped in the washer for more than 5 minutes before she was rescued. He said a customer had put coins into the machine before the little girl crawled inside, but the customer hadn't used the machine because he thought it wasn't working.

On the telephone you talk to Paul Hecker of 601 Arbor Drive in Rockland. He was on his way home from work and stopped at the Glen Rock Shopping Center to buy groceries. He heard screams coming from the Glen Rock Laundry and Dry Cleaner. He ran inside the Laundromat to see what was going on. Ms. Childs ran up to him and asked him to save the child. She asked if he had any tools, so he ran back to his toolbox in the back of his truck and got a hammer. Hecker said he took the hammer back inside and smashed the glass in the washing machine door. He then reached in and pulled her out.

A Rockland Hospital spokesperson said Jennifer was admitted yesterday afternoon and was listed in good condition. Her parents could not be reached for comment.

3. You are to write a message with a summary lead. Think about the latest information for the summary lead. Then organize the story using the hourglass format of writing. You will need to merge the two accounts of the event into one chronological account. Be sure to attribute information when it is quoted.

Middleton Police Chief Ralph Poe held a press conference at 7 p.m. last night. He said an emergency medical service team had come to an alley beside the downtown Pizza To Go restaurant yesterday afternoon after a neighboring businessman reported that there was a man in the alley who appeared to be injured.

The man, Henry Donovan, 39, of Rt. 2 Box 8 in Middleton, suffered from multiple gunshot wounds, Poe said. Paramedics took him to Memorial Hospital, where he was pronounced dead on arrival, Poe said.

Donovan's ex-wife, Regina Donovan, 34, manages the Pizza To Go restaurant and lives at Rt. 3 Box 254-A, Middleton. She and Henry Donovan, a truck driver for Keller Trucking Company, were divorced in August, 1990. He came to the restaurant yesterday afternoon to pick up their two children for a visit. Donovan arrived at the restaurant at 2:30 p.m., Poe said.

Poe said Mrs. Donovan called police at 3 p.m. and told them she thought an armed man was in the restaurant, possibly holding her children hostage.

Poe said he called in police officers, who stationed themselves at the front and back doors of the restaurant to prevent the gunman from exiting. County sheriff's deputies were also dispatched to the scene. Upon arrival, they searched the building and found no gunman. The two children, Henry Donovan, Jr., and Helen Donovan, were next door at Belinda's Bakery and were unharmed.

Police have charged businessman Bill Buchanan with first-degree murder.

After an investigation, police determined that Buchanan shot Donovan in the restroom of the Pizza To Go, then pulled his body out the back and put it in the trunk of his car, parked in the alley.

Ms. Donovan said she was sweeping the sidewalk in front of the building when she heard the shots. She realized her children were inside, and said she panicked and ran to a neighboring business to call police. While she was calling police, Buchanan went back in the Pizza To Go, got the two children and took them to the bakery next door, Poe said in the news conference.

When police and county sheriff's deputies arrived, they found no one. After the police left, Buchanan dragged the body out of his car and put it into the alley. He then called police about 4 p.m., pretending that he had found it.

"It appears Mrs. Donovan had been dating Buchanan and had recently broken up with him, saying she was considering a reconciliation with her husband," Poe said.

Buchanan is being held in the Suffolk County jail without bond. He was arrested Wednesday afternoon. His first court appearance for a probable cause hearing will be Monday.

4. You are to write a message based on the following information. Write a summary lead, then organize the story point by point. Your audience is Rockland residents.

Topic: Mobile Crime Watch
In charge, Ross S. Frick, crime prevention officer, Rockland

Frick gives the following information: "When we realized breaking and entering was up 45 percent, we knew we had to do something to offset that increase. So we are establishing the new Mobile Crime Watch. One of the things I always hear about neighborhood watch in Rockland is that nobody is in the neighborhood during the day. We need more people involved in reporting crime during the daytime.

"To accomplish this will take three parts. In the next two weeks the Police Department will train 65 Power and Light employees and local cable franchise employees during one-hour sessions. Postal workers will be trained next. All of these people are out in the community anyway. Many of them have portable telephones so they can report things. In the past they might have seen things and didn't report them to the police. Mobile watch participants won't be surrogate police officers. We don't want them to take any action whatsoever except go to a telephone. We don't want them to approach people or ask questions.

"Then we will notify residents of neighborhoods where we are starting the Mobile Watch programs so they will be aware that extra eyes on crime are in their neighborhoods. We will notify residents through flyers placed in mailboxes.

"As the final part, we hope within six months to set up a reward and award program for Mobile Watch members—the employees and residents—who help us be successful in catching criminals."

From background information, you learn that a Power and Light employee was working on a telephone pole in our county and saw people breaking into a house. He plugged his phone into the wires and police arrested the subjects.

Nearby Middleton started a similar program, called Eyes on Crime, for five years ago, and it has worked. The town has shown a decrease in all crimes except rape and murder.

REFERENCES

Richard Shumate, "Life after Kovach," *Washington Journalism Review,* September 1992.

"Newswriting for the Commercial Appeal," produced by Lionel Linder, editor, and Colleen Conant, managing editor, 1989.

Jacqueline Farnan and David Hedley, "The Mapped Format: A Variation on the Inverted-Pyramid Appeals to Readers," abstract. Paper presented at the Association for Education in Journalism and Mass Communication Conference, Atlanta, GA, August 1993.

Fred Fedler, *Reporting for the Print Media.* New York: Harcourt Brace Jovanovich, 1989.

J. Clark Weaver, *Broadcast Newswriting as Process.* New York: Longman, 1984.

5

Saying It Straight

For years, writing coaches at newspapers and magazines have worked to distill a set of qualities in writing that will catch and hold readers. Many people, such as Roy Peter Clark at the Poynter Institute in St. Petersburg, Florida, have spent a great deal of their professional careers analyzing the qualities of good writing. Authors such as William Zinsser, best known for his book *On Writing Well,* offer advice on how to strengthen and improve prose. Even communication researchers, charged with finding out what makes publications sell, have considered what qualities are valued in messages.

The research shows that the most effective is simple and forceful writing; that is, it says it straight without flourishes and pomp. This chapter

- Looks at three essential qualities in writing: accuracy, clarity, and completeness,
- Reviews five broad rules for good writing,
- Examines sentence structure, and
- Offers specific tips to improve writing.

Watchwords of Writing

No message will succeed if it does not have three essential qualities: accuracy, clarity, and completeness. We know from the discussion of audiences in Chapter 2 that they can be fickle; once they are lost, they may not return.

Writing that is accurate, clear, and complete has a better chance of holding audiences.

Accuracy ensures the credibility of writing. When the audience sees a misspelled name or an erroneous date, it doubts the accuracy of the information that follows. An audience that cannot trust a communicator will abandon him or her.

Clarity means the writer uses language that an audience understands. Simple language is preferred over complicated words. Jargon and technical language are avoided. The message comes through.

Completeness answers an audience's questions. A message that is complete satisfies the audience.

Let's look at each more closely.

Accuracy

Good communication of any kind always contains accurate information. Accuracy is comforting to audiences, which want to depend on information. Errors can occur at any stage in writing: gathering information through research and interviewing, transcribing notes, calculating figures, and creating the copy (when typos can occur). To ensure accuracy, writers must use good information-gathering techniques. They must obtain information from reliable sources and check and recheck it against other sources. Chuck Stone, syndicated columnist and university professor, notes, "If your mother says she loves you, check it out." If you find a discrepancy or an error and you don't have time to check it, follow the adage "When in doubt, leave it out."

We are all prone to committing errors sometimes. Just because a well-known person recites a fact or the fact is found in a computer database doesn't mean it is correct. The potentate may be in error, and human beings type information into databases. Name spellings, middle initials, street numbers, birth dates—seemingly trivial details—become of monumental importance once they become part of a message. Such details may be accurate in notes but then may be transcribed erroneously into copy.

If messages are wrong, people are misled. Writers and audiences rarely forget the mishap when a name is misspelled or an address is wrong. Inaccuracies in messages lead to distrust among audiences—and they can lead to libel suits. Once audience members are misled by a source, they have difficulty trusting it again.

Inaccuracies can damage good will. In an "About Town" column in a small town, a local writer reported that "Bob and Mary Allison" had been on vacation in Bermuda. Mary, indeed, had enjoyed her trip; Bob had been dead since 1988. Publication of their names in tandem was a sad event for everyone in the neighborhood, especially the embarrassed writer.

Clarity

A message that has impact will be clear and straightforward so that everyone in its audience can understand it. "Send a check for $75 by Feb. 1 if you want to ski with the Seniors Club in February" makes the requirement clear. The writing is direct and uses simple, to-the-point language.

In addition, a message needs to be so clear that no misunderstanding or confusion can possibly result. In a university memo about a memorial service for a popular librarian who died, the church was described as "the Baptist Church on Michigan Avenue near Howard University." Unfortunately, more than one church fit that description. Because the message was unclear, several people missed the memorial service, a one-time event.

Completeness

Useful messages also are complete, giving sufficient information for real understanding and guidance. A news story that leaves out an important fact can be misleading and even harmful.

Several examples of incomplete messages occurred in the coverage of the 1994 scandal concerning Jeff Gilooley, who was charged with orchestrating a criminal attack on Olympic skater Nancy Kerrigan. Many news stories identified Gilooley only as "the ex-husband of rival skater Tonya Harding." The information was true but incomplete: Gilooley was Harding's ex-husband, but he had been living and working with her for several months prior to the attack. Complete information changed the story's impact dramatically.

Keys to Good Writing

Researchers, language professionals, and experienced writers agree on five basic tenets of good writing. Anyone can apply the rules while writing and editing.

Good Writing Uses Short Sentences

Most readability experts argue that regardless of age, education, or economic status, people prefer and understand writing that uses short sentences. Human beings have little patience with long, complicated sentences that tax their brain power. Of course, not all sentences should be short. Readers would be bored. Sentence length should vary. A short sentence can have impact. A long, complex sentence can set up an idea for the audience or create a mood, and a short sentence can follow immediately, almost as a punch line. Get the point?

A study at the American Press Institute showed that reader understanding drops off dramatically if sentences exceed twenty words, and comprehension continues to drop as sentences grow longer. Only about one out of twenty people studied could clearly comprehend fifty-word sentences, a common length in newspapers and in academic writing.

Short-term memory rarely exceeds fifteen seconds, which may not be enough time to read one of the many fifty-word sentences in the *Washington Post*.

> TOKYO, Jan. 29—It surely won't be smooth and it probably won't be pretty, but the process of change—political, economic, and social—will continue apace now that Prime Minister Morihiro Hosokawa won passage tonight of the most far-reaching package of electoral reform Japan has seen since just after World War II.

By the time many readers have reached the end of that 50-word sentence, they may have forgotten the beginning!

The English language is based on a pattern of simple, subject–verb–object constructions. Most are short. Because people learn and use English this way in everyday life, they prefer this pattern in messages.

Readers would be more likely to warm up to a straightforward approach to the Japanese electoral reform, such as this one:

> TOKYO—The Japanese Parliament passed tonight the most far-reaching package of electoral reform the country has seen since just after World War II.
>
> Passage signifies continued change—political, economic, and social—for the Japanese people, a process that won't be smooth.

Journalism Professor Fred Fedler of the University of Central Florida says that simplicity makes stories more interesting and forceful. He cites as an example a prize-winning story by World War II journalist Ernie Pyle; the average sentence length was 10.6 words.

Good Writing Uses Short Words

Perhaps your high school English teacher praised you for using "penurious" rather than "stingy," or "inebriated" rather than "drunk." Then you were expanding your vocabulary, but now your audience will thank you for choosing the simpler word.

Just as they do with long sentences, readers and listeners become tired and discouraged when they face too many complex words—usually those exceeding three syllables. To be sure, you can use commonly known, longer words such as "responsibility," "establishment," "participate," and "governmental." But make sure that the longer words are the best choice, not a shorter version, such as "duty," "founding," "join in," or "federal" or "state."

When writing, select the simplest word possible to convey the meaning. For example, in a police story, avoid saying that the two men had an "altercation." Use the word "fight." Instead of "finalize," choose a word such as "conclude" or "finish." Rather than "exasperate," use "annoy" or "bother." Instead of "terminating" this paragraph, we will "end" it.

Good Writing Eliminates Wordiness

"You can almost detect a wordy sentence by looking at it—at least if you can recognize weak verbs, ponderous nouns, and strings of prepositional phrases," Claire Kehrwald Cook writes in her book *Line by Line: How to Improve Your Own Writing.* Her advice gives writers clues to where to find wordiness and where to improve sentence structure.

Author William Zinsser notes that the secret to good writing is to strip every sentence to its cleanest components. Writers must detach themselves from the information and chisel it to the bare essentials. Writers must throw out extra words and phrases—even extra sentences and paragraphs. An old adage advises, "Two words are never as good as one." Consider the simple word "new." When used in the following sentence, it is unnecessary: "Crews expect the new building to be completed within two months." All buildings under construction are new. Leave the word out.

Audiences can find the facts only when excess is trimmed. Sparse writing is more professional, more informative, more objective, and more likely to be read. Writer Stanley Elkin describes the process of eliminating excess in writing:

> *"[It's] a kind of whittling, a honing to the bone, until you finally get whatever the hell you're looking for. It's an exercise in sculpture, chipping away at the rock until you find the nose."*

Wordy writing is likely to be redundant or repetitious. No writer needs to say that a fire "completely destroyed" a downtown block; if it was destroyed, the destruction was complete. This classic often appears: "Jones is currently the manager of consumer services." "Is" means "now," and "now" means "currently." Kill the word "currently." Think about other phrases such as "past history," "acres of land," "4 p.m. in the afternoon," "at 12 midnight," "dead body," and "totally incomprehensible."

In seeking wordiness, look specifically for unnecessary adjectives and qualifiers. For example, a project can't be the "most" unique. "Unique" already means "the most" unusual. Qualifiers such as "very," "truly," and "really" can generally be cut without damage to copy.

Sometimes a statement or entire paragraph that repeats a speaker's direct quotes can be deleted.

> —Jones said he was delighted that the school would receive $40,000 to use for purchasing audiovisual equipment materials for the library.
>
> "I am just delighted that we will have the $40,000 to buy audiovisual equipment for the library," Jones said.

Delete the first paragraph. It does more than serve as a transition to the direct quote—it steals it.

As in art, too much embellishment in writing only detracts and distracts. Consider the effectiveness of the following message before and after its extra words are deleted:

> —Ninety-two years ago, the Tung Wah Dispensary attempted to cure the ailments and afflictions of the San Francisco Chinatown community from its humble outpost at 828 Sacramento Street. When the institution realized that its cramped quarters were counterproductive to the logistics

of health care, it expanded its services and relocated to 835 Jackson Street, eventually being renamed the Chinese Hospital.

Simplified, the history looks like this:

```
Ninety-two years ago, the Tung Wah Dispensary treated
sickness in San Francisco's Chinatown from its humble
outpost at 828 Sacramento Street. Cramped quarters and
expanded services led to a new location at 835 Jackson
Street, the building that eventually was named the Chinese
Hospital.
```

Without its embellishments—"ailments and afflictions," "institution," and "counterproductive"—this message is much more readable and just as informative.

Good Writing Avoids Jargon or Technical Language

In our high-tech society, so much jargon exists that it is difficult to tel! what is jargon and what is plain English. Few people recall that "input" and "output" originated in computer jargon and are therefore unwelcome in precise writing. The same is true of terms such as "bottom line" and "in the red." These accounting terms, so familiar in and out of the accounting field, still are taboo in good writing.

Examples of jargon abound in everyday life. Parents received an annual report from the elementary school. In listing the objectives for the year, the report stated:

```
"Objective Three: The mean score for the kindergarten
program will increase from 5.1 to 5.4 as measured by the
FPG Assessment Report. The lead teacher for
developmentally appropriate practice coordinated the
efforts of our kindergarten teachers to enable our program
to meet this objective."
```

For parents, what does this say? Not much. What is a mean score? What is the FPG Assessment Report? What is developmentally appropriate practice? When people see or hear such words, they stop. Confusion sets in. Parents just want to know how their children are doing in school.

Why Is Jargon Such a No-No?

First, it makes too many assumptions about audiences. Technical language reserves a message for insiders: those who are familiar with the lingo. "Outsiders" who could benefit from the information may be put off. For example, an art exhibit notice that contains artistic jargon may scare away potential visitors to the gallery. Technical terms may create a feeling that the gallery is reserved for an elite group. As a result, an audience may feel excluded or perceive the message as exclusive. For the same reason, it is also wise to avoid foreign words and phrases in published writing—unless those words are commonly used, such as voila!

Second, jargon is precise only to the insiders who use it. Once again, consider the word "input," which may be anything from telephone conversations to cash contributions. A more specific term is better.

Third, jargon usually is ambiguous. The "bottom line" mentioned in a school newsletter may mean many things: expenditures, income, or both; parent satisfaction; student learning outcomes—or almost anything. Skilled writers avoid vagueness by avoiding jargon.

Of course, whether writers use jargon or technical language depends on the audience. If they are writing for a medical publication whose audience is nurses and doctors, the language can be more specific to that profession.

Too often, though, messages for general audiences or lay people are filled with educational, legal, economic, or medical jargon. Some technical language because of its use has become more understood by the general public, such as SAT scores for Scholastic Aptitude Tests and AIDS for acquired immune deficiency syndrome. But language too often goes unexplained.

A problem related to jargon is the use of institutional language: abstract terms and phrases that may communicate well in a specific workplace or institution but that lose meaning for a general audience.

For example, medical professionals use the term "treatment modalities." That terminology is nonspecific and lacks meaning and interest, even to a well-educated general audience. Treatment modalities should be named in terms an audience can understand: a series of shots, an antibiotic for ten days, physical therapy for several months.

In a report an academician wrote "Shrinking and unstable sources of funding lead to short-term dislocations."

What he meant was "A lack of consistent and adequate funding interrupts research."

Many institutional words began as one part of speech and have been transformed into another. Teacher may ask parents "to conference" at 4 P.M.; the vice president may decide "to host" a reception. In good writing, parents will meet with teachers, and the vice president will greet guests at the reception.

It is easy to find words to substitute for institutional terms, and the simpler words are always more specific. Some general, ambiguous terms found frequently in workplaces are "input" and "facilitation." Input may mean discussion or suggestions; facilitation may be planning or sponsoring an event. Good writers find out what is meant by such terms, and they substitute simpler language.

Some terms cannot be avoided, such as the nation's gross national product (GNP). Writers must explain such words adequately when they use them. As the Associated Press stylebook explains it, "The gross national product is the total value at retail prices of all the goods and services produced by a nation's economy in a given time period."

Although jargon is conversational, it rarely is efficient in writing. When talking, you can be sure how much your audience knows about your topic; you can supplement messages with hand gestures, facial expressions, and other visual aids; and you can clarify or define confusing terms if your audience looks puzzled or asks questions.

But when you are writing, your text stands alone and must be absolutely clear. Your goal as a writer is to eliminate misunderstanding, and eliminating jargon and technical language is a giant step toward that goal.

Good Writing Comes to the Point Quickly

Chapter 3 focused on the need for writers to come to the point quickly. Perhaps this is the most problematic of writing challenges. A writer may not want to come to the point because the point is unpleasant: A company has lost money or laid off employees. A popular program has been discontinued. But audiences see through attempts to delay bad news, and they interpret them as sneaky ways to hide information. However unwelcome the message, direct communication conveys a feeling of openness and honesty.

Some writers fail to come to the point because they are in "writer's mode," self-indulgently crafting a long introduction to the main points rather than getting to those points. Readers of nonfiction are after information rather than art, and they consider the most direct messages to be the greatest masterpieces.

Still other writers have trouble coming to the point because they don't know what the point is. Critical thinking—deciding on the main goal in communicating—precedes every writing task. To come to the point, writers must know their audiences and analyze information carefully enough to know the point that audiences will want to know.

Writer and filmmaker Nora Ephron tells a story about her high school journalism teacher. In one lesson, he taught his class to recognize main points by telling them their faculty members would be attending a major conference the next day. He asked them to write a news story about it.

In the students' articles, the introductory paragraphs summarized the facts: All teachers would travel to a nearby city and hear famous speakers. After collecting the papers, the teacher threw them away and told the students, "The point is that there will be no school tomorrow."

Ephron says she never forgot the point:

It was an electrifying moment. So that's it, I realized. It's about the point. The classic newspaper lead of who-what-when-where-how and why is utterly meaningless if you haven't figured out the significance of the facts. What is the point? What does it mean? He planted those questions in my head. And for the first year he taught me journalism, every day was like the first; every set of facts had a point buried in it if we looked hard enough. He turned the class into a gorgeous intellectual exercise, and he gave me enthusiasm for the profession I never lost. Also, of course, he taught me something that works just as well in life as it does in journalism.

These five rules reiterate parts of earlier chapters. But a little redundancy and repetition are like a drill to set indelibly in student writers' minds the importance of writing copy that says it straight. Experienced writers know that in simplicity lies beauty and power.

Words

Three out of the five good writing tenets just given—short words, avoidance of wordiness, and avoidance of jargon—focus on words, the basic unit of any oral or written message. A good writer needs knowledge of language, a good vocabulary, and the sense to know when a word is inappropriate or unnecessary.

The Power of Little Words

Most of the little words in our language come from the original language that was spoken in England before Roman and French invaders added their vocabulary to the mix. The English common folk retained their own words for everyday things, and they borrowed from Latin and French only when they had to.

As a result, the things nearest and dearest to us still are called by their original English names: home, fire, food, and mother, for example. And it is these words to which English-speaking people still respond emotionally. The word "home" has much stronger emotional appeal than the cooler, more technical word "domicile," which is borrowed from Latin. Likewise, "food" sounds good; "nutrients," a Latin-based word, is another matter.

How Little Words Are Successful

Professor and writing coach Carl Sessions Stepp says that people respond to small words because they usually are "first-degree" words, or words that are immediately understood. Everyone has a single, readily available mental picture of "home," along with a host of meanings and feelings associated with that mental picture. But few people can respond so completely to "domicile." The writer who uses "mother" taps the audience's rich reserves of emotion and information.

Stepp points out that larger, multisyllabic words, many of which have origins in other languages, are "second-degree" words. Such words are abstract rather than concrete. They produce no immediate images in the minds of readers or listeners and are often ambiguous when other information is given. Take, for example, the word "nutrition." Does it mean food substances, or measures of vitamins and minerals? It is a second-degree word because the audience needs more information for full understanding.

Consider other second-degree words, such as "facility" and "output." Compare them with these first-degree words: "school" and "grades."

Stepp argues that writers are more likely to appeal to audiences if they choose first-degree words and avoid second-degree words. In writing, we deal with many second-degree words that are part of science, technology, education, and almost every other field. Writers need to remember to define such words in first-degree terms whenever possible, as in this sentence:

```
Nutrition—the kinds of foods patients eat every day—is the
topic of a workshop for nurses at Sibley Hospital April 14.
```

Little words are more heart-warming and more easily understood. They also save space, time, and the reader's energy. They are more readable. And audiences respond to readable copy with overall approval, giving high marks to writers and to the entire publication.

Let's revisit the Associated Press article about the Dallas drug bust that follows. The language couldn't be much simpler. Most fourth-graders could read the story with very little trouble.

Crime, Fear, Poverty All Part of Life in America

Young Woman's Eyes Reflect Despair of Violent Nation

BY JULIA PRODIS

Associated Press

DALLAS—Her eyes are the color of earth, and as vacant as the lot next door.

She's sitting on a concrete step holding a baby that's not hers. Her 16-year-old friend is lying face down on the sizzling sidewalk beside her, his arms arched awkwardly behind him, his hands cuffed in plastic police ties. A girlfriend is similarly contorted at her feet.

"What's your name?" a police-woman asks this hot August day in Dallas.

In a low, slow whisper, she answers, "Latasha."

"La-what?"

"La-Tasha," the thin, moonfaced 19-year-old says with slightly more effort, her blank gaze never looking higher than the holster holding the officer's 9 mm semiautomatic.

Minutes ago, eight muscular members of the Dallas drug enforcement squad, wearing black boots and bulletproof vests, had stormed the faded yellow bungalow behind her. It took two heaves of "the slammer" to break down the door, blocked only by an empty bookcase.

Shrieks from inside, then blurs of motion as the young man bolted out the rear and the woman ran toward the back fence. Latasha Smith never said a word, and the baby didn't cry.

She has the dull look of someone who had seen this rerun too many times. Her look of despair, so deep it turns everything gray, is the same look that flattens the faces of the young and hopeless in poor, violent American neighborhoods everywhere.

Neighborhoods where crack heads fear friends and neighbors more than the cops. Where homes are so filthy detectives can't pick up evidence without something crawling on it. Where neighbors scatter when someone screams for help.

For Americans who say crime is their gravest concern, these calloused Latashas and their criminal friends stir angry fear. But for Latasha, it's just another day.

The baby with cocoa skin and wavy brown hair spits up on Latasha's chest as she rocks negligibly back and forth. Indifferently, she wipes his face with her droopy white tank top.

"Who's payin' for that baby?" the policewoman asks.

"It ain't MY baby," she retorts.

"It's my baby," says the 16-year-old boy, squirming awkwardly on the sidewalk. As he strains to lift his head to speak, the pebbles clinging to his cheek dribble to the ground.

Latasha tells the officer she has three children of her own and she's on welfare. She quit the last job she had washing dishes because she didn't like it. Her children are scattered with relatives and friends today.

"Did you grow up like this baby is growing up?" the reporter asks.

"My daddy shot my momma dead when I was 2." She speaks flatly, like a kid bored with homework. She was raised by her grandfather.

She doesn't explain why she is at this house that isn't hers holding somebody else's baby.

An undercover officer recently bought drugs at this house. The police had come back to clean it up and close it down—one of nearly 400 Dallas dope houses stormed this year.

After running background checks on the three, the sergeant in charge decides to arrest the handcuffed youths on drug charges and ticket Latasha for failing to appear in court after being cited for driving without insurance.

"Do you ever dream of a better life?" the reporter asks.

She shrugs.

She doesn't watch the van carry her two friends away. She just sits in front of the house with the For Rent sign and the broken door, holding someone else's baby, and stares blankly at the vacant lot next door.

Language can be a little grander and still be simple. Consider this excerpt from *Newsweek*'s issue "The First Sixty Years," marking the magazine's 60th anniversary in January 1994. Author Tillie Olsen described the 1930s:

> ...At least a million transients—a third of them between 18 and 24 years old—were on the move, riding the "rattlers" to someplace that might be better.
>
> "Hoovervilles" were the human dumpheaps where nameless Frank Lloyd Wrights wrought their wondrous futuristic structures of flat battered tin cans, fruit boxes and gunny sacks, cardboard and mother earth, encrusting the banks of the rivers or mushrooming under the viaducts. Dog-kennel size, dog-kennel life. Sometimes shelter was any hole in the ground, covered with an old army coat or bit of canvas.
>
> From *Newsweek,* Jan. 3, 1994, © Newsweek, Inc. All rights reserved. Reprinted by permission.

Olsen uses words that are simple, descriptive, and familiar to convey the situation of homeless people during that decade.

The Right Word

Wordsmiths like the late Theodore Bernstein and the late John Bremner have long decried the lack of precision in language. Bremner lamented what he called "the surge of literary barbarism" in English usage. Both stressed the importance of knowing language and definitions. In his book *Words on Words,* Bremner wrote

> *To love words, you must first know what they are. Yes, words are symbols of ideas. But many words have lives of their own. They have their own historical and etymological associations, their own romantic and environmental dalliances, their own sonic and visual delights.*

To language craftsmen like Bremner, writing is a love affair with language.

A careless writer describes a basketball player as "an intricate part of the team." Perhaps his footwork is intricate, but what the writer really meant to say was "an integral part of the team."

A letter from a university provost to a newspaper columnist thanked her for "the prospective" she gave to a local issue. The provost meant "perspective."

In the 1994 attack on figure skater Nancy Kerrigan, the bodyguard and the ex-husband of Tonya Harding, Kerrigan's competitor, were charged. In hearing the first reports, a woman commented on the impact on Tonya Harding, "She certainly will be astigmatized by what these men have done." As it turned out, Harding needed more than glasses.

In a news story, a student quoted a professor as saying, "The meeting will be a great opportunity for faculty members to mingle with their piers." Professors overboard!

Language needs to be specific and correct. Television personality Archie Bunker spouted malapropisms: words that didn't say what he meant. Oriental was "ornamental," and distinguished was "extinguished." We laughed. As writers, we don't want our audiences laughing at us—unless we mean for them to chuckle.

Similar Words

Words that sound alike or are spelled alike are troublesome for writers. Among the most common are "principal" and "principle," "affect" and "effect," "its" and "it's." Such words are particularly troublesome today, when writers depend heavily on computer spell-checkers. Few programs will know the difference between "naval" and "navel" or "stationary" and "stationery." The resulting confusion can be misleading and embarrassing. Writers must be comfortable in reaching for a good dictionary or other reference book to check correct spelling and usage. Other references, such as those listed at the end of this chapter, are valuable for writers who are choosy about words. Appendix C discusses spelling in the computer age.

Writers should pay heed to synonyms. Many writers haul out the thesaurus when they are weary of using a word too often. But a synonym may not be specific. One editing teacher advises against using a thesaurus and prefers a dictionary. Remember that repetition of a word or words throughout a message is acceptable. Repetition can unify a message. Say "bank" throughout a news release about the opening of a financial institution's 78th branch bank. It unifies the release, and "bank" is more specific than "facility."

Word Choice

While taking care with word usage, writers should strive to choose words that are universally accepted and understood. If they are unsure about a word or its use, they should consult a stylebook or a dictionary. The *Associated Press Stylebook,* for example, adds cautionary notes about how specific words included in its entries should be used. The note might warn that the word is offensive or derogatory. Dictionaries will include in the definition whether the word is below the normal standard for literate writing. Dictionaries also will indicate spellings of words and correct usage, as in the case of synonyms.

If a dictionary or a stylebook warns against usage of a word, writers should use it only if they have a compelling reason. They may also have to explain in a note at the beginning of the article or the broadcast that the message contains offensive language. Using profanities and vulgarities is discussed more fully in Chapter 10 on quotations and attribution.

Sentences

Sentences should be complete. Each must have a subject and a verb and must state one complete idea, thought, or meaning. Granted, some writers use short but incomplete sentences for emphasis, such as "The day he left was cold and in the dead of winter. January 22, to be exact." Sentence fragments or stray phrases generally have little place in straight writing, and beginning writers should avoid using them.

This is a fragment: "Cold and in the dead of winter."
This is a sentence: "The day he left was cold and in the dead of winter."

Sentence Types

Grammarians define different types of sentences on the basis of structure.

- A simple sentence is one independent or main clause. It can have more than one subject and verb, object, and modifying phrase.

  ```
  Five people died Wednesday in a skiing accident in
  France.

  A local businessman has won a national award for
  implementing an innovative employee benefits program.
  ```

- A compound sentence has two or more simple sentences that may be joined by a conjunction such as "and" or "but" or by punctuation such as a semicolon.

  `Fire destroyed Tuesday a historic landmark in downtown`
  `Midland, but the owners said they will rebuild the`
  `bookstore on the site.`

  `Many people have changed their diets to cut out high-`
  `fat foods; others have ignored warnings that a high-fat`
  `diet can cause heart disease.`

- A complex sentence has at least one independent or main clause and other clauses that are dependent upon the main clause.

  `When the school board meets Monday night, it will vote`
  `on a controversial multicultural plan that some`
  `elementary school students' parents fear will focus on`
  `sexual orientation as well as on ethnic diversity.`

- A compound-complex sentence is a compound sentence with at least two independent clauses and one or more dependent clauses.

  `The Democratic candidate for lieutenant governor has`
  `raised almost $600,000 for his campaign, which has been`
  `hard fought against the Republican incumbent, and he`
  `expects supporters to contribute even more after he`
  `completes a three-day tour across the state.`

Vary Sentence Types

Good writers use a variety of sentence types, but they prefer the simple sentence. A good guideline is to use many simple sentences and to use compound sentences formed from short simple sentences.

Writers use complex sentences because of the need for attribution and identification. But they work hard to avoid compound-complex sentences, saving them to express ideas that are difficult to state any other way.

Here's a good example of effective sentence variety from a *USA Today* story about young adults in Iran:

> Suddenly a parade of BMWs screeches to a halt in front of a ritzy apartment building.
>
> Out jump dozens of young women, with only their faces showing over their black full-length veils.
>
> They enter blowing kisses to the well-groomed crowd, and they race toward a back room, giggling.
>
> Minutes later, they emerge in revealing bustiers, leather miniskirts, black high heels, gold earrings, and lots of Chanel No. 5.
>
> "Everything you see in a Los Angeles club you see here," says Hooman, 27, a Western-educated importer.

Notice that the first two sentences are simple and the third is compound. The fourth also is a simple sentence; even though it is a long list, it is easy to read because of its simple structure. Only the last sentence is complex, integrating three separate thoughts: You see many things in a Los Angeles club, you see those things here, and the attribution by Hooman, an importer.

Studies show that people of all ages and levels of education prefer simple sentences, in which subjects come before verbs and verbs before the remainder of the sentence. A series of simple sentences relaxes your readers or listeners and prepares them to encounter something more complex when it occurs in your text, as it inevitably will.

Look at the variety in this excerpt from *Newsweek*'s 60th anniversary issue. Author John Updike wrote about the 1950s:

> Many Americans were happy in the '50s—but not as happy, looking back, as we should have been. The American economy was the world's behemoth. The imbalance of trade was over a billion dollars in our favor, instead of more than a hundred billion in annual outflow. Ten dollars bought a four-course meal in Paris, instead of a demitasse and a stale croissant. At home $10,000 bought a house, and a quarter bought a gallon of gas. You could walk most city streets without a qualm at 2 in the morning, and as to family values—boy, did we have family values! Divorce rates dropped, as did the age when people got married. Wives

churned out new Americans at the highest birthrate in decades. Night after night, we clustered around the television set watching "Father Knows Best," "I Love Lucy," "Leave It to Beaver," "The Pat Boone Show" and "The General Electric Theatre..."

Common Sentence Errors

In constructing sentences, some writers forget the rule of parallel structure. In writing, all parts of any list or series must be parallel—that is, if the first element in the list starts with a noun, all others must be nouns as well. For example, the structure of this sentence is not parallel:

```
Previous legislative agendas included the Family
Preservation Act, child protective services, and
extending to school boards the right to ban corporal
punishment.
```

Nouns in the list, "act" and "services," are not parallel with the verb form "extending." The sentence should be rewritten to read

```
Previous legislative agendas included the Family
Preservation Act, child protective services, and the right
of school boards to ban corporal punishment.
```

When writers start with a specific verb form, such as an infinitive with "to," they must keep the same format. The structure of the following sentence is not parallel:

```
The banquet is an occasion to reward corporations for
"family friendly" policies and recognizing volunteers and
the media.
```

It should be rewritten to read

```
The banquet is an occasion to reward corporations for
"family friendly" policies and to recognize volunteers and
the media.
```

Another common sentence error is the incorrect placement of modifying phrases or clauses. Such misplaced elements can lead to humorous and misleading sentences, such as the following:

```
After wheeling me into the operating room, a mask was
placed over my face.

The bank makes low-interest loans to individuals of any
size.

Mrs. Rogers was arrested shortly after 3 p.m. at the home
where the couple lived without incident.
```

Once spotted, modifier problems are easy to repair. Good writers train themselves to check modifier placement: Did the mask really wheel me into the operating room? Does the bank discriminate based on height and weight? Did the couple really live in the house without incident? The questions can be cleared up by quick rewriting:

```
After I was wheeled into the operating room, a mask was
placed over my face.

The bank makes low-interest loans of any size to
individuals.

Mrs. Rogers was arrested without incident shortly after 3
p.m. at the home where the couple lived.
```

A good sentence can never be interpreted to mean more than one thing. Linguists say it has a "single reading"—meaning that the reader never needs to go back and read it again to understand it. If the reader goes back, it should be to savor the quality of the writing. Good writing aims for a single reading, so that readers move unobstructed through messages to meaning.

Paragraphs—Short Paragraphs

Words become sentences, and sentences become paragraphs. English composition books devote entire chapters to the topic of writing good paragraphs. But, as mentioned in Chapter 4, when writers are concerned with transmitting information quickly, their ideas about paragraphing change. A paragraph is a whole presentation or argument on a topic in an essay for an English composition or literature class, while in mass communication, a paragraph is a single fact, thought, or "sound bite." That single thought or idea may take several sentences to explain. In newswriting, paragraphs are often short to break up blocks of gray copy. Just as they do with short sentences, writers should vary their paragraphs.

Effective use of three grafs instead of one paragraph is shown in this sports story by *USA Today* writer Chuck Johnson:

> —Some major league players are in line to get rich quick over the next 10 days.
>
> The filing period for salary arbitration runs today through Jan. 14. A total of 113 players are eligible. Salary figures will be exchanged Jan. 18, and arbiters will hear cases Feb. 1–20.
>
> Atlanta, Montreal, St. Louis and Kansas City, with eight players each, have the most eligible to file.

Newspaper and magazine writers start a new graf to signal a new fact or a change of speaker—and sometimes just to give the reader a break. Readers appreciate white space in a publication, and frequent "graffing" gives such visual relief by making space—literal and figurative—between ideas.

New Speaker Equals New Paragraph

One of the most useful functions of frequent graffing is that it effectively signals a change of speakers. Notice how *Washington Post* writer Paul Taylor moves smoothly from one quote to another, just by starting new grafs:

> —"Political advertising is so wretched that most of it wouldn't be approved by our own self-governing boards," Alexander Kroll, chairman and chief executive officer of Young & Rubicam, said at a recent ad industry luncheon here.

"I think we need to ban political ads," Jay Chiat, chairman and chief executive officer of Chiat/Day/Mojo, which creates ads for Nissan and Reebok, said in an interview.

"The worst thing that has ever happened to the advertising business is political advertising," said Malcolm MacDougall, chairman of the MacDougall Co.

With quotations, the short bursts provided by one-sentence grafs add a lively, conversational air to newswriting and keep the reader moving down the page. "New speaker, new graf" is a newswriter's rule that can add clarity to all writing. The technique can be accomplished in any writing.

Most writing can benefit from shorter paragraphs. Bite-sized paragraphs of newswriting may not be appropriate in all settings, but leaner paragraphs tend to streamline messages of all kinds.

Where We Are

For many beginning writers, thinking about rules stymies them from the start. But let's summarize what we have said so far about good writing.

1. Good writing uses short sentences.
2. Good writing uses short words.
3. Good writing eliminates wordiness.
4. Good writing clears away redundancy, jargon, and institutional language.
5. Good writing comes to the point quickly.
6. Good writing has a mix of sentence types.
7. Good writing has short paragraphs.

When listed, the rules seem more manageable.

The Way to Clearer Writing

Writing often moves from the general to the specific as writers refine their sentences. This chapter is following such a path. At the outset, we discussed broad principles of accuracy, clarity, and completeness. We then looked at the basic tenets of good writing and the components of any piece of writing: words, sentences, and paragraphs.

Now for the specifics. Additional guidelines can help you say it straight. Keep the guidelines in mind as you write, but don't be so tied to them that you stop after every sentence to analyze whether it meets the standards of good writing. Go ahead and write, then go back and apply the guidelines in editing.

Write the First Draft As You Would Say It

Writing coach Robert Gunning said writers should write the way they talk. He argued that all writing would improve if people simply talked and wrote down what they said. Gunning was onto a great idea: First drafts are most effective when a writer puts down on paper what he or she would tell someone about a topic. The result: text that is conversational, that uses simple language, and that is easy to revise into a well-organized written message.

Author Tom Wolfe made his fiction writing career by writing the way he talked. You can see his style in the following section.

Colorful Description

In his speech to the American Society of Newspaper Editors, author Tom Wolfe noted the phenomenon of the trophy wife, what the successful CEO believes he deserves as a perk. He described the courtship ritual, adding his characteristic style, this way:

> *. . . the sight out on the discotheque floor of the 57-year-old CEO with his trophy wife-to-be. He's wearing his hard-finished worsted navy blue chalk-striped suit. He's wearing his medium spread-collar white shirt . . . and he's wearing his hair combed back over his ears in little sloops known as the 57th Street biggie look. His trophy wife-to-be, his lemon tart, is out there, and she's wearing a pair of Everlast boxing trunks. She's got on a man's strap style undershirt. She's got a hairdo that looks as if a Snapper lawnmower's gone over her head . . .*
>
> *And he's beaming at her with red eyes through these walnut shell eyelids. . . . He's desperately trying to do the robot or the eel or the sadomacho until the onset of dawn, saline depletion, or myocardial infarction—or whichever comes first. And after all, why shouldn't he? Because what are Mom and the Cutlass Sierra and Buddy and Sis up against a love like this? That first night on the disco floor,*

she wore a pair of boxing trunks while leather punks and painted lulus, African queens and sado Zulus paid her court. I grow old, the 1990s way. Deaf but from a Max Q octophonic beat. Stroked out but on my own two feet. Disco macho for you, my new cookie.

Don't Begin at the Beginning

After seeing a four-car collision, the typical observer arrives home and blurts out, "I saw an incredible wreck on Highway 501. Four cars collided; all the drivers were injured, and one car burned." Only then will the observer back up and give background: "I was in the left lane, coming home from the mall," and so on.

Like urgent conversation, writing needs to jump straight to the point, then fill the reader in—just as we discussed in Chapter 3 on writing leads. This technique gives writing a conversational tone and at the same time gets to the ever-so-important point of the message.

Starting with salient facts is a natural way to tell about important information. Unfortunately, it is a form that most people forget after years of reading stories and writing essays, both of which usually start with formal introductions. If your goal is to say it straight, say it—your main point—soon in your message. Suspenseful beginnings work best in drama.

Consider Writing and Editing to Be Two Separate Tasks

When you spill out your conversational first draft, write it without stopping to edit. Mixing writing and editing wastes time and effort. If you edit as you go (and most amateurs do), you may fuss over a sentence that you eventually eliminate. At the very least, you will interrupt your own thought processes and conversational flow. So write first. If you pause to ponder sentence structure or information, that's okay. But don't wander or stray from the effort.

Some beginning writers lack the confidence to sit down and write. But author Joel Saltzman points out that we all are more competent wordsmiths than we think:

When you're talking, odds are that 98 percent of the time you don't even think about grammar. You're doing fine and it's just not an issue . . . I am suggesting that you don't worry about it right now; because the more you worry about grammar, the less you're going to write.

After you finish your outpouring of prose, let the copy cool by taking a short break before you begin to edit. This separates the writing and editing processes and allows you to see your copy in a different way. If you edit or rewrite immediately after your draft is finished, you will read what you think you wrote rather than what is actually on the page. More about the editing process is covered in Chapter 6.

Stick with Subject–Verb Order

Most human languages prefer to place subjects before verbs, and ours is no exception. Curious people want to know who did something, then what they did (and to whom or what). Keep these audience interests and preferences in mind when you write. Subject–verb–object order generally gives the sentence action.

```
A man wearing a stocking mask robbed the University dining
hall late Tuesday night and locked the dining services
manager in a closet.

A massive earthquake registering 6.8 on the Richter scale
rocked Japan early Tuesday morning.
```

Readers get confused if subjects and verbs are scrambled, regardless of how artistic the result may be.

```
"Came he swiftly to her bower?"
```

Not in the information age.

Choose Active Verbs

We learn that verbs are action words, but not all verbs are active. Some show no action at all, such as the verb "to be" in all its forms (is, am, are, was, were, be, being). Such verbs are less interesting and harder to picture than are active verbs.

Writers prefer active verbs because they contain more information and sensory detail. "He was president" is vague compared with "He dominated the country as president." Good writing is filled with active verbs that evoke images in the mind of the reader or listener.

```
Lightner whacked the ball with such force that it sailed
over the outfield wall—his first home run of the season.

Babies cried, children clamored, balls thunked into
holes, tickets ching-ching-chinged into eager
hands while the Chuck E. Cheese theme song warbled
in the background.
```

Choose the Active Voice

When writers use active verbs, they write in active voice.

"Mattingly hit the ball." The subject, Mattingly, performs the action. The object, the ball, receives action. This sentence format is called active voice, and it is the natural order of English. "A man wearing a stocking mask robbed the University dining hall" carries more action than "The University dining hall was robbed by a man."

Every now and then, a sentence has no obvious subject and must be written in another format, called the passive voice. Take, for example, this sentence: "The law was changed several years ago." It is in passive voice. The recipient of the action, the law, has been moved into the subject position— probably because a long legislative process kept the writer from isolating a single person or session responsible for changing the law.

Research shows that people prefer active sentences over passive ones. The sentence "Congress passed the bill" is easier to read and comprehend than its passive equivalent, "The bill was passed by Congress." Skilled writers prefer the active voice and use passive sentences only when necessary. In our example about Mattingly, a passive structure would hardly have the same impact: "The ball was hit by Mattingly."

Sometimes writers use passive sentences for emphasis even when the subject is apparent: "The anticrime bill was passed by Congress." Here the writer wants to focus on the bill rather than on Congress.

Generally Put Time Elements After the Verb

Because verbs are stimulating to readers, they should come before less interesting elements. Audiences need to know when something happened, but they can wait to find out. Time element, a necessary but often dull part of a message, can be relegated to a place after the verb. Some writers prefer to put it immediately after the verb. Here are a few examples:

```
Former Mayor Barry Anderson was married Tuesday morning in
a small private ceremony.

Grant applications requesting up to $100,000 for research
on learning disabilities may be submitted through June 15
to the National Institutes of Health.
```

Sometimes, however, the time element carries importance and needs to go elsewhere—even first in the sentence.

```
Wednesday a 14-year-old youth collected $125,000 that he
found in a paper bag a year ago. The money was never
claimed.
```

In this example, the beginning and end of the sentence set up the time span: On Wednesday the youth cashed in after waiting a year.

```
Beginning this weekend the city planetarium will offer
extra weekend shows to expand its offerings for people who
work and school children.
```

Right away, people know that an event is coming soon.

Be Specific Rather Than General

Always give the most specific information you can. Significant details enlighten and delight readers and pack information into a few words. Instead of saying that Madonna went on a shopping trip, tell what she bought: a case of mascara and two string bikinis. Inquiring minds want to know! Instead of saying that a reporter had a messy desk, try

```
On his desk Howard had a can of unsharpened pencils and two
potted ferns, both of them dead.
```

Watch out for words that have almost a generic quality, such as "facility." Be specific: bank, gymnasium, recreation center, high school. Use the specific noun.

Author Tom Wolfe has a marvelous talent for combining simple words into run-on, colorful, entertaining description, as you have just seen in the excerpt from his speech to the American Society of Newspaper Editors in 1990.

Appeal to the Senses

An audience, whether it is reading or listening, still can use the full range of senses as it absorbs information. That means writers must pay attention to their senses when gathering information. Writers can report the facts or describe the scene without being subjective—a fear that many beginning writers have and that keeps them from being descriptive in their writing.

Writing that appeals to the senses—that creates mental pictures, aromas, and sensations—is more memorable and more appealing; it transports the audience to the scene of the message. Once captured, the audience is likely to remain in the writer's world long enough to get the message.

Through writing that appeals to all the senses, *Washington Post* feature writers Patrice Gaines and DeNeen L. Brown take readers to an inner-city housing project in the following passage:

> Three days after lethal gunfire exploded at a nearby schoolyard and two hours before the mayor was to visit, maintenance men and female prisoners were cutting grass, trimming trees, and picking up litter at Fort Dupont Dwellings, a cluster of scarred, two-story brick buildings with Plexiglas windows.
>
> A school-crossing guard and some mothers who had just walked their children to school Tuesday morning were amused by all the raking, sweeping, and grooming. They found it especially comical—worthy of

loud, cynical laughter—that workers were cutting grass in front of buildings where no one lived.

"They do nothing until somebody gets shot, then they pacify us with two days of cleaning up," said a 53-year-old grandmother. For 28 years, she has lived in this apartment complex that was built in the 1940s to be a stopover for families expected to move out and up.

Fort Dupont Dwellings was home to Launice Smith, the 4-year-old girl who died yesterday after being shot in the head Saturday afternoon at a pickup football game at Weatherless Elementary School. The 300 block of Ridge Road, where Launice lived, is called "Little Vietnam" by some because of the popping sounds of gunfire nearly every night.

The reader sees the scarred buildings and dim Plexiglas, hears cynical laughter and gunshots, and even smells the freshly cut grass. No one would doubt the authenticity of the writers' description, which sets the scene and mood for the audience.

One need not be a feature writer to use sensory appeal. It works well in everyday forms of communication, such as directions to the company picnic: Instead of "Turn right two blocks after the fork in the road and proceed to 15ll," how about this:

```
Look for a grove of tall pines two blocks after the fork in
the road; turn right and go to the red mailbox marked 1511.
You'll smell pungent smoke from Marvin's famous barbequed
ribs.
```

With such sensory appeal, it's doubtful that anyone will get lost.

Use Statistics Sparingly and Powerfully

We live in an era when numbers make powerful messages: A basketball arena will cost $29 million. A pharmaceutical company will lay off 1,600 workers.

Audiences become insensitive if they are bombarded by alarming numbers, regardless of how striking those numbers may be. Statistics of any kind should be delivered one at a time in good writing. Never let two numbers touch in written copy; avoid putting numbers close to one another except in direct comparisons:

```
Women work 88 hours per week doing home and workplace
chores, while men work about 60.
```

Another good rule of thumb is to limit yourself to no more than three numbers in any one paragraph to avoid overwhelming your reader or listener. *USA Today* reporter Jack Hovelson shows how it is done:

> Minivans—among the USA's most popular vehicles—have terrible bumpers, says an insurance group that runs low-speed tests every year.
>
> That's expensive and potentially dangerous news for the 1.1 million consumers who buy minivans each year.
>
> Mazda's MPV—the worst—will cost about $3,200 at the repair shop if you back into a pole at just 5 mph, according to the Insurance Institute for Highway Safety.

Professor Philip Meyer, who has been a consultant at *USA Today,* suggests that in any statistical report, one or two numbers stand out as being crucial. The important numbers should appear early in your message, and others may be summarized in lists or tables outside the written text.

Translate Statistics into Everyday, Tangible Terms

People have little intuitive understanding of large numbers. The citizen who learns that a sports arena is to cost $29 million is left with many questions: Is that a good price for an arena? How many new schools would that buy? How much will my county taxes increase?

Good writers provide an understanding of big numbers in several ways. One way is to compare one number with another:

```
The $29 million price tag compares with the $18.2 million
cost of an arena built in 1989 in Seattle.
```

Another way to present numbers is to give them in terms the average person deals with each day. Few of us can visualize $29 million, but many people can understand a 3.5 percent tax increase to fund the stadium.

The clearest way to present costs is to use an individual citizen as an example:

```
A person owning a home with a tax value of $154,000 will
pay about $200 more each year in taxes to finance the
arena.
```

The same approach is used in the *USA Today* story on minivan bumpers, which cites shop costs of $3,500 for an average fender bender. Such writing allows the audience to understand personal gains or losses that may be obscured in reports of large numbers.

Make Sure Your Calculations Are Accurate

Many writers jokingly state that they went into communications because they couldn't do math. But any writer who uses numbers must be sure they are correct. Errors can be embarrassing for both the subjects and the writer.

In a news story about salary increases at city hall, a reporter looked at the current year's salary for the city attorney: $35,000. The proposed salary for the next fiscal year was $39,000. The story said the city attorney would get a 10.25 percent pay increase. The actual increase was 11.4 percent. The reporter erroneously divided the difference of $4,000 by the new salary rather than the current salary. Other city employees were upset that the city attorney was getting 10.25 percent compared with their 4 percent. When the real difference eventually was published, the unhappiness grew. (And the city attorney expressed his anger that the figures were published at all, forgetting that the salaries of public officials are public record.)

When in Doubt, Leave It Out

Unless you are able to check the accuracy of a spelling or a surprising fact, leave it out. Accuracy is linked, in the minds of audience members, with quality—with company quality, publication quality, and writer quality. Your reputation is riding on what you write.

Some errors are painful to people in the community. A university magazine noted offhandedly that a famous scientist had discovered a new kind of plant. His research assistant, who in fact had made the discovery and received credit for it in scientific journals, called the reporter to correct the error. Few people will ever see a small correction notice, but people like the offended research assistant will remember the slight for years.

Multiple copies of a mistake are always embarrassing, whether in an office memo or a front-page story. Such mistakes also may lead to legal problems. Appendix A gives libel guidelines for writers.

Rewrite Long Introductory Phrases

Audiences are eager to get to the point, and long introductory phrases slow them down. Long phrases also interrupt the subject–verb–object pattern that readers and listeners prefer.

Avoid this:

```
Because the Redskins had been waiting all season for a
victory, several players refused to be interviewed.
```

Prefer this:

```
Several Redskins players refused to be interviewed after
waiting all season for a victory.
```

Eliminate Long Strings of Prepositional Phrases

Any group of two or more prepositional phrases makes a sentence seem to meander rather than flow. Too many prepositional phrases strung together within a sentence are undesirable but easy to fix. Prepositional phrases are among the movable parts of any sentence; they also may be placed in new (short) sentences.

Avoid this:

```
The school's marching band will appear in a series of
performances on three consecutive Tuesday afternoons on
the athletic field near the gymnasium on the school campus
beginning this Tuesday.
```

Prefer this:

```
The school's marching band will present a series of Tuesday
afternoon performances beginning this week. The band will
play on the athletic field near the gymnasium.
```

Look for unnecessary prepositional phrases everywhere in writing. Take this:

```
Marilyn Jacobs, one of the writers of the letter, said the
group wants action immediately.
```

and edit it to read:

```
Marilyn Jacobs, who helped write the letter, said the group
wants action immediately.
```

Avoid Making Everything Look IMPORTANT

Some writers like to add emphasis by underlining text or by using capital letters, exclamation marks, and even quotation marks. Frequent use of such elements detracts from professional polish. Once in a while, everyone needs to add emphasis. Save it for when it "*REALLY*" counts.

Avoid this:

```
NOTRE DAME Varsity Cheerleaders Harry Allen and "Bitsy"
Howard placed first in "couples" competition at a national
cheerleading event Saturday.
```

Try this:

```
Notre Dame varsity cheerleaders Harry Allen and Bitsy
Howard placed first in couples competition at a national
cheerleading event Saturday.
```

Clear Out Euphemisms

Most of us were taught to use euphemisms in polite conversation—to say "expecting" rather than "pregnant," "plump" rather than "fat," and "passed away" rather than "died." In fact, we like euphemisms because they are handy substitutes for embarrassing words.

Avoid this:

```
The guard said that two residents of the correctional
facility had gone to "their just reward."
```

Prefer this:

```
The guard said that two prisoners had died.
```

Using the straightforward words "prisoners" and "died" instead of the longer euphemisms keeps the sentence short and the reading easy.

Good writing requires specific information. No euphemism is precise and meaningful enough for good writing. In fact, some euphemisms are designed to be imprecise—to mislead or give false comfort. Never forget that "protective reactions strikes" are "bombings" and that "peacekeeper missiles" are "nuclear warheads." Both terms came into vogue with the politically correct language fad of the 1960s. Politically correct terms generally are longer and less accurate than the synonyms they replace. For example, a drunk is a "person of differing sobriety," and a loser is an "individual with temporarily unmet objectives." Writers have to draw the line between what is acceptable taste and what is a surrender to faddish writing. Those who aren't in the politically correct circle may wonder what on earth the writer is saying. Once euphemisms are removed, the meaning is clearer.

Keep Writing Readable

Readability is defined most simply as the level of difficulty of a given message. Readable, or high-readability, writing is easy to understand. Several ways to measure readability have been found, most of which are based on (1) sentence length and (2) concentration or number of multisyllable words.

One common readability measure is the Fog Index, developed in the 1940s by Robert Gunning for United Press International wire service. To compute a Fog Index, (1) calculate the average number of words per sentence in a given message and (2) count the number of difficult words, or those with three syllables or more, in a 100-word sample from the message. Add these two figures together and multiply by 0.4.

The resulting number—the Fog Index for the writing in question—corresponds to the number of years of education a reader would need to read and understand the copy. For example, a publication with an average of 22 words per sentence and 15 difficult words in the 100-word sample would have a Fog Index of 14.8. That means its readers would require some college education to read the piece comfortably.

Let's see how that works on the Patrice Gaines' piece about Fort Dupont Dwellings. Seven sentences have 199 words or an average of 28 words per sentence. Words with three syllables or more in the first 100 words number 6. Add 28 to 6 and multiply by 0.4; the answer is 13.6. The Gaines' piece does not have high readability because of the long sentences. Only 6 out of 100 words have three or more syllables, so her preference for simple words keeps the readability between high school and college level. That is consistent with the *Washington Post*'s overall style.

Most readability experts agree that clear writing is geared to the eleventh-grade level. Even people with a great deal more education seem to be most comfortable reading at the lower level. Journalism Professor Fred Fedler notes that most wire service copy is written at about the tenth-grade level.

The *Wall Street Journal*'s Fog Index routinely falls into the eleventh- to twelfth-grade range, despite the complicated nature of financial reporting. A clever marketing strategy is operating here: Dow Jones knows that to make business reports palatable, they must be readable.

Be Aware of Misinterpretations

As writers edit their copy they need to be aware of all possible interpretations of what has been written. They need to know an audience's language tastes for effective communication. Language choices can alter meaning for the reader or put a different slant on a message—often a slant that the writer never intended. Sometimes the results are comical, such as a ship was "birthed" instead of "berthed" at a nearby naval station, or a mother who wants "piece of mind." Think about the sentence "Donations may be given by church members of any size." The size of the donations, not of church members, is the issue.

A prepositional phrase in the wrong place can change the meaning. Lacey Smith died of a head wound at Memorial Hospital at 4 p.m. Wednesday. What the writer meant was that Lacey Smith died Wednesday afternoon at Memorial Hospital after suffering a head wound. Smith had the head wound before arriving at the hospital; Smith was not wounded by hospital personnel. "The thief was muscular with a round face about 5 feet 3 inches tall." How tall was the thief?

You, as the writer and editor, must also review writing for bias (discussed in Chapter 7) and for "funky" or trendy language that just ain't good writing.

Watch Out for Language Trends

Writers should be circumspect of popular trends in writing. As we noted earlier in the discussion of avoiding euphemisms, the politically correct movement, especially in the early and mid-1990s, substituted a myriad of words and phrases for ones that had been part of common language. In many cases, the new language was wordy and less precise.

Using such "pop" language excludes segments of the audience that may not be cued to the lingo. Certainly language evolves. Each time a new edition of Webster's dictionary comes out, new words are included. Many of us can remember when "ain't" was not in the dictionary. Dictionaries list and define words that are common in the English language, but a dictionary is just one of many sources writers use.

One trend that has caused extreme pain to language experts has been the conversion of nouns to verbs. "Host" has become "to host," and "conference" has become "to conference." With computer networks increasing the use of such terms, they soon will be standard parts of the language. Many already are accepted usage, but some writers still cringe when they hear them.

Another trend that offends many writers is the addition of "ize" to create new words: "prioritize," "finalize," "maximize," "accessorize." Again, while the words have found their way into everyday usage, language professionals try to find better and more accurate verbs.

How the Rules Apply

Overwhelmed by so many rules? Keep them in the back of your mind while you do the most important task of all: Write! Then go back to your draft and apply the principles. Remember: You'll never need all the rules at once.

For practice, let's take a real-life letter, with names and places changed, that defies the guidelines in this chapter. It is neither clear nor correct; it is wordy and indirect. In short, it's a mess.

```
Mr. and Mrs. Joe Dighton
103 Roberts Road
Silver Springs, Md. 20901
```

Dear Joe and Patti:

I do hope you enjoyed your recent visit to THE CLIFFS retirement community and THANK YOU for taking the time to look at our community. I thoroughly enjoyed visiting with you and Patti last evening and do hope you folks will decide to become a part of "Our Family."

While Rand McNally has named us the second best place in America to retire because we have the 20th lowest cost of living, third best health care and ranked us a bargain in housing costs. They also ranked us as the Nation's safest community, boasting a practically nonexistent crime rate. Nestled in the foothills of the Blue Ridge Mountains in Swain County, North Carolina, and surrounded by two scenic rivers and a national forest is a location that provides the best of GOD's creation for spending lazy days of fishing, swimming boating, hiking or hunting. If you prefer our tennis/swimming complex or 18-hole championship golf course designed by Dan Birch is most enjoyable.

Our developer has endeavored to create a community for middle class America based on traditional family values centering on a family atmosphere and our backgrounds are varied from physicians, engineers, farmers, government employees, retired military and the list goes on . . .

```
If I can be of further assistance or you have friends—or
know of someone—looking for what we have to offer please
give me a call.


                    Sincerely,

                    Donna Sales

                    Marketing Director
```

Needless to say, Joe and Patti were unimpressed by the letter from The Cliffs. What can you fix, now that you have all this chapter's advice on writing? Can you help Donna Sales to "say it straight?"

Here's a list of some problems with her letter:

- Too much is made IMPORTANT by Overuse of Capitalization.
- Donna has made an error in logic: The letter is to both Joe and Patti, but the writer stumbles in saying, "I enjoyed talking with you and Patti."
- Too many statistics are mentioned too quickly, and they do not appear in parallel form. Also, they are not comprehensible: Is the resort 20th from the highest cost of living—meaning that it is expensive—or is it 20th from the lowest cost?
- Joe and Patti's hometown, Silver Spring, is misspelled in a way that most Silver Spring residents find particularly tiresome. (Silver Springs is a place in Florida where people ride in glass-bottom boats.)
- Most sentences begin with long introductory phrases.
- Most sentences are too long, complex, and confusing.
- The second paragraph is too long.
- The letter is wordy throughout and has a Fog index of 14.8.

You may want to add to the list, but let's focus on simplifying the language, shortening the sentences, lowering the Fog index, and clearing up the confusion. Here's a rewritten version:

```
Patti and Joe Dighton
103 Roberts Road
Silver Spring, Md. 20901
```

Dear Patti and Joe:

I hope you enjoyed your recent visit to The Cliffs. Thank you for taking time to look at our community. I enjoyed visiting with you both and hope you will decide to become part of The Cliffs family of residents.

Rand McNally has named us the second best place in America to retire because of our reasonable costs for high-quality health care and housing. It also has ranked us the nation's safest retirement community.

The Cliffs, nestled in the foothills of the Blue Ridge Mountains in Swain County, N.C., is bounded by two scenic rivers and is next to a national park. This is an ideal location for retirement, providing the best of God's creation for your days of fishing, swimming, boating, hiking, or hunting. You may also enjoy our tennis and swimming complex or our 18-hole championship golf course, which was designed by Dan Birch.

Our developer has created a community with traditional family values and a warm, family-like atmosphere. Our residents have backgrounds in professions, including medicine, engineering, farming, and military and government service.

Please give me a call if I can answer your questions about The Cliffs, or if I can help any of your friends who are looking for what we have to offer.

Sincerely,

Donna Sales
Marketing Director

If Patti and Joe had received the revised letter, they might have given The Cliffs another look.

The long sentences are divided, and the long paragraph splits naturally into two. The result is a more inviting letter. The new Fog index is 10.9, which Gunning would applaud. Most importantly, The Cliffs appears to be a well-run enterprise. And the only difference is in the writing.

The following exercises will require you to apply the guidelines in this chapter, just as we did in The Cliffs example. When you have completed them, take a message you constructed during the last week and try to rewrite it more clearly and simply. Most writers find it difficult to rewrite and edit their own work. Chapter 6 will review the stages of editing to make the task more manageable.

EXERCISES

- Change the words used incorrectly in the following sentences.

    1. The perspective budget for the coming year will include raises for the city's firemen.
    2. An incoming ice storm will effect whether we can drive to work tomorrow.
    3. The state historical society will reenact signing the state constitution in the Capital.
    4. The country's navel force has been reduced.
    5. His desire for money is his principle guiding force in business.
    6. The coach said the team ignored his advise to make it a passing game.
    7. Jiminy Cricket said Pinocchio should let his conscious be his guide.
    8. The engineer eliminated the High Road sight because it sloped to much.
    9. Returning the stolen car to it's owner is the best decision.
    10. The most affective writing follows good writing principals.

- Edit the following sentences to make them shorter and to the point.

11. In order to expedite the delivery, the company will add a third delivery truck for its routes on Monday.

12. We will have pizza for dinner whether or not you choose to come.

13. She is presently employed as the assistant to the president, but she expects to make a decision whether or not to change jobs by the end of the year.

14. If they are willing to pay the difference between the economy pack and the family pack, customers will learn that the family pack will save them more money in the long run.

15. Students voted Thursday to conduct a poll to determine the status of living conditions in dormitories.

16. Clarendon Park residents will march Saturday to protest the city council's decision to annex the neighborhood over residents' objections.

17. If the school maintains lines of communication and makes the alumni feel as if they are still a part of the school even though they have already graduated, the school should have no problem reaching its fund-raising goal.

18. The residents of the neighborhood said they would petition the city council to reconsider again the decision to allow beer sales before 11 a.m. on Sunday morning which would be against the wishes of many church-going citizens.

19. Fifteen scholarship winners, who were chosen because of their high academic achievement, will be given $15,000 in scholarship money to use at the college of their choice after they graduate from high school.

20. Child-care experts disagree over whether or not children should be spanked as part of a parent's disciplinary techniques or whether or not putting children in a time-out away from activities is punishment enough.

• Correct the grammar and punctuation problems in the following sentences.

21. He will likely have the money to attend the fund-raising gala and becoming a sponsor.

22. The organization's goals are to educate the medical community about the disease; attract 400 new members this year; support those who have the disease and encourage more research.

23. As an environmentalist, his efforts focused on the University's South Loop Road plan to save trees, green space and the University's student–family housing development.

24. She paid $35—half the savings in her piggy bank, for the Rush t-shirts at the concert.

25. Setting the meeting for 2 p.m., the time should be agreeable to all participants.

26. The committee of financial consultants and economic experts have to develop a plan to reduce the corporation's debt.

27. Irene uses coupons when she goes to the grocery store; saving $3 to $4 each trip.

28. It is a difficult plan for a politician to explain to their constituents.

29. The program offers workshops for child day care teachers on positive discipline as well as conducts community issues forums and workplace seminars.

• Eliminate redundancy by editing.

30. Susan is currently director of marketing sales.

31. He served as past president of the Rotary club.

32. The elementary school will need 25 acres of land for a multipurpose building, playground, and ball fields.

33. Fire completely destroyed the town hall in the month of June.

34. The future outlook for the economy indicates interest rates may rise slightly.

35. The circus will be at 3 p.m. Sunday afternoon and 7 p.m. Sunday night.

36. Due to the fact that more than two-thirds of the people did not respond, the picnic will be canceled.

37. She climbed up the tree in order to get a better look at the defendant.

38. John went on to say that any student's effort should be recognized.

39. The Broadway show will close down six months after it first began.

- Edit the following story to eliminate redundancy and wordiness. Simplify words where possible.

A group of local parents have asked the administrators of the town recreation program to close a town swimming pool unless safety conditions at the pool are improved next summer.

Parents said they are particularly upset over the drowning death of a 5-year-old boy in the shallow end of the pool in August.

In a letter addressed to the assistant town manager, Renee Lovelace, the parents also said that they were concerned because the pool had no black lifeguards. The swimming pool is located in a predominantly black neighborhood in the town.

"We are especially upset about the treatment of children at the pool last summer," said Irma Middleton, one of the writers of the letter. "We would rather drive our children to other pools than have them go to a pool where they are not safe."

The letter said that the town needs to hire a black pool manager who is a strict disciplinarian. The town also needs to hire black lifeguards.

The letter writers also noted that when the child drowned to death last summer, three lifeguards were on duty at the pool.

"There's no earthly reason why a child should drown in a pool with lifeguards on duty," said Middleton.

Lovelace said the town would take under consideration the parents' concerns. She was in agreement that more black lifeguards should be hired, she added.

```
The town's pools are scheduled to reopen after
Memorial Day weekend.
```

- Correct any punctuation problems in the following sentences:

    40. "I'm very impressed with Clinton," said Judy Aronson, a post-doctoral fellow at UNC Hospitals, "he seems like he's thought things out."
    41. Retired nursing assistant Phoebe Alston feels the campaign had too much mudslinging.
    42. People were asked, whom did they vote for and why.
    43. Greg Dreher, 18, a University freshman said he was voting for Bush because he thought the economy would suffer at the hands of Clinton and other Democrats.
    44. Tracie Ray, 20, a junior from New Jersey, said the committee of young Republicans had their obvious favorite.
    45. Heather Jones, a sophomore from Broadway, said, "I'm not happy with the campaigns at all and I voted for Clinton because he maintained a sense of honesty in the campaign."
    46. People came out to vote in high numbers, and poll workers said they had to remain long after the polls were closed.
    47. Martha Ellison said, "Voting is a privilege. I have never missed a vote, and I hope I never will."
    48. A low voter turnout is not understood in countries where people have just received the vote said the media analyst.

REFERENCES

Henry Beard and Christopher Cerf, *The Official Politically Correct Dictionary and Handbook.* New York: Villard Books, 1992.

Theodore M. Bernstein, *Dos, Don'ts and Maybes of the English Language.* New York: The Times Book Co., 1977.

John Bremner, *Words on Words.* New York: Columbia University Press, 1980.

E. L. Callihan, *Grammar for Journalists.* Radnor, PA: Chilton Book Company, 1979.

Claire Kehrwald Cook, *Line by Line: How to Improve Your Own Writing.* Boston: Houghton Mifflin, 1985.

Lauren Kessler and Duncan McDonald, *When Words Collide*. Belmont, CA: Wadsworth Publishing, 1992.

Ernie Pyle, *Here Is Your War,* New York, Pocket Books, 1945.

Tom Wolfe, excerpt from transcribed speech to American Society of Newspaper Editors, Washington, DC, April 1990.

William Zinsser, *On Writing Well*. New York: Harper & Row, 1976.

6

Editing and Polishing Writing

Dear God, I like the Lord's prayer best of all. Did you have to write it a lot or did you get it right the first time? I have to write everything I ever write over again. Lois.

So goes a letter in *Children's Letters to God,* a collection by Stuart Hample and Eric Marshall. Lois has learned a lesson early and is way ahead of many writers. Many student or beginning writers assume that a writing job is finished once they get a message down on paper. But experienced writers know that writing is only a first step, and a small step at that.

The first writing is called a first draft because whatever is written initially—be it a letter, a memo, a news release, a televised announcement, or a radio ad—is never as clear and polished as it could be, and it is never the finished copy.

A first draft is a rough, almost private stage of writing. North Carolina novelist and English professor Doris Betts tells students, "Handing in your first draft is like passing around your spittle"—in other words, unprofessional and offensive.

Between the first draft and the finished product comes editing. The first draft should be as good as you can create it. Just because you will edit does not allow you to be sloppy or careless on the first go-round. Editing will refine and improve that first effort.

This chapter looks at

- The stages of editing,
- The importance of style,
- Basic style rules, and
- Copyediting symbols.

Editing, Editing, Editing

Editing is essential before any letter is mailed, article printed, news release distributed, or advertisement aired. All writers must know how to edit. As Claire Kehrwald Cook notes in her book *Line by Line: How to Improve Your Own Writing*:

> *In correcting your own work, you have a free hand. You don't need editorial delicacy and diplomacy. You only need editorial skills that will enable you to look objectively at what you have written. If you can master them, you can do more to improve your writing than anyone else can.*

As a writer you are responsible for editing and revising your own work. Eventually, you may be an executive who must communicate policies to staff members, or you may be the sole information specialist within a nonprofit organization. No one else is likely to fix your writing and improve it.

You may work on a newspaper staff or in a large corporate communications office where others will edit your work. No matter where you are, you must know how to edit. You are the originator, the one who must shape and streamline the initial draft. The draft must be clear, accurate, and complete when it leaves your hands.

To be sure, many writers have the help of an editor. An editor can catch inconsistencies and grammatical errors and can ask questions to make the draft more complete. But an editor may not be familiar enough with the subject to find all inaccuracies, or may be harried because of a deadline and not have time to correct all flaws.

As you gain experience as a writer, you also will be asked to edit, judge, and revise the work of others. You may be promoted to an editing position or solicited by others who know less than you do about good writing skills.

Editing is hard work, and it is time consuming. But it has to be done.

The Fear of Editing

Student writers—and even experienced writers—usually dread editing. Editing their own writing seems tedious—just more work. Thinking about rewriting discourages writers whose goal is to be finished with the assignment. The emotional reaction to continued work may stymie their efforts to review.

Some writers view editing as a negative process. When editors comment, the writer may see the remarks solely as criticism, and the editing process is seen as negative feedback. Editing should be considered an integral part of the writing process rather than a separate critique. Rewriting does not mean that what was written first is bad; it means that the work has promise and can be improved.

Many experienced writers, seeing an advertisement they produced or reading the lead on their news story, have sighed and said, "If only I had used this word instead of that, it would have been so much better." Experienced writers are always trying to improve their work and rewrite it. They seek skilled, critical editors who can make their work shine.

William Strunk wrote *The Elements of Style,* a brief but pointed book on how to improve writing. Much of the material is still pertinent more than seventy years after it was written. Strunk's student, E. B. White, is responsible for remembering the book from class and having it published. White wrote the foreword and never forgot the advice of his mentor. He once noted to an interviewer that he rewrote essays as many as fourteen times before they were published. He spent three years writing the popular children's book *Charlotte's Web* and almost twelve years writing *Stuart Little.*

Anyone who reads *The Elements of Style* can see that each word is carefully selected to say just what Strunk and White mean: There's no fat and no redundancy. *The Elements of Style* was first published in 1935, although Strunk had used the same material in a class he taught eighteen years earlier. Despite its age, the little book's wisdom and guidelines are invaluable to anyone who wants to be a serious, competent writer and editor.

The Stages of Editing

Less experienced writers often have more difficulty determining which words must be removed to keep prose tight, accurate, and clear. They don't know how to begin. Assessing each word's contribution to the overall meaning and then changing or cutting prose can be wrenching. To ease the pain, writers should consider editing as a process to be done in stages. Specific tasks in each stage allow writers-turned-editors to be focused and thorough.

Editing follows five basic steps. Each stage is a separate operation and must be completed before the next stage may be done successfully.

1. Without stopping, READ the written piece from start to finish to consider the prose. Get the full sense of the information. Without making changes, go on to the second stage of editing.

2. Be sure the structure will reach audiences. Does the content satisfy audience needs? Does the lead communicate directly to the audience? Does important information reach the reader quickly enough? Is any essential information missing? At this point, more research and rewriting may be required.

3. Check for accuracy. Checking for accuracy is an intense, time-consuming job. In a professional office, writers have help from editors or fact-checkers. But regardless of who helps, writers are ultimately responsible for the accuracy of their work.

4. Review the language. Are the words simple, clear, and direct? Are the sentences active and easy to read? Are redundancies eliminated? Is the message free of poor grammar, spelling errors, bias, jargon, and institutional language?

5. Read the piece through for overall quality and reader appeal. This stage is what some people equate with the term "editing." It is the final cosmetic once-over. Editors may also find here errors that were inadvertently edited in during the earlier stages.

Editing for content, structure, accuracy, and correctness, as described in Stages 1 through 4, is critical before the final stage. A message must be read fully in Stage 1 before its structure can be analyzed in Stage 2. And its structure must be established before the content is checked for accuracy and correctness in Stage 3. Language, spelling, and grammar are examined in Stage 4, almost the last stage.

Some writers may question the sequence of the stages of editing. But the reasoning is quite simple: It is efficient. If Stage 4 came first, editors would toil over sentences for spelling and grammar, then possibly delete them later during content editing. It's far better that such sentences go first. More importantly, however, the stages allow for the most critical tasks to be done first in case the writer/editor runs out of time. For example, it is more important to write a compelling lead than to smooth out a transition, and it is more important for the piece to be complete and accurate than even to be free of spelling errors.

Editors should be flexible as they move through the stages of editing. If they see a problem that needs to be fixed, regardless of the stage, they should do so then. Editors who wait may forget to make the repair.

A Closer Look

The stages of editing have been outlined only to show how editing and revision are necessary routines in writing. Let's look at how each keeps writing complete, clear, concise, and accurate.

Stage 1: Reading the Copy

The first level of editing requires reading through the entire piece uninterruptedly as if you were a consumer who had never heard of the subject. This is usually a stage most writers skip; yet it is critical for them to step back and see the message as a whole, as audiences will see it.

"But why should I read my own writing before I start to make changes?" a student writer may question. "I collected the information. I wrote it. I know what is there." Within that statement lies the danger. Because a writer may be so familiar with a topic and its components, he or she may overlook whether the meaning is clear to someone new to the subject.

In the first stage, the ideal scenario is to put away a piece of writing for a few days and come back to it. Then you can look at it with a fresh eye: with the eye of an editor rather than the eye of a writer. But you may not have that luxury. If you are pressed for time, get up, walk around, have a snack, and get some fresh air. Then return to your writing. You will see it from a new perspective.

When you sit down for the first reading, don't read with pen in hand, ready to make specific changes. In the later stages of editing, you will make repairs. Focus on how you feel and what you learn as you read your own

piece. Read aloud to slow down and to hear what you have actually written—not what you think is there. The most common errors detected by
reading aloud are awkward language, inadequate explanations that confuse
the meaning, and too much prose on a particular topic.

As you read and detect weaknesses, you can make simple notes in the
margin, such as "fix," "delete," or "explain." You will find, after your first
reading, that you are eager to get on with improving your writing.

Stage 2: Examining Structure and Substance

Now pick up the pen to make more detailed notes. In reviewing the structure
and substance, you may find that additional research and rewriting are needed.

Consider the audience. Does the message attract the audience's attention
and meet its needs?

To attract the audience, the lead must be effective. Remember from
Chapter 3 that the lead is the first paragraph or first several paragraphs of
your message. Ask

- Does the lead adequately set up the article?
- Are all the points raised in the lead answered in subsequent paragraphs?
- Is the lead itself interesting and written in a way to attract an audience
  into the message?

The lead gives the audience specific cues about the substance of the
message. To maintain your credibility with your audience, you do not want
to promise a certain message in your lead and then not deliver it.

At the same time, be sure the lead reflects the story's content. Consider
this lead on a feature story about campus security:

The four local teen-agers who died in a fiery car crash last Thursday
morning had been drinking, bringing to four this year's total of fatal
accidents involving teen-agers who were drinking and driving.

This lead, which focuses on the deaths, hardly lets a reader know that
the focus of the story is actually a continuing problem with teen-age drinking at parties where alcoholic beverages are served. The reader has been
misled.

If the lead and the message do not match, you will need to rewrite. The new lead on the above story would state

```
Teen-age drinking and driving have reached a crisis, said
Rockland's police chief today, in confirming that the four
teen-agers who died last Thursday had been drinking.
```

To hold the audience with the message, a writer must look at the overall organization and ask

• Is the message developed logically? Do facts follow in a clear sequence?

• Is the transition from one point to another effective? Each paragraph should be tied to the previous one.

• Are paragraphs organized so that each contains one thought or idea? Readers will be confused if too many thoughts are packaged into one paragraph. Start a new paragraph—basically a unit of organization—with each new quote or each new idea.

• Are there statements or sentences that stop you because they are out of context?

• Do all the quotes add to the message? Would it be better to paraphrase or omit some?

Again, the answers to these questions may require rewriting.
To determine if you need more information, ask

• Is the message up to date? Are the latest statistics used? For example, a television news story on child abuse must have this year's figures on reported cases, not figures from two years ago or even last year. Your audience wants to know how serious the situation is today. If those numbers aren't available, you need to say so, and why.

• Are any questions raised that aren't answered? Each message must be complete. In a news release about its earnings, a company that says it is privately held must define what privately held means. A message that is written and not aired may need some description so readers can mentally picture the action.

The answers to the questions in Stage 2 are guidelines for how much reporting and rewriting must be done so that copy is complete and flows smoothly and logically.

Stage 3: Checking for Accuracy

No aspect of writing is more important than accuracy. Professors often quip, "If your mother says she loves you, check it out." Employees may ridicule an executive who includes inaccurate information in memos. Readers turn away from publications and advertisements where they repeatedly find errors. Students lose faith in textbooks when they uncover wrong data.

The bottom line is trust: If your audience doesn't trust the validity of any part of your message, it will question the accuracy of the entire message. Once it loses trust, the audience will be less willing to believe in future communications from you and may move to other media, never to return.

Research has shown that even one error in a newspaper can cause readers to doubt the rest of the paper and to have less faith in the reporter's abilities. Accuracy, therefore, can build or break your reputation, not just the reputation of the medium that carries the message.

Steps to Ensure Accuracy

• Let your copy cool before checking for accuracy. Take a break for a few minutes so you can approach it with a clear mind. If you read it immediately after Stages 1 and 2, questionable material may not stand out.

• Check name spellings. Review your notes. Doublecheck with the researcher or another writer. Use a telephone book, city directory, or other printed reference. Correct names are essential to avoid confusion—and even legal trouble—when people have the same or similar names. For example, in writing about a nightclub singer named Delsie Harper, a reporter inadvertently left off the D, and the newspaper immediately got a call from a church deacon named Elsie Harper.

• Use reputable sources to confirm information. For example, the city budget director will have more knowledge on changes in the next fiscal year budget than will an anonymous citizen who calls a newspaper to complain.

• Make sure quotes that contain opinion or outrageous claims are attributed, such as this one: "Women get what they deserve," a self-proclaimed antifeminist said today. The quote has some credibility with the attribution but would have more if the antifeminist were named.

- If quotes are libelous—that is, damaging to a person's reputation—either make sure they can be defended or cut them. A person's barroom allegation about his next-door neighbor's drug use is not protected by law and should never be published. You may quote a witness's remark in a trial, however, because what occurs in court proceedings is protected. See more about libel in Appendix A.

- Question statistics. For example, a story reports that the president received positive approval from "more than half" of the nation. The actual statistic was 53 percent. The margin of error, or accuracy of the poll, was plus or minus 3 percent. Adding 3 percent to 53 percent means as many as 56 percent of the country support the president. But subtracting 3 percent from 53 percent also means that as little as 50 percent of the nation approve of him. And 50 percent is not more than half.

- Recalculate percentages. Your boss may tell that the company CEO will get only a 7.6 percent pay increase. Check it. A raise from $150,000 to $172,500 is a 15 percent pay increase, not 7.6 percent. The inaccuracy would hardly make other employees confident in the public relations department and its message.

- On technical subjects when there is doubt about an explanation, call an expert source and read your material to that person for comment.

Getting information right is also important because inaccuracies are audience-stoppers. When radio listeners hear statistics that they question, they puzzle over the error and no longer hear what you have to say. The best-constructed message framed in the finest form means nothing if your information is wrong or even confusing.

Stage 3 is devoted to ensuring that information is accurate. A list of specific steps to ensure accuracy in Stage 3 is given here. What if you cannot check a fact? Enlist someone else, such as a reference librarian, to verify what is in question. If you cannot verify information and you are working on a deadline, leave it out. If the information is vital to the message and it can't be checked, the message will have to wait. Never publish information if you have doubts about its accuracy.

Stage 4: Using Clear Language

Editing is hard. It means giving up words. Student writers may have been rewarded for using polysyllabic words found on high school vocabulary lists, or they may have written at length to fill an English requirement for a term paper. Early in life, writers develop a bad habit of writing long. Such writers have a difficult time determining what words to cut to keep prose tight, to the point, and clear.

Consider these questions during this stage:

- Is the copy clear and easy to read?
- Are words simple, direct, and easy to understand?
- Are jargon and institutional language eliminated? (Remember the discussion from Chapter 5 on saying it straight.)
- Is redundancy gone?
- Are sentences short and to the point?

Part of Stage 4 is looking at spelling, grammar, and punctuation. In the technological age, many writers use computers that have spelling and grammar checking systems. No system, however, takes care of mechanical errors, and few spelling programs adequately check troublesome synonyms, such as affect and effect, red and read, naval and navel, stationary and stationery, trustee and trusty, lead and led, and so on. Appendix C is a guide to how to spell in the computer age.

Just as you have to check spelling, you have to review grammar. Chapter 8 discusses common grammar problems; consult the reference books listed at the end of that chapter for additional help.

In Stage 4, writers must be on the lookout for jargon. Such language should be replaced immediately with clearer terms, so that, for example, "organizational inputs" become "suggestions from parent groups," and "facilitation of new methodologies" becomes "trying a new survey."

In this stage of editing, you also need to pay careful attention to word choice. Remember: The right word enhances audience understanding and willingness to pay attention, whether the message is read or heard. "Let your conscious be your guide," may not affect listeners. And some readers might not even notice the confused choice of "conscious" instead of "conscience." Those who do notice will not be impressed. If necessary, review the discussion of word usage in Chapter 5.

Stage 5: Giving the Piece the Last Once-over

In Stage 5, read the entire piece through. At this point, no major reworking should be needed. Check, however, for any editing errors that may have crept in during earlier stages. The final reading is the last check to make sure that Stages 1–4 have produced a message that is complete, accurate, comprehensible, pertinent, and interesting. This is the time to congratulate yourself.

After completing Stage 5, you may send your copy to your editor or to a corporate executive for review, if you are in an organization or business. If you are an advertising copywriter, the message will go to the account executive and then to the client. In print media, the story will go to an editor and in broadcast, to a news director. If you are a high school principal, your memo may be reviewed by the school system's superintendent before it is sent to parents. If you are a student, the article is turned in to a professor or instructor.

But don't think that turning in your piece ends the editing process. The copy may come back for another round of editing and changes before publication.

Watching Style

Part of good editing is ensuring consistency throughout writing. Using a consistent style guarantees that a certain pattern in word usage, titles, punctuation, abbreviations, grammar, and spelling persists. If IBM means International Business Machines in the first sentence of a television broadcast, it will mean the same thing later on. If Dr. means doctor on the first page of the newspaper, it will not mean "Drive" as part of someone's address in the obituary page. Consistent usage builds credibility and reduces chances of audience confusion.

Many media organizations follow a style that guarantees consistency. Most newspapers and public relations firms follow the Associated Press style found in the *Associated Press Stylebook*. Other media outlets, such as publishing houses and newsletters, have adopted their own stylebooks. For example, the *Washington Post* and the *New York Times* have their own style manuals. Many universities and publishing houses use *The Chicago Manual of Style* or the style manual of the Modern Language Association.

No one is ever expected to memorize stylebooks, but writers and editors must be familiar with their content. When a question arises, they need to know where to find the answer. Writers will find that certain rules are used so often that they become second nature. For example, most writers become familiar with the capitalization rule for titles: Professional titles are always capitalized before a person's name but never after a name. For example, University President Bill Sandler said classes would end early Tuesday because of the threat of a blizzard. After his name, the title would read like this: Bill Sandler, university president, said . . .

Basic Style Rules

As noted earlier, some publications and media organizations have certain style rules that writers must follow. The most broadly accepted rules are those set out by the *Associated Press Stylebook,* which is periodically updated.

Over the years, certain rules have remained consistent and are part of good writing.

TITLES. Titles should precede names unless they are long and bulky. William McCorkle's name is not lost if a short title is used before it, such as University President William McCorkle. But his name would be hard to find if his title were University Associate Vice Chancellor for Student Affairs and Services. When an individual has a long title, put the title after the name: William McCorkle, university associate vice chancellor for student affairs and services.

When titles precede names, they are capitalized. After names, they are not.

Most titles are always written out. The only time some are abbreviated is when they precede a name. The *Associated Press Stylebook* indicates which titles can be abbreviated, for example, governor as Gov. Sheila Aycock and lieutenant governor as Lt. Gov. James Ramsey. Titles that are never abbreviated include president, attorney general, professor, and superintendent. Most military titles can be abbreviated.

Stand-alone titles are always written out, and they are never abbreviated or capitalized. The president said he would turn over the files to the Justice Department. The pope will visit the United States in May.

Vice president is not hyphenated.

CAPITALIZATION. The general rule is to capitalize proper nouns that refer to a person, place, or thing. Sacramento is the capital of California. Mayor Harmon Bowles agreed to lead the town's Christmas parade. Easter is usually in late March or early April.

ABBREVIATIONS. Be stingy with abbreviations. They can sometimes lead to awkward moments or pronunciation, as when you try to read "superintendent" as "supt."

For states, the Associated Press gives the following abbreviations: Ala., Ariz., Ark., Calif., Colo., Conn., Del., Fla., Ga., Ill., Ind., Kan., Ky., La., Md., Mass., Mich., Minn., Miss., Mo., Mont., Neb., Nev., N.H., N.J., N.M., N.Y., N.C., N.D., Okla., Ore., Pa., R.I., S.C., S.D., Tenn., Vt., Va., Wash., W.Va., Wis., and Wyo. In text, do not use the Postal Service list. Eight states' names are never abbreviated: Alaska, Hawaii, Idaho, Iowa, Ohio, Texas, and Utah. Abbreviate states' names when they are used with the name of a town or city, as in Birmingham, Ala.; otherwise, write them out.

You can abbreviate months when they are used with a specific date: Nov. 12, 1948. Write November 1948, however. Never abbreviate March, April, May, June, or July.

Don't abbreviate the days of the week or the words "assistant" and "association."

ACRONYMS. Use acronyms sparingly. Many people don't know what AMA stands for. It could be American Medical Association, but it also could be something else. The *Associated Press Stylebook* lists some acronyms that can be used on first reference because people are familiar with them; some examples are FBI, CIA, A&P, CBS, AIDS, TNT, and UFO. With all others, write them out; on second reference, use words such as the bureau, the agency, the grocery store chain, the network, the affliction, the explosive, and the object.

NUMBERS. The general rule is to write out numbers zero through nine and use numerals for numbers 10 and higher. Always spell out numbers at the beginning of a sentence, however. In writing numbers above 999,999, write out the words "million" and "billion" rather than using all those zeroes. For example: To clear the site, the construction crew moved 1.2 million cubic yards of dirt. Congressional aides discovered the budget would require an additional $1.4 billion in revenues.

The Associated Press lists two dozen or so exceptions to the rule, but the main ones are these:

Age. Always use a numeral for age. She has a 3-year-old daughter and an 85-year-old mother.

Percent. Always use a numeral. He estimated 9 percent of employees are truly satisfied with their jobs.

Time. Always use a numeral. The guests will arrive at 9 p.m. Classes start as early as 8 a.m.

Dates. Again, use numerals. He was born Jan. 3, 1926.

Temperatures. Use numerals for all temperatures except zero. The weather service predicted the coldest weather in 15 years for the weekend, noting that temperatures would drop to 2 to 3 degrees below zero.

Dimensions. Always write height and weight as numerals. The average height of the team's basketball players is 6 feet 4 inches. The record-breaking carrot weighed 5 pounds.

Money. Write dollars and cents as numerals. The price of an egg is about 7 cents. Hemming the dress will cost $7.

Copyediting Symbols

When you send your copy to a higher level for editing, you may get back a printed copy with editing marks on it. Many people, despite computers, still feel more comfortable working with a hard copy, or words on paper, that they can edit with a pencil or pen. They can see the original all at once and have a better feel for the changes they have made.

Knowing copyediting symbols is important because not all communicators have access to computers. Some may still type messages and then edit by hand. Media professionals must be able to translate copyediting symbols into changes, and the editing shorthand can save copyeditors time.

Here are some of the common editing symbols.

Paragraph mark	¶ The president met with House leaders about his proposed budget.

Capitalization	Police Sgt. william T. cassidy
Lower case	The teacher picked 15 Apples.
Delete letter, word	She gave them to the stμudents.
	She gave them to ~~to~~ the students.
Delete punctuation	"Are you going?," she asked.
Transpose letters	She adrdessed 2,345 invitations.
Transpose words	The robber a had gun.
Insert punctuation	Marcia her sister, is a pianist.
Insert letters, words	Marian chose chosticks for eating.
	Marian chopsticks for eating.
Add a space	Four players are needed for bridge.
Write out	The meeting will be Tues. night.
Abbreviate	Governor Rex Casey died today.

Look at the following sample from a church bulletin to see how it was edited
by use of proper copyediting symbols.

Copyediting Symbols in Practice

At a meeting last month, The Longview Church board
of deacons decided it would hire an asst. director of
special projects.

The Church has focussed much efforts of its on

programs for the homless and needy, said the Rev. paul

Jacobs. The activities are more then he can can handle

along iwth his minsterial duties he said.

Applications can be sent to the Church before

September 1.

Wrap Up

In the age of technology, many writers would like to rely on spelling and grammar checkers, and word and sentence checkers, to polish and refine their writing for them. They would willingly latch onto any aid to reduce the tedium of editing. But no flawless mechanical way to edit exists.

No book on how to improve writing can stress enough the critical role of editing and the acceptance by writers that editing is essential. Remember the words of Doris Betts: We would hardly want to serve spit to our audiences.

The stages of editing discussed in this chapter give writers a more methodical approach to editing. Following the stages will produce better writing. Ensuring the right structure will improve your ability to reach audiences. Guarding the language will increase audience comprehension and retention. Paying attention to spelling and grammar will reinforce the strength, clarity, and credibility of your writing. Adhering to a set style will give your writing consistency. Being aware of bias will make your writing acceptable. Writers who are serious about their craft and their audiences will take the time to apply the guidelines and to edit, edit, edit.

EXERCISES

- Read the following story. Edit it, using the five stages of editing. Make a list of questions for any missing information that would require more research. Follow Associated Press style, and use proper spelling and grammar. Watch out for redundancies. The audience is readers of the campus newspaper.

```
All of the faculty members from the School of
Journalism and Mass Communication will be attending on
Thursday of this week a regional meeting of the
Association for Education in Journalism and Mass
Communication in Greensboro.

     The meeting will commence at 10 a.m. in the morning
and conclude at 2 p.m. in the afternoon following a noon
luncheon.

     In the morning, sessions will offer journalism
educators the opportunity to have discussions on
current issues addressing journalism and mass
communication.

     At a luncheon program, professor Walter Blayless
will be speaking on the topic of cigarette advertising
and the effect on the nation's young people of today.

     The meeting sponsored by AEJMC is exemplary of the
several regional meetings the organization holds across
the country each year. The annual meeting is always
held in August each year at different locations around
the country.
```

Compare your editing steps to the following:

In Stage 1 editing, you learned that the faculty members would be at a meeting on Thursday, the focus of the meeting.

In Stage 2, you would consider the lead. You might wonder: What will happen to classes if all the faculty members are gone on a weekday? More research and interviewing would need to be done. The research might require you to write a new lead geared for the student audience. It would say

```
Students in the School of Journalism and Mass
Communication will not have class Thursday because
faculty members will attend a professional meeting in
Greensboro.
```

In Stage 3, you would check for accuracy. You would check the spelling of Walter Blayless and the organization. You would also doublecheck to make sure that the meeting is in Greensboro. In Stage 4 would come the most work. The first draft is wordy. Phrases such as 10 a.m. in the morning and 2 p.m. in the afternoon would be shortened to 10 a.m. and 2 p.m. Blayless will be speaking on the topic of cigarette advertising could be tightened to Blayless will speak on cigarette advertising. Stage 5 would be the final reading for overall quality.

Your edited copy might look something like this:

```
Students in the School of Journalism and Mass
Communication will not have class Thursday because
faculty members will attend a professional meeting in
Greensboro.

    A regional meeting of the Association for Education
in Journalism and Mass Communication will begin at
10 a.m. and end at 2 p.m.

    Educators will discuss issues in journalism and mass
communication during the morning sessions.

    The luncheon speaker, Professor Walter Blayless,
will talk about cigarette advertising and its effect on
youth.

    AEJMC has several regional meetings each year. The
annual meeting is in August in different U.S. cities.
```

• Copyedit the following sentences according to Associated Press style. Also check for any grammar, spelling, or punctuation errors. Use copyediting symbols to save time.

1. Lieutenant Governor Stanley Greene was stripped of his powers by the N.C. Senate.

2. William Williams, Dean of the Graduate School of Journalism, will speak to students about graduation requirements on Wed. afternoon.

3. The students are expected to begin the test at 9:00 A. M. Tuesday.

4. The President lives at 1600 Pennsylvania Avenue, but his mail is delivered to the U.S. Post Office on Twenty-second Street.

5. The state Senate is expected to enact a bill to require polio vaccinations for children under the age of two.

6. The airport in Medford, Oregon was closed yesterday after an Alaskan airlines jet made an emergency landing on their runway.

7. The Atty. Gen. has a B. A. in history from American University.

8. The Soviet block countries sponsored the Friendship Games rather than attend the 1984 olympics in Los Angeles.

9. The city and county used thirteen busses to transport the children to the July Fourth picnic.

10. Water freezes at 0 degrees Centigrade.

11. Three houses on Sims street were destroyed by the fire, which began at 112 Sims Street.

12. Following the Federal Reserve action, three banks announced a one percent increase in the prime rate, putting it at six percent.

• Copyedit the following sentences according to Associated Press style. Also check for any grammar, spelling or punctuation errors. Use copyediting symbols to save time.

13. U.S. Senator Jesse A. Helms (R–North Carolina) used to be city editor of The Raleigh Times.

14. John L. Harris, 48 years old, of 1632 Winding Way Road was charged Tuesday with cocaine possession.

15. The champion wrestler measured six feet six inches tall and won 4/5 of his fights.

16. Army Sergeant Willie York was charged with misappropriating $1,000,000 dollars in construction equipment.

17. Hurricane Diana, blowing from the East, caused millions of dollars in damages to the east coast of the United States.

18. Colonel Max Shaw, who has served as a national guardsman for more than twenty years, is Ed's commanding officer.

19. Ability with a frisbee is not a valid measure of IQ.

20. We heard the kickoff announced over the radio at the laundramat.

21. The stockings were hanged by the chimney with care, in hopes that Kirs Kringle soon would be there.

22. Travelling the 30 miles, or 60 kilometers, to Kansas City, we got 32 miles per gallon in our new minivan.

23. The five-year-old boy got on the wrong bus and was missing for 2 hours.

24. Sarah sold two hundred and two boxes of Girl Scout cookies to her neighbors on Sweetbriar Pkwy. and Pantego Ave.

REFERENCES

Claire Kehrwald Cook, *Line by Line: How to Improve Your Own Writing,* Boston: Houghton Mifflin, 1985.

William Strunk, Jr., and E. B. White, *The Elements of Style,* 3rd ed. New York: Macmillan Publishing, 1979.

Lauren Kessler and Duncan McDonald, *When Words Collide,* Belmont, CA: Wadsworth Publishing, 1992.

The Associated Press Stylebook and Libel Manual, ed. Norm Goldstein. New York: The Associated Press, 1992.

7

Recognizing Bias and Stereotypes

Understanding bias means considering your own background as well as the backgrounds of others. Many people believe they can write about other people without allowing any personal bias to creep into their stories, news spots, or news releases. But stepping outside personal bias is rarely accomplished because most people are unaware of how ingrained their beliefs and attitudes can be. Bias is not just overt, as racial prejudice or political beliefs are. It is subtle. And it comes from who you are.

Consider your background. Did you come from a suburban middle-class home where you attended a school with little ethnic diversity? Did you speak a language other than English at home? What is your family's ethnic or racial background? Did you grow up in an urban ethnic neighborhood—Italian, African American, or Laotian?

Did you live in a subsidized housing project, in an inner city, or in a small town of 5,000 people or less? Maybe you grew up on a farm or ranch and your nearest neighbor was a half mile away. Did you attend private or public schools?

What is your gender? Do you or does someone in your family have a physical or mental disability? What is your religion? What political party do you claim?

All these aspects of your background and many others built your attitudes and beliefs. As a communicator you must become aware of your attitudes and beliefs to curb the bias that is still evident in many stories produced by the mass media today—and the bias that keeps many stories from appearing.

Bias often surfaces in stereotypes that show up in adjectives, or nouns ascribed to certain groups. People form stereotypes from their perceptions of individuals' or groups' behavior and from their experiences and those of friends and relatives. Think about the label in the sentence "Jane is a typical college student who wants to have a good time and study as little as possible." As a student you wouldn't want people to ignore your attributes and view you as a lazy, party-animal student. The generalization isn't fair to you or most other students. As a writer you must learn to confront such stereotypes and avoid perpetuating negative overgeneralizations about groups.

In this chapter, we will discuss

- How writers can begin to recognize bias,
- How bias in writing affects specific individuals and groups, and
- Specific tips on how to avoid bias in writing about individuals and groups.

The Bias Habit

Journalists' cultural values can affect their ability to be truly fair. Because of the way the brain processes information, people must categorize and label people and events. Walter Lippmann referred to this phenomenon in 1922:

> *The real environment is altogether too big, too complex and too fleeting for direct acquaintance. We are not equipped to deal with so much subtlety, so much variety, so many permutations and combinations. And although we have to act in that environment, we have to reconstruct it on a simpler model before we can manage it.*

The adaptive process means that people do not see as many perspectives as possible, or they develop a view that does not fit reality. Most importantly, in this adaptive process, people will select the information that confirms their attitudes and beliefs, according to journalism researchers H. Stocking and P. Gross, who add that people may not even be aware that they process information with a cognitive bias. They do not have to make a conscious effort to be biased; in fact, they may be trying to be unbiased, as journalists do in attempting objectivity.

Bias in Writing

Groups such as journalists construct a shared view of "reality" because of the similarities in the way they view the world. Timothy Crouse in his book *The Boys on the Bus* explained the close working relationship among political reporters on the campaign trail:

> *It was just these womblike conditions that gave rise to the notorious phenomenon called "pack journalism" (also known as "herd journalism" and "fuselage journalism"). A group of reporters were assigned to follow a single candidate for weeks or months at a time, like a pack of hounds sicked on a fox. Trapped on the same bus or plane, they ate, drank, gambled, and compared notes with the same bunch of colleagues week after week.*

As early as 1950, one famous study showed how wire editors rely on their own personal values to select the news. David Manning White reported that "as 'gate keeper' the newspaper editor sees to it (even though he may never be consciously aware of it) that the community shall hear as a fact only those events which the newsman, as representative of his culture, believes to be true."

It is important to remember that bias surfaces in many arenas. Adjectives and nouns are ascribed to people because of where they live, their political beliefs, their sexual orientation, and their religion. Bias attributes certain characteristics to women, men, people with disabilities, children, older people, and members of ethnic and racial groups. Labels are dangerous. They are offensive and usually imply inferiority. They do not describe individuals, nor do they apply to groups. Writers who don't think perpetuate negative stereotypes and myths.

How Myths Are Perpetuated

More than thirty years after the beginnings of the civil rights movement in the United States, inequities based on race and ethnic background persist. Mass media have both helped and hindered the effort for equal rights in this country. On one hand, they give voice to various social movements and allow the message of equality to reach a mass audience. On the other hand, they also perpetuate misinformation and ignore a myriad of other ethnic groups.

One problem is that most people who run the mass media are not from diverse ethnic backgrounds. Most are of Western European descent, and a large majority are male. They have little context, therefore, to help them know what it is like to be an African American, Native American, Asian American, Latino, or other person of color in the United States. (Only about 7 percent of journalists nationwide are from these groups.) Too often, stories about those communities are reported with an outsider's perspective, resulting in misinformation or stereotypes. In other cases, the stories may not be reported; the group may be invisible to the journalist.

Consider some of the overt examples of this problem during the 1992 riots in Los Angeles. In an on-air conversation between a KABC anchor and a TV reporter, the following exchange took place after live video showed some Latinos looting:

"Tell me, do these people look like illegal aliens?"

"Yes, they do."

Maria Elena Durazo, president of the Hotel and Restaurant Employee Union, Local 11, called the media presentation of Latinos "extremely offensive" because "illegal alien" was often used to refer to Latinos.

The mass media also portrayed the whole riot situation as a "black–white" conflict rather than showing how it affected all groups in Los Angeles. Several estimates showed that actually Latinos were involved in more than 50 percent of the arrests. Rueben Martinez, senior editor of *L.A. Weekly* and co-host of KCET "Life and Times," explained that although national television emphasized black–white conflict, "this was an Asian, Latino, black, Anglo thing as the city of L.A. is now."

Asian Americans were also shut out of much of the coverage of the riots. Dean Takahashi, then president of the Asian American Journalists Association, criticized the *Los Angeles Times* because Asians received few interviews in an opinion poll of 900 people after the riots.

Andrea Ford, an African American journalist for the *Los Angeles Times,* explained that the coverage before the riots predicted the kinds of reporting problems during the riots.

> *I don't think you can expect the media to suddenly become responsible and thorough at the time of crisis if it hadn't been before the crisis occurred. . . . If you pick*

up the L.A. Times *on an average day, you would believe this community was overwhelmingly white, that it was overwhelmingly upper to middle class, and in terms of international reporting, the world consists of Europe, South Africa and Japan. . . . If you look at certain people of color, you would believe they were all in jail, and they were all gang members.*

Breaking the Bias Habit

Today, writers and reporters are trying, through better awareness, to overcome the cultural bias implanted in the news. But old habits die hard. How can you learn to sift through the information you will be writing and present the least biased and stereotypical coverage?

Society itself is giving writers some help. Today a multicultural approach is being integrated into numerous aspects of society, from school textbooks to television advertisements. All types of cultures in the United States are gaining a voice. As someone disseminating information, you can learn to tap into these cultures for stories and diverse insights.

Media can have an impact in breaking the bias habit. As newsrooms become more diverse, the types of stories aired or printed will continue to become diverse. Reporters can describe people as individuals, not cast them in broad terms ascribed to a group. Reporters can also become circumspect when using language and learn what terminology individuals and groups prefer. Many organizations, such as the Asian American Journalists Association and Special Olympics, have developed guidelines on language use.

Considering Specific Groups

John Mitrano, executive director of the National Organization of Italian Students and Educators, noted in a survey:

While there is usually a grain of truth to stereotypes, over time, these become no longer salient. With the twilight of ethnicity upon us in third and fourth generation families, new portrayals must be used to depict groups accurately. Television shows, movies, and advertisements must emphasize the qualities that we see ourselves as having. We must also become vocal and mobilized when we do not like the way we are portrayed.

Many words and images applied to specific groups have historically negative and derogatory connotations. Writers must be aware of them and avoid them.

Racial and Ethnic Groups

If asked to make a list, most people could come up with derogatory terms used to describe specific racial and ethnic groups. Writers must avoid terminology that perpetuates beliefs that all members of any group look alike, talk alike, think alike, or belong to the same political party.

Some language, while it may seem loaded with bias, can be appropriate when used in a historical context or with cultural sensitivity, noted Pale Moon Rose, president of the American Indian Heritage Foundation. Terms such as "redskin" and "brave" are acceptable if used appropriately and in a historical context.

Linda Cook Roberts, who won an International Association of Business Communicators Gold Quill for an affirmative action communication program, developed the following guidelines for writing about racial and ethnic groups:

• Avoid presenting members of racial or ethnic groups as if they are all the same. Too often, for example, African American neighborhoods are presented as "drug-infested." This assigns a negative status to a whole people and their neighborhoods.

• Refrain from using descriptive words that strengthen racial or ethnic stereotypes. Consider this sentence from a *Washington Post* article on less well-known Washington, D.C., monuments.

And he chose an unusual man to help: Benjamin F. Banneker, a free black man who was a math whiz and self-taught in astronomy.

• The word "unusual" clouds the sentence with a potential stereotype: the implication that African Americans are not helpful, are not intelligent in math, or are unable to learn astronomy on their own.

• Describe race or ethnic origin only when it is pertinent. In an article about Jessica James becoming the vice president of a local bank, it is not relevant to mention that her great-grandparents were born in slavery.

• Understand the problematic racial and ethnic undertones of some language. For example, the term "minority" is problematic in an international sense because people of color make up the majority of the world's population, and changing demographics in the United States means that some ethnic groups are the majority in certain locations. Remember also that "minority" always refers to a group rather than to certain individuals; it is best to use "members of minority groups" rather than "minorities."

• Never use a patronizing focus or treat a member of an ethnic group as a token. Ivan Penn, a reporter for the *Baltimore Sun,* was the first African American to serve as editor-in-chief of the student newspaper, the *Diamondback,* at the University of Maryland. But he describes himself first as a reporter, as a University of Maryland alumnus, and as a former *Diamondback* editor.

• Integrate coverage of ethnic groups into all aspects of articles or broadcasts instead of doing periodic "special" editions.

• Look for a diversity of sources when writing. An American Indian might be interviewed about political struggles instead of the meaning of a ceremonial dance.

Sexism

Women have risen to powerful jobs in both the public and the private sectors, but they have not gained enough power to transform their image in the media. Many writers thoughtlessly use language that treats women as inferior or that is demeaning or insulting. They are referred to as girls or mothers and are described by their physical attributes such as "attractive" or "brunette" or "shapely."

For example, Carol Moseley Braun, an African American woman from Illinois, successfully ran for the U.S. Senate in 1992. A *Washington Post* feature referred to her in its lead as "a celebrity with a problem." It then revealed that her problem was having to find pantyhose at a hotel gift shop. A story about a male candidate probably would never focus on his troubles in buying an undershirt.

Consider this lead from the *Durham Morning Herald,* now known as the *Herald-Sun:*

STOVALL—Janet Parrott presides each month at a table of men who are each old enough to be her father.

She is blonde, freckled and five months pregnant. An outsider is surprised to learn she is mayor of the small Granville County town of Stovall.

Most of the information in this lead, which appeared in the *Durham Morning Herald* in Durham, N.C., is irrelevant to Parrott's ability to govern as mayor. Of course, readers can sense the unusual aspect here, and that news value is appealing. Janet Parrott is a different mayor because she is a woman governing in a group of men. But her physical traits of being blonde, freckled, and pregnant have little relevance to the story. Gender stereotypes—"blonde, freckled and five months pregnant"—made for clichéd writing and revealed both a personal and a cultural bias. Writers should consider whether they would apply description uniformly and write that a town's male mayor is a blond, freckle-faced expectant father.

Beginning writers should also be aware that some other writers and editors are sensitive to the use of gender-specific nouns such as "chairman," "fireman," "stewardess," and "mailman." When possible, use "chairwoman," "firefighter," "flight attendant," or "postal service worker" or "letter carrier." Writers should also know their publication's policy about courtesy titles. Many organizations have eliminated courtesy titles such as Mrs., Miss, and Ms. before women's names. The last name is used on second reference.

Sexual Orientation

Writers should also avoid perpetuating negative images based on sexual orientation. Gay and lesbian rights movements since the mid-1960s have worked diligently to recast gay and lesbian portrayals in society. Until the mid-1970s, most news stories that referred to gays and lesbians did so only in the context of police reports. Gay and lesbian issues have been addressed in the schools, in the workplace, and in the military. Despite increased coverage, some editors and reporters still produce stories that present homosexuality as deviant, and negative stereotypes continue.

Writers and broadcasters must be careful not to make value judgments when a source is gay or lesbian or when the subject deals with homosexuality. Saying, for example, that a source "confessed" to being gay communicates negative, secretive feelings about homosexuality that your openly gay source will resent.

A person's gender or sexual orientation should be ignored in a message unless it is relevant. People's sexual orientation may be part of the fabric of the message but should be woven in as part of who they are, not presented as their complete identity. For example, gays and lesbians are well-known actors and leaders in fields such as science, politics, and medicine.

Madeleine Blais of the *Washington Post* wrote a multidimensional profile of Jim Graham, the director of the Whitman-Walker Clinic in Washington for people with AIDS. The article successfully described Graham's life and the clinic's life without making sexual orientation the focus. One paragraph described Graham's coming to grips with his alcoholism and his coming out to his wife. At an Alcoholics Anonymous meeting, Blais reported, "he told her that on the night before their wedding he had sex with a man who kept asking him if he knew what he was doing getting married. He wanted to ask her forgiveness." The reporter's work was done without bias.

Writers should never make assumptions about people's sexual orientation or people's sentiments toward gay and lesbian issues. Some people favor equality for all people. Remember that many people who are not gay or lesbian support gay and lesbian rights, just as many Caucasian people support civil rights for people of color.

Disabilities

Unless you or someone in your family has a physical or mental disability, as a writer you may tend to forget people with disabilities exist. Among the derogatory labels applied to the disabled are "crippled," "deformed," and "invalid." The Disabilities Committee of the American Society of Newspaper Editors noted a list of terms to avoid, including "special," which is seen as patronizing; "stricken with or suffers from" instead of "a person who has" a specific disability; "victim of" rather than "a person who has" AIDS or cerebral palsy.

Unlike other groups that receive discrimination because of social norms, people with disabilities face discrimination both from attitudes and from real barriers created by society's architectural and communication barriers. Maybe you have never seen a person who uses a wheelchair in your local grocery store because there is no curb cut in the sidewalk in front of the store or no ramp at the door of the store. Maybe you have had little interaction with a profoundly deaf person because you do not know where to find a Telecommunications Device for the Deaf (TDD), which would allow you to call the person on the phone.

Many people, including writers, forget that people with disabilities constitute a vital, and numerous, part of our society. Estimates are that 12 to 15 percent of the population, about 37 million people, has some form of disability. Therefore, a significant number of today's audiences either have a disability or know someone who does. Yet, people with disabilities receive only sketchy news coverage or are rarely written about. Writers are missing readable, audience-enticing stories about civil rights violations, new technology, legislation, and changes in business practices. An enterprising reporter could mine such story topics indefinitely.

The late John Clogston, a journalism professor at the University of Northern Illinois, said that writers often portray people with disabilities in one of three demeaning ways: They imply that people who have a disability are somehow less human than other people; they present them as medically defective or somehow deviant or different in society; or they go overboard in trying to portray them positively, thus making them superhuman or "supercrips," as Clogston called them.

Writers have a tendency to focus stories on the individual rather than the issues surrounding a disability, and they tend to wrap people with disabilities in pity and sympathy. Joe Shapiro, who covers social policy and disability issues for *U.S. News and World Report,* suggests that "instead of writing the sad story about the 10-year-old boy saving money to buy his mother an electric wheelchair, write the sad story of a health-care system that doesn't provide the funding to get the needed chair for that mother."

Writing about People with Disabilities

Lucille deView, syndicated columnist on aging for Knight-Ridder/*Tribune* and the writing coach for the *Orange County Register* in California, recommends the following tips for writing about people with disabilities:

• Let people with disabilities speak for themselves in your writing, not a friend or family member.

• Recognize the individuality of all people.

• Look beyond the individual to the issue if possible. If someone who uses a wheelchair is also an athlete, you might ask about the accessibility of local gymnasiums, swimming pools, and outdoor sports facilities.

• Look beyond the person's disability and get a well-rounded view of his or her life. Having a disability is just one small aspect of who a person is. He may collect antique sheet music, or she may have been a police officer during the 1960s.

• Ask about language. Ask which terms they prefer for publication. Do not assume that because they use a term, it is acceptable to all. Someone may refer to herself as a "cripple," but this is a derogatory term and should not be used.

• Avoid assigning superhuman traits. People with disabilities participate fully in aspects of life: They have all types of jobs, and they have spouses and families. If they are athletes, it is because they enjoy physical activity. Find out about the societal barriers they may have faced in achieving their goals, just as you do in any interview.

• Mention a disability only if it is pertinent to the message. It is not relevant to mention that a business owner uses a wheelchair unless he or she is talking specifically about access issues or other disability-related issues.

Be careful about writing that someone succeeded "in spite of" a disability—a phrase often viewed by the disabled as extremely patronizing. Some writers may contend that "disability" implies that individuals are not able, and if they succeed, then the news value of emotional impact and conflict are there to attract readers. Never assume that an accomplishment by a person with a disability is unusual.

In general, people specializing in coverage of disability issues recommend two easy rules in writing about people with disabilities. First, avoid clichés and clichéd constructions. Use value-neutral terms, that is, words that don't stereotype. Avoid saying that someone is confined. The person gets out of the wheelchair to sleep and to bathe. To that individual, the wheelchair is liberating. It is more accurate to say the individual uses a wheelchair. Second, never inject pity or a condescending tone into copy.

Ageism

Older people may also face stigmatization by society, and the mass media play a role in that process. In some instances, older people are labeled as forgetful, senile, rigid, meddlesome, childlike, feeble, fragile, frail, gray, inactive, withered, or doddering. Such adjectives may describe older people at some point in their lives or may be medically appropriate. But if such words are used indiscriminately, they demean older people and perpetuate inaccurate stereotypes. With the repeal of mandatory retirement, older people continue to work into their 70s and even 80s if they choose. They do most things that younger people do.

Consider an example from a *Texas Monthly* profile on then Texas Governor Ann Richards in 1992. The story was written because of rumors that she might one day run for president. At the outset, appearance stereotypes were broken: Richards was pictured on the cover in a white leather outfit sitting on a motorcycle.

The article presented the 58-year-old governor, who is also a grandmother, in a multidimensional way—not as an older woman who happens to be governor but as an effective, dynamic governor who happens to be an older woman. Her bouffant white hair is a sign of age and a symbol of her political personality. Her hair style, which was popular in the 1950s, successfully contrasts with her liberal feminist beliefs. Her age is relevant only as a part of who she is.

Lucille deView suggests that writers avoid these myths about older people:

• Older people can participate in a variety of activities, so don't adopt a "gee whiz" attitude toward their abilities. Most people over the age of 50 continue the physical activities they enjoyed when younger, whether swimming, hiking or playing tennis.

• Older people should be seen as individuals, not as members of a senior age group in which people are believed to have the same interests and abilities. Older people's interests are just as varied as those of individuals in other groups.

• Older people are not stereotyped in appearance. They dress in numerous fashions, and not all older people have physical problems or even gray hair.

• Age does not mean loneliness or loss of sexual interest. One study showed that 74 percent of older men and 35 percent of older women live with spouses. Another 23 percent of older women live with relatives or unrelated people, and 7 percent of older men do the same, according to Mary Spencer's *Truth about Aging: Guidelines for Publishers.* Although more people 65 years of age and older are living alone, they often choose that path for more independence.

DeView says that writers should focus on realistic presentations of older people. Some older people have no financial problems, while others struggle financially during their later life. Not all older people have ill health or are unable to cope with poor health. Although 45 percent of older people have serious medical conditions, they may not severely limit their participation in society. Only about 5 percent of older people live in nursing homes.

Children also may be portrayed in an unpleasant light. Not all children are immature, naive, whining, sneaky, dishonest, or lazy. Children mature and develop at different paces. Some are responsible, creative, athletically gifted, loving, aggravating, and mean. Each must be considered individually and be allowed to ascribe traits to himself or herself, as did one 5-foot teenager, who described herself as being "vertically challenged."

Overcoming Bias in Writing

Even after a discussion of bias such as the one in this chapter, traces of insensitivity can still creep into writing. You need to be constantly aware of your own background and attitudes to understand when and how bias might surface in writing, to recognize it, and to exorcise it.

Writers, reporters, and broadcasters today must be trained to avoid the flaws of their predecessors in the mass media. They must learn to question their own beliefs and assumptions to understand better the diverse ethnic groups within society.

Today's writers, through better awareness, are trying to overcome cultural bias by sifting through information and presenting the least stereotypical and biased picture possible. Messages—from school textbooks to television advertisements—use a multicultural approach that presents all kinds of people as equals. But despite education, old biases die hard for many. The writer of the story on Mayor Janet Parrott did not hide her bias that men are usually leaders. Every time a bias is confirmed by a writer, it is strengthened for readers.

Beginning and even experienced writers sometimes pass along stereotypes, such as the dizzy blonde or the dumb jock, because they think people like and understand such shorthand portrayals just as they like cartoons. Therein lies the danger. Because mass media professionals present distinctive images of people and groups, they can determine how consumers view people and groups who are not like themselves. Thus, writers must work responsibly in disseminating information rather than misinformation.

Make sure that what you write or broadcast does not perpetuate negative stereotypes. Stereotypes communicate inaccurate information and can undermine the quality of your work. Sensing stereotypes and avoiding them is a critical step on the path to better writing.

EXERCISES

1. Describe yourself culturally and ethnically. List any physical disabilities or other pertinent differences. Make a list of words or phrases, both negative and positive, that you have seen used in reference to your special traits. Compare your list with those of others in your class, and compile a directory of words to avoid when writing, and why. Explain the connotation of each word. Make a list of acceptable words or phrases.

2. What is the ethnic makeup of your college or university? The town or city where your school is located? Do a five-day content analysis of your local or student newspaper. Count the number of stories each day in the news, sports, and features sections. Count the number that focus on an ethnic group or an issue related to an ethnic group. At the end of the five days, calculate what percentage of the newspaper's stories related to ethnic groups. Do the percentages match the groups' makeup in the university's or town's population? Was coverage positive, negative, or neutral? What types of stories do you believe are missing?

3. Do a similar content analysis of the evening news broadcast, locally and for a national network. Count the total stories and the number concerning ethnic groups. Give your impressions about whether the general coverage was positive, negative, or neutral.

4. Read the Janet Parrott story and rewrite the first four paragraphs to avoid bias.

    STOVALL—Janet Parrott presides each month at a table of men who are each old enough to be her father.

She is blonde, freckled and five months pregnant. An outsider is surprised to learn she is mayor of the small Granville County town of Stovall.

After serving eight years in the town's highest office, she is still somewhat surprised herself.

"I've always been interested in the town," she said, "but I never set out to be mayor."

These days, she handles things better than she did starting out at age 24. "It's not a handicap to be a woman anymore," she says. "In fact, it has its advantages."

She was mayor before Isabella Cannon was Raleigh's mayor. At a League of Municipalities meeting in 1979, Mrs. Parrott received a few raised eyebrows.

Paul Munn, one of the town commissioners, says she is effective in getting help from the town board.

"When I get into a situation I can't handle, I'm not ashamed to say 'please help me,'" she said.

A Stovall native, she fell naturally into the job. After graduating from high school, she took a job as town clerk, tax collector, water bill collector, and "whatever else," in 1973.

When Mayor Harold Culbreth left the mayor's office in 1979 to return to school, he asked her to run.

That was a shock.

"I couldn't picture myself being mayor. The job is essentially the same as what I was doing, but it's a whole different ballgame when you have that title attached to your name."

The day after she took office, she was admitted to the hospital for three days with ulcers.

Since then, Mrs. Parrott has learned a lot.

She doesn't burst into tears when the town encounters major problems. A few months ago, when the town's wells dried up, she was on the phone to Raleigh and had a National Guard tanker truck hauling water into town the same day.

Twenty-four hours later, she fell asleep while on the phone asking for aid from Congressman Tim Valentine. She had been awake the whole 24 hours.

"I am conscious that this is a big responsibility," she said. "What I do can affect the people I love and have lived with all my life. . . .

"When we were out of water, it was a tragedy to me. I had friends who were cancer patients at home and needed water, and elderly people who would have to walk somewhere to find water. I was feeling responsible for it, even though there was nothing I could have done to prevent it."

Reprinted with permission from the *Herald-Sun* Newspapers.

5. You have the opportunity to interview the incoming student government president, a son of two Cuban refugees. List five objective questions you could use to begin the interview, then list two effective questions you could ask to determine his experiences with cultural differences in the United States.

6. Examine the front page of your local or student newspaper for cultural bias of any kind in headlines, stories, cutlines, or bylines. Look for specific language that carries bias or stereotypes. Note how the writer could have avoided bias. Write four to five paragraphs on your findings.

REFERENCES

A. Arluke and J. Levin, "Second Childhood." *Public Communication Review.* 1:2, 1992.

Timothy Crouse. *The Boys on the Bus.* New York: Random House, 1993.

"Focus on Racism in the Media." *Extra!* July/August, 1992.

M. Johnson and S. Elkins. *Reporting on Disability, Approaches and Issues.* Louisville, KY: Advocado Press, 1989.

Walter Lippmann. *Public Opinion.* New York: Harcourt, Brace and Co., 1922.

J. Pickens, ed. *Without Bias.* New York: John Wiley and Sons. 1982.

H. Stocking and P. Gross. *How Do Journalists Think? A Proposal for the Study of Cognitive Bias in Newsmaking.* Bloomington, IN: Eric Clearinghouse on Reading and Communication Skills, 1989.

Comments by Pale Moon Rose and John Mitrano from surveys of ethnic and racial groups, Fall 1993, by Jan Johnson Elliott, associate professor, University of North Carolina at Chapel Hill.

"Women's Lifestyles: A Special Report." *Scripps Howard Editors Newsletter.* Cincinnati, OH: Scripps Howard Newspapers, Spring 1989.

8

Testing Your Grammar

Our world is fast-paced and fast-changing—hardly the kind of place you would expect to need something as tedious as a lesson on grammar. But today's communicator cannot afford to slow down audiences, and faulty grammar does just that.

Consider the reader who encounters *its* where *it's* should be. For a split second, he will pause and wonder about the error, the writer, and the publication. Sometimes the musing reader will stop reading entirely because of the slowdown or because of the reduced credibility or appeal of the flawed message.

People don't have to be grammar experts to stop and wonder about correctness. For example, any unusual use of "whom" or "who" may cause a reader to reflect rather than read on. "Now what was it we learned about whom?" the reader muses, and the tempo of reading is lost.

The television viewer may cringe when the news announcer says, "The committee will reconvene their meeting tomorrow morning." She knows a committee is an "it," not a "their." She has paused to correct the sentence and at the same time has lost the remainder of the announcer's message.

Research has shown that when messages are perceived to be error free, they also are thought to be credible and well written. The perception of quality carries over to the writer and to the publication. In other words, publications free of errors are thought to be of high quality, produced by quality folks. Grammar problems fall within the category of errors.

If audiences are freed from grammatical distractions, they move comfortably through a message. Such comfort and ease are essential for effective communication in the information age, where distractions are abundant. In today's cluttered communication environment, writers have little control over such audience-stoppers as busy schedules and competing media. But they can control distractions that exist within messages. Editing for common grammar problems will eliminate one important source of audience turnoff.

This chapter will

- Test your knowledge in a diagnostic quiz,
- Discuss five problem areas where grammar problems usually occur, and
- Test your proficiency in each problem area.

But My Grammar Is Good . . .

Most of us who pursue writing as a career consider ourselves to be language experts, and in general, our grammar and language use are far above average. Even educated people have problems, however. Evidence of grammar problems is found in mistakes made daily by adults in business letters, memos, and reports as well as in newspapers and on the airways. An ad proclaims, "There's no down payment and no service charge!" To be grammatically correct, it should say, "No down payment and no service charge ARE there." A newsletter states, "Children will be grouped by age, irregardless of grade in school." There is no such word as "irregardless," which is simply an aberration of "regardless."

Educated, employed people regularly make grammar mistakes that other educated people will recognize. Writers need to learn what their most frequent grammar errors are and how to correct them. A first step in checking your grammar is to know what errors you are most likely to make.

Grammar Problems

Author Katherine C. McAdams, an associate professor at the University of Maryland, has developed "The Grammar Slammer," a workshop on grammar problems. It identifies five areas in which real-life errors are most likely to occur:

- Punctuation, especially commas, semicolons, colons, apostrophes, dashes, and hyphens.
- Subject and verb agreement.
- Correct pronoun choices that agree and that also avoid gender bias, such as "Each student has his or her book" rather than the more common and erroneous "Each student has their book."
- Correct sentence structures, especially when sentences use modifiers or require parallel structure.
- Word use—that is, using words (such as regardless) correctly. Often this area involves spelling problems and confusing words that sound alike, such as "affect" and "effect" or "vain" and "vein."

This chapter follows the format of the Grammar Slammer workshop, giving a short lesson on each of the problem areas and following that lesson with some exercises. The approach is designed for writers who are bright, motivated, and capable of learning quickly.

The lessons provide a quick fix rather than an in-depth lesson. The lessons are designed to refresh and renew rather than to re-educate. Going through the grammar lessons will help you to identify your grammar deficiencies. You then can be on guard for your particular problems when writing and editing. You may find that you have many weaknesses in language skills and understanding. If so, you will want to study the books recommended at the end of this chapter or take a grammar course.

Test Yourself

To determine which areas you need to work on, take the following diagnostic quiz. Record your answers on a sheet of paper.

Grammar Slammer Diagnostic Quiz

The following sentences contain errors in grammar and punctuation. No sentence contains more than one error. Read each sentence. Circle the error. In the space provided at the end of each sentence, indicate which part of the sentence has the error by noting the number that follows the error. Sentence 1 is an example.

1. If the regular season is any indication (1), Maryland should be considered (2) a top challenger (3) for the championship; having

downed (4) defending regional champion Kentucky twice in the (5) invitational tournament (6) _____4_____

2. The list of candidates (1) being considered as successors (2) for the University Chancellor have (3) been trimmed (4) to approximately 50 names, including (5) four UMCP officials. _____

3. The computer did not (1) seem to be (2) working today, it kept rejecting (3) the operator's (4) instructions. _____

4. The following afternoon, (1) Wednesday, October 25 a Royal (2) Indian Air Force DC-3 (3) put down in the abandoned dirt strip of Srinager Airport. (4) _____

5. Traditionally expected to be in control of their surroundings, (1) the insecurity makes freshmen (2) uncomfortable in their new situation. (3) _____

6. Franco's body (1) will lay in state (2) until services are held (3) at the chapel. (4) _____

7. Hopefully, the council will pass (1) a new noise ordinance (2) before the students return (3) to campus in September (4) _____

8. Among those who attended services for Rein were Dick Crum, head football coach at (1) UNC-CH, (2) Joab Thomas, chancellor at NCSU; John Caldwell, (3) former NCSU chancellor; and (4) Paul Deitzel (5), athletic director at LSU. _____

9. She predicted that (1) neither Howard Baker (2) or George Bush (3) would receive the Republican nomination. (4) _____

10. In its advertising, (1) the Acme Company claims that they are in business (2) only (3) to do good. (4) _____

11. Millie Rosefield, chair (1) of the Rockland Historic District Commission ran (2) fifth in the Nov. 6 race (3) for four council seats. (4) _____

12. One of every five (1) of the state's residents (2) live in the sort of poverty (3) that drove Erskine Caldwell to write. (4) _____

13. Three-fourths of the business district (1) in Long Beach, N. C. was destroyed (2) by Hurricane Hugo, (3) which struck the coast in 1989. (4) _____

14. Many a boy use to believe (1) that he could acquire (2) practically superhuman strength (3) just by eating the right cereal. (4) _____

15. Jones said the parade would feature the homecoming queen, (1) the marching band will play, (2) a pep rally, and (3) as many floats as possible. (4) _____

What's wrong with the following sentences? Correct each error.

16. Several people, all of them eager to give their opinions and all of them pressing forward to meet the governor, who was conducting interviews with voters in the area.
17. I like ice cream and cookies, I don't like cakes with icing.
18. Rosalie complained, and she had no heat.
19. Being a weight-lifter, his muscles were well developed.
20. The alligator is hunted for their skin.

Several of the following words are misspelled in a way that a computer spell-checking can't resolve. Circle the misspelled words and write the correct spelling for each in the space provided.

1. principal (of a school) _____
2. sherriff (a law officer) _____
3. marshall (an officer of the law) _____
4. seperate (to divide) _____
5. stationery (you write on it) _____
6. recommend (to suggest) _____
7. roommate _____
8. sieze (take control) _____

Answers for the diagnostic quiz are included in Appendix D at the back of the book.

Grammar Problems

Look at the problems you missed on the diagnostic quiz. You should have an idea of what grammar problems you need to review. The discussion of each problem is followed by exercises. Test your proficiency and move on. Record your answers on a sheet of paper. To check your work, look at the answers in Appendix D.

Problem 1: Punctuation

Perhaps no problem looms larger than that of punctuation. Few people actually know the rules and regulations of punctuation use. Most of us end up, much of the time, using the "feel good" school of punctuation, saying "I just feel like I needed a comma," or "A semicolon just felt right."

Professional communicators must give up their "feel good" philosophy of punctuating. The first rule of punctuating professionally is this: DON'T PUNCTUATE UNLESS YOU KNOW A RULE. When you even think of adding a mark of punctuation, stop and think about whether it may be justified by the rules in this chapter. If not, you probably don't need to punctuate at all. This leads us to the second rule of punctuating professionally: WHEN IN DOUBT, LEAVE IT OUT. If you are not sure about where to place a comma, for example, don't put one in a sentence.

One more tip before we move into rules: If you find that you are punctuating excessively, that is, using more than three punctuation marks within any given sentence, it's probably time to rewrite that sentence. Sentences that require many punctuation marks, even if they are all correct, are usually too long and complex to be easily understood by readers. So the third rule of punctuating professionally is that LESS IS MORE. Less punctuation leads to clearer, more readable copy.

Commas

Literally hundreds of comma rules exist. But the nine listed here, distilled by high school English teacher Mary Penny in the 1940s, have been found over the years to take care of most everyday comma problems.

RULE 1. Use commas in compound sentences when clauses are separated by a conjunction such as and, but, for, nor, or yet.

- She managed the restaurant, but he did the cooking.

Note: In such sentences, leaving out the conjunction leads to an error known as a comma splice, whereby a comma is left to do the work of joining two sentences: She managed the restaurant, he did the cooking. Like weak splices in rope, commas are not strong enough for this task. A period or semicolon is needed to make a correct sentence:

- She managed the restaurant. He did the cooking.
- She managed the restaurant; he did the cooking.

RULE 2. Use commas to separate elements in a series. Such elements usually are adjectives, verbs, or nouns. *Note:* Journalism departs from traditional rules of punctuation by leaving the comma out before a conjunction in a series of elements.

Book or English composition version:

- The tall, dark, handsome man hailed, lauded, and applauded Ben, George, Maude, and Rebecca.

Journalism version:

- The tall, dark handsome man hailed, lauded and applauded Ben, George, Maude and Rebecca.

RULE 3. Use commas when attributing from quoted material. Commas set off words of attribution from the words of a one-sentence quotation unless a question mark or exclamation mark is preferred. Use them also in words of saying:

- He said, "Hello." or "Hello," he said.

RULE 4. Commas follow introductory matter.

After an introductory adverbial clause:

- When the team was forced to kick, the coach sent in his best players.

After two or more introductory prepositional phrases:

- In the spring she returned to College Park. (no comma)
- In the spring of 1981, she returned to College Park. (comma)

With a phrase that contains a verbal (that is, a verb as a modifier):

- Singing as she worked, Mary answered the phone.
- Kicked by a horse, Don was more than stunned.
- To cure hiccups, drink out of the far side of a glass.

RULE 5. Commas follow the salutation of a friendly letter and the complimentary close of any letter. Commas follow capitalized elements, such as

Sincerely and Very truly yours, and a colon follows the salutation of a business letter.

- Dear Reese,
- Dear Dean Cleghorn:

RULE 6. Commas follow all items in a full address or date.

- July 16, 1962, is his date of birth.
- She has lived in Manteo, N.C., all her life.

RULE 7. Commas surround nonessential words or phrases.

- Well, we will just have to walk home.

Commas set off appositives, which are words or phrases that rename a noun. Appositives amplify a subject.

- Betty Brown, his mother-in-law, has been married four times.

Commas set off nonessential modifying clauses and phrases.

- The president-elect, suffering from laryngitis, canceled his speech.

RULE 8. Commas surround words of direct address.

- Betty, please pass the butter.
- I can see, Fred, that you are lazy.

RULE 9. Commas indicate omitted verbs, usually expressed in another part of the sentence.

- Talent often is inherited; genius, never.

Semicolons and Colons

Miss Penny added three more rules to her list to take care of another widespread punctuation problem: the correct use of semicolons and colons. Miss Penny's rules 10 and 11 explain the two uses of the semicolon—the ONLY two uses. Rule 12 explains the use of colons.

RULE 10. Semicolons connect two complete sentences if sentences have a related thought. Use of a semicolon is usually done for drama.

- The brown-eyed, dark, and vivacious model, at age 25, seemed destined for quick success; on Dec. 11, 1991, her apparent destiny was altered.

RULE 11. Semicolons are used in a list separating items that require significant internal punctuation.

- He visited Richmond, Va.; Raleigh, N.C.; Greenville, S.C.; Birmingham, Ala.; and Baton Rouge, La.

RULE 12. Colons precede formal lists, illustrations, multisentence quotes, and enumerations.

- The following students received scholarships: Jim Johnson, Juanita Jones, Martha Taylor, Tiffany Eldridge, and Teri Sampson.
- He answered her with a parable: "A man once had six sons. Five of them . . ."
- Clinton listed the steps in his recovery program: First, to raise interest rates; second, to reduce spending . . .

Slammer for Commas, Semicolons, and Colons

Now, using Miss Penny's list of twelve rules as your reference, complete the following exercise. REMEMBER: The most important rule is that you DON'T punctuate unless you know a rule. Defend each mark of punctuation that you use by citing one of the Penny rules in the space provided. Record your answers on a sheet of paper.

Rule or Rules

_____   1. Although we watched the Super Bowl we don't know who won.

_____   2. John Blimpo an egocentric man dropped his hat in the fruit salad.

_____   3. Guitars have six strings basses four.

_____   4. The tall dark handsome man listed his hobbies as reading fishing painting and writing.

_____   5. To Whom it May Concern

The spelling and grammar test will be given on March 2 3 and 4 1981 in Room 502 of the Journalism Building

Grammatically yours

J. School Dean

_____   6. Dad go ahead and send the money now.

_____   7. The women's basketball team were down by four points at half-time however they came back to crush their opponents.

_____   8. Congress passed the bill but the debate took several weeks.

_____   9. Well just be in by daybreak.

_____   10. Her blind date was a real disappointment he talked loudly and constantly about his pet snake.

_____   11. She was elected on Nov. 3 1972 in Baltimore Md. the city of her birth to serve as mayor.

_____   12. She named her courses for the fall semester journalism English political science history and French.

Check your exercise by looking at the answers in Appendix D. Then go on to tackle some other troublesome marks of punctuation.

Hyphens and Dashes

Remember that hyphens and dashes, although often confused, are different.

The hyphen differs from a dash in both use and appearance. The hyphen is shorter (- as opposed to —), and it comes, without additional spaces, between two words that are combined to express some new concept, such as polka-dot and part-time. Hyphens are useful joiners that bring some creativity to language.

Rather than joining phrases, dashes are useful in separating them—usually where that separation can be heard. Dashes are sometimes used to replace commas to ensure that a pause is audible and even dramatic. Although charming, he was—on the other hand—a thief.

Here is a list of guidelines for using hyphens and dashes correctly:

1. Never use a hyphen after a word ending in "ly."

• The newly elected president stepped to the podium.

2. Use a hyphen to connect two or more related modifying words that do not function independently.

- Todd always ordered the blue-plate special.
- Todd dreaded any face-to-face confrontations.

3. The dash is a punctuation mark that one hears. It is a noticeable pause. Choose a dash instead of a comma so that the audience can "hear" the pause.

4. Dashes work where commas would also work. The only difference is that the dash adds drama—and an audible break in the text. Because dashes may substitute for commas, they are used to set off nonessential material.

- The murderer was—if you can believe it—a priest.

5. Too many dashes in any text may be distracting and even irritating to readers. Limit dashes to only the most dramatic of pauses. In most cases, such as this example, commas will suffice.

- She is—as most of you know—a punctuation expert.
- She is, as most of you know, a punctuation expert.

Problem 2: Subject and Verb Agreement

Few writers make obvious errors in subject and verb agreement, such as "I is interested in cars" or "The class know it's time to go to lunch." But most people struggle with the following subject–verb agreement problems.

1. Collective subjects can be confusing. Some nouns that appear to be plural—such as Girl Scouts, checkers, economics—are treated as singular units.

- The Girl Scouts is a fine organization.
- Checkers is an ancient game.
- Economics is a difficult subject.

Some, however, have Latinate endings and remain plural, although spoken language tends to make them singular, such as media and alumni. They require plural verbs.

- The media have raised the issue of the senator's competency.

2. The pronouns each, either, neither, anyone, and anybody are always singular, regardless of what follows them in a phrase. Take, for example, this sentence:

- Either of the boys is an excellent choice for president.

The phrase "of the boys" does not change the singular number of the true subject of this sentence: the pronoun "either." Following are some other examples of correct usage.

- Neither has my vote.
- Either is fine with me.
- Each has an excellent option.
- Anyone is capable of helping the homeless.

3. A fraction or percentage of a whole is considered a singular subject.

- A quarter of the pie is gone.
- Sixty-seven percent of the voters is needed to withhold a veto.

4. Compound subjects, in which two or more nouns function as the subject of a sentence, can lead to agreement problems. To solve such problems, substitute a single pronoun such as "they" or "it" for the sentence's subject or subjects.

For example, transform this problem sentence: The students and the teacher is/are waiting for the bus. By use of substitution, the subject becomes "they": They are waiting for the bus.

Some other examples:

- The opening number and the grand finale thrill the audience. (they thrill)

- There are no down payment and no service charge. (they are not there)

5. When subjects are structured with either/or and neither/nor, use the verb that responds to the subject closest to it, as in the following cases:

- Either the leader or the scouts pitch the tent.
- Either the scouts or the leader pitches the tent.

Slammer for Subject–Verb Agreement

Check your knowledge of subject–verb agreement by taking the following quiz. On a separate sheet of paper, write the verb that agrees.

1. He did say he would look at the sheet of names, which includes/include the owners of two apartment buildings.
2. Their number and influence appears/appear greatest in West Germany.
3. Experience in the backfield and the line gives/give the coach a good feeling on the eve of any opening game.
4. A first offense for having fewer than 25 cartons of untaxed cigarettes results/result in a $500 fine.
5. Before you make a final judgment on this student's story, consider the time and effort that has/have gone into it.
6. Who does the teaching? Full professors. But so does/do associates, assistants, and instructors.
7. She said they would visit the Peaks of Otter, which is/are near Lynchburg, Va.
8. The news media is/are calling for a peace treaty that is fair to everyone.
9. The United Mine Workers exhibit/exhibits solidarity during strikes.
10. There is/are 10 million bricks in this building.
11. The president said that students today are too job-oriented and neglect the broader areas of study that constitutes/constitute a true education.
12. Five fire companies fought the blaze, which the firefighters said was/were the longest this year.
13. Each of the 100 people believes/believe in God.

14. It is/are the boats, not the swimmers, that stir up the dirt in the lake.
15. The editor told the staff there was a shortage of money for the newsroom, a shortage she said she would explain to the board of directors, which decides/decide all matters on the budget.
16. One of my classmates typifies/typify student apathy.
17. Drinking beer and sleeping is/are the most important things in my life.
18. Dillon said he has insurance for everything except the buildings, which is/are owned by Thomas F. Williams.
19. Approximately 51 percent of the U.S. population is/are female.
20. There is/are only one way to beat taxes.
21. Neither the professor nor her two assistants teaches/teach this course in a style students like.
22. Each student is/are responsible for getting the work done on time.
23. All students considers/consider that an imposition.
24. The General Assembly and the governor disagrees/disagree on the solution.

Check your answers against those in Appendix D. The next grammar problem is about correct pronoun use.

Problem 3: Correct Use of Pronouns

Pronouns are little words—he, she, you, they, I, it—that stand for proper nouns. Look at this sentence:

International Trucking is hiring 20 new drivers because it is expanding in the Southeast.

In this sentence, the word "it" is used to substitute for International Trucking. Pronouns help us avoid needless repetition in language by doing the work of the larger nouns, which are called antecedents. In the example above, "International Trucking" is the antecedent for the pronoun "it."

Pronouns must agree with their antecedents, as in the following examples:

- Marianne said she (Marianne) would never color her (Marianne's) hair.
- Baltimore became a model city after it successfully restored the water-front.
- Journalism is a popular major, and now it prepares students for many careers.

Following are guidelines to ensure correct pronoun choices.

1. Watch for collective subjects—groups that are treated as single units—and use the correct pronoun.

- The committee gave its report.
- The United Mine Workers gave out a list of its legislative goals.

2. When using singular pronouns, use singular verbs.

- Each of the rose bushes was at its peak.
- Everyone in the audience rose to his or her feet and chanted.

3. Use correct pronouns to handle issues of sexism in language. The generic person is no longer "he."

- Each of the students had his or her book.
- The students had their books.

4. Be attentive to stray phrases or clauses that come between pronouns and antecedents and cause agreement problems.

- He presented the list of candidates being considered for the office and told the committee to choose from it.
- The list of candidates for the position has been trimmed.

5. Use reflexive pronouns only when a subject is doing something to herself/himself or themselves.

- Jan introduced herself to the new chancellor.
- Henry never could forgive himself.
- The relatives had the chalet to themselves.

Slammer for Pronouns

To ensure agreement of pronoun and antecedent, write the appropriate pronoun in each of the following sentences. Use a piece of paper to record your answers.

1. Each student had (his or her/their) assignment completed before class.
2. General Foods plans to change (its/their) approach to marketing baked goods.
3. Larry introduced me and (him/himself) to the governor.
4. The jury took (their/its) deliberations seriously.
5. The Board of Directors set a date for (their/its) annual retreat.
6. The Redskins (is/are) my favorite team.
7. Neither the Terps nor the Crimson Tide (was/were) having a winning season.
8. Neither of the teams (was/were) victorious.
9. The alumni voted to charge $1 an issue for (their/its) magazine.
10. Any of the three finalists (is/are) an excellent choice.
11. The six-member committee voted to reverse (its/their) decision.
12. The librarian's collection fascinated him, and he asked to borrow from (her/it).
13. The media (is/are) ignoring Perot's speeches.
14. Each of the students could handle the job by (himself or herself/ themselves).
15. Everyone in the audience rose to (his or her/their) feet for the ovation.

Check your work against the answers in Appendix D, and prepare to tackle the biggest pronoun problem of all: the WHO/WHOM dilemma.

Who and Whom

The word "whom" has all but disappeared from spoken English, so it is little wonder that few of us know how to use it correctly. Even though usage is changing, writers of published materials still need to know the rules that govern the distinction between who and whom.

1. Who is a substitute for subjects referring to he, we, or she, or the nominative pronoun.

- Who saw the meteor?

The statement He saw the meteor, as a question becomes Who saw the meteor? "Who" is substituted for the subject "he." Relative clauses work the same way when "who" is substituted for a subject. In the sentence He questioned the man who saw the meteor, "who" substitutes for the subject of the clause He saw the meteor. This is confusing because the entire clause serves as an object of the verb questioned. But the function of the clause does not change the role of a pronoun; in this sentence, the role of "who" is as the subject of the verb "saw."

2. Whom is a substitute for objective pronouns such as him, her, or them.

- Whom did he question for hours?
- He questioned her for hours.

The statement He questioned her for hours, as a question becomes Whom did he question for hours? "Whom" is substituted for "her" as the object of the verb questioned. Substitution works the same way in relative clauses. In the sentence Marcella was the one whom he questioned for hours, "whom" substitutes for the object "her" in the clause He questioned her for hours. Again, it is the role of the pronoun within its subject–verb structure that determines whether it is subject or object, and therefore who or whom.

That and Which

Another fine distinction between pronouns is the difference between that and which. Again, the spoken language no longer follows strict rules regarding these subordinate conjunctions, but careful writers need to observe the following guidelines:

1. That is a restrictive pronoun, indicating that the information it precedes is essential for correct understanding of the sentence.

- Dogs prefer bones that improve their dental health.

The use of that tells us that dogs prefer only this specific kind of bone.

2. Which precedes nonessential material; therefore, it typically appears with commas (the ones used to set off nonessential information).

- Dogs prefer bones, which improve their dental health.

The use of *which* tells us that bones improve dogs' teeth.

3. *That* and *which* are not interchangeable. As you can see in the example sentences, the meaning of the sentence is affected when the comma is added in the second sentence and *that* becomes *which*. In the first sentence, dogs like only bones that are good for them; in the second, dogs like bones better than other things, and bones just happen to be good for dental health. The second sentence is far more logical.

Slammer for Who/Whom and That/Which

On a sheet of paper, write the appropriate pronoun in the sentences below.

1. Alvin, (who/whom) everyone adored, absconded with the family fortune.
2. Betty, (who/whom) was the apple of his eye, followed him to Mexico.
3. The FBI agents (who/whom) Alvin had avoided for several months finally arrested him.
4. Veronica, Alvin's sister, (who/whom) needed the money desperately, refused to post bond.
5. Alvin, (who's/whose) health was delicate, wasted away in prison.

Select the appropriate pronoun, then note the proper punctuation as needed in the following sentences.

1. Betty bought a gun (that/which) was on sale and set out to free Alvin.
2. She headed north from Mexico in a car (that/which) had more than 130,000 miles showing on its odometer.
3. The car (that/which) had New Jersey license plates was quickly spotted by police in Texas.
4. The Texans (that/which/who/whom) spoke in a slow drawl told her she was wanted in New Jersey for conspiring with Alvin.
5. She pulled out the gun (that/which) she had in her glove compartment and started shooting.
6. The policeman (that/which/who/whom) was standing closest to her car died after he was struck by a bullet.
7. Other officers took Betty's gun (that/which) now was empty of bullets.

8. They also arrested Betty and placed her in a jail (that/which) overlooked the Rio Grande.

Check your answers against those in Appendix D and move on to the next grammar problem: modifier placement.

Problem 4: Modifier Placement

To solve modifier placement problems, place modifying clauses and phrases closest to what they modify, as shown below.

Wrong: Swinging from an overhead wire, we saw a kite.

Better: We saw a kite swinging from an overhead wire.

Wrong: When wheeled into the operating room, the nurse placed a mask over my face.

Better: The nurse placed a mask over my face after I was wheeled into the operating room.

Wrong: We saw a herd of sheep on the way to our hotel.

Better: On the way to our hotel, we saw a herd of sheep.

Slammer for Modifiers

Modifiers are placed with what they modify. Rewrite the sentences below on a piece of paper, and correct misplaced modifiers. Some sentences are correct as written.

1. The waiter served ice cream in glass bowls which started melting immediately.
2. The Simpsons gave a toy robot with flashing eyes to one of their sons.
3. We saw a herd of sheep on the way to our hotel.
4. Most people have strawberry shortcake topped with mounds of whipped cream.
5. The house is one of the oldest in Rockville, where Mrs. Rooks taught ballet.
6. Flying at an altitude of several thousand feet, the paratroopers could see for miles.
7. I could not convince the child to stop running into the street without yelling.

8. After the first act of the play, Brooke's performance improves, the critic said.
9. While watching the ball game, Sue's horse ran away.
10. The museum director showed me a spider with the orange diamond on its belly.
11. The bank approves loans to reliable individuals of any size.
12. After being wheeled into the operating room, the nurse placed a mask over my face.
13. Riding in a glass-bottom boat, we saw thousands of colorful fish.
14. Aunt Helen asked us before we left to call on her.
15. Do it yourself: Make up a sentence suffering from modifier malady. Then correct it.

Check your work against the answers in Appendix D, and prepare for the final grammar problem: word usage.

Problem 5: Correct Word Usage

English is a language enriched by words borrowed from other languages, resulting in a rich vocabulary—but also in many cases of unorthodox spelling and idiosyncratic usage. It makes little sense to have both affect and effect in the same language, functioning so similarly but not identically. And why do we distinguish between pore and pour, or flair and flare? Who cares?

Careful writers have to care because subtle usage errors can cause big misunderstandings. In addition, correct usage leads to credibility; readers have confidence in error-free reading.

The number of troublesome words in daily use is so great that no attempt is made to list them all here. Instead, we have included as Appendix B Professor Thom Leib's Abused Word List, a catalog of usage problems that most often plague writers. Get acquainted with the Abused Words List by working on the following exercise.

Slammer for Abused Words

Use Appendix B to help identify correct usage for each of the following troublesome words.

Hopefully

Affect vs. effect

Less vs. fewer

It's vs. its

Lie vs. lay

Sit vs. set

Comprise vs. compose

SUGGESTED READINGS

Theodore M. Bernstein, *Dos, Don'ts and Maybes of the English Language.* New York: The Times Book Co., 1977.

John Bremner, *Words on Words.* New York: Columbia University Press, 1980.

E. L. Callihan, *Grammar for Journalists,* 3rd ed. Radnor, PA: Chilton Co., 1979.

Lauren Kessler and Duncan McDonald, *When Words Collide.* Belmont, CA: Wadsworth Publishing, 1992.

9

Research and Observation

Writing begins with an idea. During a trip to the ocean, a writer is fascinated with the porpoises that periodically surface and roll as they travel offshore. She wants to write about porpoises. But she needs more information than just her observations to write a factual, accurate, complete, and entertaining article. She must learn more.

Gathering information is like detective work. As a sleuth you start with a clue. Step by step you add pieces until you have enough information to reconstruct events and solve the case. As a writer you add to your knowledge until you can create an accurate and complete summary of the topic.

Writers, like detectives, gather information from research, interviews, and observations. Research allows writers to study what others have already found out. That information may be in books, magazines, statistical abstracts, encyclopedias, data banks, or any number of other written sources. In today's information age, writers can access hundreds of documents that have been stored in computer databases—and even thousands if they have time.

Armed with facts retrieved in research, writers can move to interviews. They identify knowledgeable, expert, and relevant sources to add personal comment on the topic. Sources' quotes enliven the recitation of facts. Interviewing is discussed in Chapter 10.

Writers also note their observations. Student writers are sometimes reluctant to include their impressions for fear they will appear too subjective and not objective. They must overcome that fear. In the porpoise story, the writer would be remiss not to describe the rolling action as the sleek, gray mammals break water a hundred yards off the beach. Audiences want to know what the animals look like and how thrilled the author is at seeing a school of several hundred porpoises dotting the waves as they surface for air.

In this chapter you will learn

- How to think about topics, formulate questions, and test early results,
- What basic resources to consult,
- The wealth of information in government documents,
- How to be wary of factual errors endemic to print and electronic sources, and
- How observation is a part of gathering information.

Getting Started in Research

Writers start out as generalists; they know a little about a lot of subjects. Some develop specialties or subject areas they prefer, whether they are newspaper or electronic media reporters, public relations practitioners, or advertising copywriters. They may cover general assignment topics or report on special beats such as business, medicine, sports, the environment, children's issues, government, religion, or the media.

Whether they are generalists or specialists, writers need to do research. A medical writer may know medical terminology, but if he wants to do a piece on wholistic treatment of cancer, he must become knowledgeable about the topic. A television station's government reporter must learn the newly elected members of Congress before she goes to the opening session.

Writers need to find information that is accurate, relevant, and up to date. Time is their greatest enemy. Most writers have deadlines and have limited time to devote to research, particularly if they write for daily newspapers. So they need to find information quickly and efficiently.

Barbara Semonche, a former newspaper librarian, is the librarian at the School of Journalism and Mass Communication at the University of North Carolina at Chapel Hill. She has developed a dozen guides for students in the quest to find information. She notes:

You can be certain of two things: either you will find useful information efficiently or you will not. You will find too much information or too little. Your success will depend to a certain extent, upon the quality of your search strategies. The other part is finding the best reference sources.

Developing a Strategy

To be successful in research, you need a strategy to find information. Once you have defined your topics, you must make a list of questions, identify obvious sources, conduct searches for additional sources, review those sources for additional leads, refine their questions, then interview.

You are a medical reporter and want to write a story on childhood immunizations. You first list information you need to know, like the following questions:

Initial question list for story on childhood immunizations

Who has to be immunized?

What are the state laws?

What shots do children have to have?

At what ages do children get which shots?

Are there any reactions to the shots?

How much do the shots cost at a doctor's office?

Can children get shots at public health clinics? How much?

Where are the clinics here? What are the hours for immunizations?

How many children register for school and aren't immunized?

Is this a problem locally?

Have any other diseases surfaced locally?

Why do parents not get their children immunized?

Additional questions after research

What are the risks to children who aren't immunized?

Do children ever die from immunizations?

What are the reactions parents can expect?

How many children in the state aren't immunized properly when they start school?

How many immunizations are given each year in the state? In our county?

What childhood diseases are appearing again?

How much of the cost of immunizations does the government pay?

Do we consider some diseases eradicated?

Thirty years ago children suffered from mumps, measles, and even polio. Now children can be protected even against chicken pox. Are we too complacent about a resurgence of diseases?

Are there any diseases left that children need to be protected from?

If a certain number of children are immunized, does that protect other children, as in the herd effect?

What factors prevent parents from having children immunized at the proper time?

The obvious sources would be newspaper and journal indexes, articles and information in databases, pediatricians, and local health department and school officials. As you do research you uncover articles that name experts in the field, identify agencies that oversee immunizations, and show a reappearance of some childhood diseases.

Eventually your source list grows to include state health officials, state statutes that stipulate which immunizations children must have to enter school, officials at the Centers for Disease Control, legislators who allocate funds for immunizations, parents, and even children. You refine your list of questions for each source and prepare to interview your sources.

Your search strategy is similar if you are writing a story for the alumni magazine on a graduate whose first novel has been published. She is an assistant professor at a college in another state. Before the interview, you need to find information on the author. The first part of the strategy is to start close to home: the university's alumni files and the yearbooks for the time the author was on campus. Old telephone books will tell you where she lived.

You then might consult general biographical reference books. Your alumna might be notable enough to be included in *Who's Who*. But you discover she's not. If you can find no accessible biographical history, you will have to rely on a strategy that includes interviewing former professors, roommates, colleagues, friends, and family members. You may have to call the English department where she teaches and have someone send a curriculum vitae. You may have to consult newspaper indexes in her home state to find specific articles about her. If one source indicates an organization to which she belongs, you may need to look for references on that organization. Articles about the organization may include material about your up-and-coming author.

Basic Reference Sources

Although computers have assisted the information-gathering process, some older researchers prefer looking up facts in printed material. Every student writer needs to know the basic documents that can aid in research. To find sources, writers should consult indexes that tell where information is located. For example, *Biography Index* would tell a researcher where to find information on Malcolm X. Directories such as the *Gale Directory of Publications and Broadcast Media* and the *Encyclopedia of Associations* provide data on companies and organizations.

A multitude of reference books exist—and many are online in computer databases. Some are general reference books such as encyclopedias or the *World Almanac,* which is updated annually. Some furnish interesting or unusual data, such as *Famous First Facts,* which lists "firsts" alphabetically, and *Acronyms, Initialisms and Abbreviations Dictionary,* which can clarify the meaning of the acronym M.A.S.H. Or you may find speech material in publications such as *Familiar Quotations.* Others contain addresses that might be helpful such as *Standard and Poor's Register,* which lists officers of major corporations and their addresses and telephone numbers. The best place to launch your research is the online catalogue of your college or university library. The online catalogues permit searching by keywords, singly or in combinations, which greatly increases the ease and speed of getting useful results.

References by Type

Researchers and writers use hundreds of sources. Listed here are some types of publications that writers traditionally have relied on for information.

BIOGRAPHICAL SOURCES. Such sources list information about well-known people. Some are specific, such as *Who's Who in American Politics* or *Who's Who in the United Nations.* The information will include birthdate, parents' names, education, career, awards and achievements, and family data. Among other biographical sources are *Who's Who, Contemporary Newsmakers, Current Biography, Contemporary Authors,* and *Who's Who among Hispanic Americans.* More than 100 biographical dictionaries exist, each focusing on a special group or profession. The one for journalism is *Biographical Dictionary of American Journalists.*

STATISTICAL INFORMATION. *Statistical Abstracts of the United States* is one of the most widely used reference books. It provides information from the number of police officers in Albuquerque to the number of houses with indoor plumbing in Lincoln, Nebraska. Data are based on information collected by the federal government and other sources. *Census of Population of the United States* is published every ten years after the *U.S. Census* is conducted. Census information also is available in CD-ROM and on the Internet. *Editor and Publisher Market Guide* contains data on cities, such as the number of shopping malls a city has and whether its water is fluoridated. Most states compile statistical books, particularly those dealing with vital statistics: births, deaths, marriages, and divorces. Writers can find information on states, counties, cities, and even sections within cities that is especially helpful if they are looking for the local angle on a story. For international information, writers can consult the *United Nations Demographic Yearbook.*

A word of note: Many statistical books do not come out quickly. For example, a state's 1996 statistical data may not be published until May 1997 because of delays in reporting year-end figures and in producing the copies.

POLITICAL AND GOVERNMENT INFORMATION. The *U.S. Government Manual* contains information on departments and agencies in the executive branch. *Congressional Quarterly* publishes a weekly report that catalogues the voting records of Congress and major political speeches. States annually publish manuals that contain information about branches of government and legislatures, summaries of the state history, the state Constitution, and biographies of major state officials. Information on foreign governments and leaders can be found in reference books such as *Statesman's Yearbook* and *Current World Leaders.*

GEOGRAPHIC DATA. Writers may need to locate cities, towns, and countries. They can refer to the *Times Atlas of the World* and *Rand-McNally Commercial Atlas.* A gazetteer, such as the *Chambers World Gazetteer,* will describe an area and its location, population, and history.

BUSINESS INFORMATION. Writers may need data on a company or an industry, and students may need information on a potential employer. Among available resources are the *Dun and Bradstreet Reference Book of Corporate Managements, Standard and Poor's Register,* and Moody's *Manuals.*

Writers should always remember basic sources such as telephone books, city directories, and maps. They should rely on assistance from reference librarians to direct them to current and complete indexes and other references. Many beginning writers waste time trying to find information on their own when they could do research much faster if they would ask for direction. Librarians can help writers expand the lists given here.

Pitfalls in Research

The hunt for information may be complex. Librarian Barbara Semonche warns that not all information is in a compact, convenient form. At the start of a search, students may discover people with the same name, such as William Perry. A William Perry was a football player also known as "the Refrigerator." Another William Perry was secretary of defense under President Clinton.

Information may be dated. Some biographical reference material is not cumulated, and you may have to look in earlier editions. Students and other researchers must remember that not every reference includes every individual, and those that do may not have all the facts about an individual. Researchers must look at many sources to find complete information. Searching for information is rarely one-stop shopping. But using many sources helps uncover discrepancies and inconsistencies about information and also helps ensure that information is as accurate as possible.

Writers should look continuously for other sources. The research game is a detective hunt. Names or sources mentioned in an article or in references can be lead to nuggets of information elsewhere. The only constraints will be time and deadline pressure.

Government Sources

Local, state, and federal governments produce millions of pages of documents every year. Documents range from official findings, such as federal Food and Drug Administration studies, to county tax records and the disposition of local traffic cases. Most government documents are open and accessible to the public. Many are free by mail upon request, and others are available at the city hall, the county courthouse, a regional federal repository, or the Library of Congress. They provide a wealth of information for writers and curious citizens.

Writers should find out where federal depository libraries are located in their states. More than 1,400 exist across the country and contain thousands of federal documents. The 52 regional depositories house all federal documents available to be deposited but not necessarily all federal documents that are produced. A writer can ask a librarian in a federal depository to obtain material from a regional depository via interlibrary loan.

Public Records

When government documents are produced in the course of business, the documents are considered to be public. The documents have been created by government, which is supported by taxpayers' money. Researchers, writers, and anyone who wants the documents can request to see them or to have copies made. All states have laws that pertain to what is and what isn't a public record. The general rule most journalists follow is that any document is considered to be a public record unless the agency or individual who has the document can cite the section of state statute that prevents its disclosure. If the agency cannot, it must relinquish the information. Media writers should know what the open records laws are for their particular state. State press associations can provide the law and its exceptions. Publications such as *The News Media and the Law,* published by the Reporters Committee for Freedom of the Press, can be consulted. The Electronic Frontier Foundation is a valuable resource and can be accessed via Internet.

Agencies can charge a reasonable fee for photocopying documents. Most states have regulations pertaining to computer storage of public documents and reasonable charges for making copies or providing access to computerized information. Some news organizations have the computer capability to tap directly into state databases, such as those that maintain drivers' license records.

Freedom of Information Act

In 1966 the U.S. Congress passed the federal Freedom of Information Act (FOIA). The act became law in 1967 and has been amended twice. The law is much like state laws regarding public records. Anyone is allowed to make a written request for information from any federal agency, but not all information is available. The act provides broad exemptions, such as information relating to national defense or foreign policy, internal personnel rules and practices of an agency, personnel and medical files that would constitute an invasion of privacy, information compiled for law enforcement purposes, and geophysical information such as that related to well locations.

The media have worked continually to reduce the number of exemptions. Michael Gartner, former president of the American Society of Newspaper Editors, once lamented in a speech on national Freedom of Information Day that the name "Freedom of Information" implies that government is holding information hostage. He objected to many of the restrictions, particularly those that prevent publication of what the United States broadcasts to third world countries over the Voice of America.

The act sets out the procedure for requesting information, the time required for an agency to respond, appeals procedures, and fees. Individuals must pay the cost of photocopying the information but can request waiver of that cost if the release of the information is in the public interest.

Writers or individuals seeking information under the act may be frustrated. Delays can occur even when procedures are followed. The request must be specific and must be sent to the proper agency. When the information is uncovered, a reporter may receive sections or entire pages inked out to protect exempted information. The reporter pays the cost of photocopying all pages—even the blackened ones.

FOIA searches are time-consuming and can be costly, but many journalists have used them to find information and to produce fact-filled stories. For example, *USA Today* investigated the salaries and perquisites for college coaches. It filed more than 1,000 requests for information under the FOIA and state open records laws to secure facts used in the series. The newspaper found that men's coaches earned more than women's coaches—and sometimes more than the governors of their respective states.

Computer Databases

Technology has changed the way writers transmit and share information. Telephone lines, most of which are multifaceted fiberoptic cables, transmit data bits via facsimile machines and modems. Distance is irrelevant. A public relations practitioner in Detroit can write a statement and fax it to a company official at a conference in Switzerland. A reporter can write a story on a laptop computer during a meeting and zap it in a matter of seconds via a modem and telephone to the city desk thirty miles away. The technology has moved beyond delivering only text to sending photographs, maps, and other visuals in color.

Technology has also changed the way information is stored. People who began writing careers in the mid-1980s and earlier have seen a phenomenal change in the way they seek information. In the "old days" before 1985, most treks for information ended in libraries—newspaper, city or county, university—or wherever resource books were housed. People consulted encyclopedias, data books, statistical abstracts, articles, scholarly journals, and newspaper clip files. People handled paper to get information. They viewed older editions of newspapers on microfiche.

What Are Databases?

Writers today still use paper sources. But more and more they can avoid trips to the library and call up information in a matter of seconds while sitting at their computers in the office or at home. Newspapers, books, magazines, library holdings, and even job banks are online for writers who have modems attached to their computers. People can find bibliographical citations and information on individuals or agencies. They can access local computer databases or broader networked systems that combine databases.

Even government has entered the computer information age. In early 1995 THOMAS, a new congressional online access system, became available. Information-seekers can access the *Congressional Record,* congressional legislation digests, and directories of congressional members' electronic mail. More libraries are getting online access to a gateway service to the Government Printing Office that allows direct access to copies of bills and other material printed there.

Computers allow any organization that produces information to store it so that it can be accessed by others. New companies have formed to serve as liaisons between holders and seekers of information. Other companies have been launched to create and store information. Those who want the data pay those who have access to or possess the specific information. The information is stored in databases.

Since 1990 the number of databases has grown rapidly in number, diversity, and relative ease of access. Services that access many online sources include those owned by the media, such as America Online, a service owned by Simon & Schuster publishing company; VU/TEXT, which is operated by Knight-Ridder Newspapers, Inc.; and Dow Jones News/Retrieval, which has full text articles of the *Wall Street Journal* and business information on thousands of companies. Information on commercial services is shown here.

Some Commercial Services

America Online (800-827-6364). AOL has more than 2 million customers. The software is provided free, and users have access to e-mail and the Internet. AOL includes information for news junkies, stock quotes, airline reservations, radio and television listings, games and entertainment, travel and shopping, encyclopedias, and even college courses online.

CompuServe (800-848-8199). Basic services range from news to financial to health information. Premium services have additional charges. Users can get electronic mail accounts. Media include Reuters, the Associated Press, major daily U.S. newspapers, CNN, and Australian, French, and German newswires.

Prodigy (800-776-3449). Software is free. Prodigy has upwards of 2.5 million subscribers and doesn't charge to send or receive Internet or e-mail. The service has AP wire stories and photos; major newspapers, including *Newsday,* the *Los Angeles Times,* the *Atlanta Journal and Constitution,* the *Tampa Tribune; Sports Illustrated for Kids;* and affiliations with some 30 TV networks, including HBO, ESPN, and CBS.

To use commercial systems, subscribers pay a fee to secure logins and passwords to enter the systems. They also pay for the service on a time basis, that is, a fee for each minute they are using the system, much like the per minute charges on telephones. Fees for the services have decreased, but they still remain high and comparatively expensive for most individuals. Discounts are available to educational institutions, such as colleges and universities, but a school may still pay as much as $300 a month for one to three passwords to log on to an electronic system. Colleges and universities may buy a specific number of passwords or accounts and make them available to students at a central location, such as a library. Student fees pay the cost, and only enrolled students can access the databases.

Computers, with or without the aid of a commercial service, add speed and convenience to the research process. Schools of journalism and mass communication have recognized that students need skills in using databases, and many have begun to offer courses on electronic information retrieval.

Pitfalls of Databases

Newcomers to databases may be so overwhelmed by the ease and efficiency of retrieving information that they overlook the drawbacks. Anyone using a database must be aware of these facts:

- Databases require an equipment investment in a computer, a modem, and a telephone line.

- Databases may not be complete. Many government documents and historical information are not stored in databases.

- Databases may not be up to date. Although information may be accessed quickly, it may not be as current as a researcher would like. Lag times exist for adding new information to databases.

- Information in databases is not necessarily accurate. People add information to databases, and they are prone to making errors. Writers must double-check the accuracy of what they find in databases.

- Information may be costly. As noted earlier, signing on to a service is expensive. Users may pay $30 or as much as several hundred dollars per hour to access information, depending upon which service they are using and whether they have a discount.

- High demand may make it difficult to sign on. Writers may be frustrated if they repeatedly hear busy signals or are told that all access lines are in use when they try to log onto a database.

- Users may have to wade through a lot of junk to find what they want. Computer networks are so accessible that people are pushing information out without regard to the quality of writing or the content.

What Students Need to Know

Most students entering college today are comfortable with computers and are eager to experiment with new software. Developing a familiarity with one system eases the transition to other programs. Technology changes so quickly that college students today have computer skills unknown to those who graduated five or even three years ago. Faculty members assign and review work via electronic mail. Students write to friends on e-mail.

For many students, e-mail is the first step in accessing information. Through a commercial service or their universities, students can obtain an e-mail address that allows them to exchange messages with anyone else who has an address. Information is available through e-mail. For example, e-mail discussion groups exist. Discussion groups are organized by topic, such as "journalism," and information is sent to all subscribers on the mail list. Usually an editor or moderator controls what goes out to the group. Apart from discussion groups, students can get information via e-mail about other sources, such as government. By sending an e-mail message to a specific address, students and writers can add themselves to lists and receive continual updates. As with any source, however, information should be double-checked if it is to be used in any writing. The cautions regarding databases also apply to information obtained through e-mail.

At first, using computer databases may prove frustrating and confusing. But with coaching, students can become empowered. Students who have computer information retrieval skills will have access to hundreds of databases. They can learn to access the approximately 50,000 specialized bulletin boards. They can access the library collections via computers and modems without leaving their dormitory rooms. They can check job banks via the information highway and even put out requests for information and see who responds.

Colleges and universities have offices of technology that provide classes on how to set up e-mail accounts and how to use resources such as Internet. Students have many avenues to learn about the constantly changing technology. They can learn what databases are available on their campuses. Companies that sell computer products provide instruction. A little enterprise will put students in touch with the experts who can keep them current.

Many books on how to use databases and networks have been published. One helpful publication for students is Nora Paul's *Computer Assisted Re-*

search: A Guide to Tapping Online Information, published by the Poynter Institute for Media Studies in St. Petersburg, Fla. The cost is $3.

How to Use a Database

Databases provide information in two basic ways: citation format or full text. A citation format summarizes the information: title, author, publication, date of publication, and a 25-word summary. A citation database, such as DIALOG, contains references from newspaper and magazine indexes. The citation allows writers to screen quickly dozens of articles, then select the ones that are most relevant and then find the full text of the desired articles. The writer can read the entire article on the screen using a database service such as Nexis/Lexis, which has about 8 million complete articles from publications, including newspapers and magazines, and get printouts or store noteworthy articles in a computer folder.

Online bibliographic databases were launched in the mid-1960s. Full-text databases that contained selected newspaper, magazine, and wire service articles debuted in the late 1970s. Of the approximately 1,600 daily newspapers in the United States, only 200 or so are available in full text online. A good place to discover what publications are available is Bibliodata's "Full Text Sources Online."

Obviously, scanning lists and reading articles via databases is much faster than searching indexes for individual publications and then searching for the publication and the desired article. Writers who use databases don't have to handle microfilm or old print copies as they once did to find information.

How do researchers find articles on specific topics? They can search the databases by menu, key words, or a combination of both. A menu gives a series of choices, just like a menu in a restaurant. Writers select the menu item they want. Each new menu offers a new set of choices, and writers move through the process until they have a "hit," or an article they want.

With key words, writers type in words that identify their topic. For example, a television reporter is developing a story on teen violence. He wants to know if teen-agers are being charged with murder in greater numbers today than 10 years ago. To search a database, he could type "teen" when asked for a key word. The database would tell him how many articles contain the word "teen"—probably hundreds. To narrow the offerings, he would type two key words: "teen" and "violence." He would use the connecting word "and," which limits the search because all articles must contain both words. The list would be shorter. From there he could continue to narrow the search by adding words such as "murder," "guns," "deaths," etc. Using the connecting word "or" would add to the number of articles pulled up by the database. For example, if the reporter typed in "teen" or "violence," the database would find all articles with violence, even those involving adults, and all articles on teens, even those that mentioned teens and fashions and cars.

Now and the Future

The *Gale Directory of Online Databases* lists more than 8,000 databases in the United States. Many databases are networked—that is, interconnected—to form large databases. Some such as Bitnet for universities and educational institutions serve specific audiences.

The dominant name that most people have begun to connect with access to computerized information is the Internet, a growing network of smaller computer networks, including those in universities, government, and businesses. The idea behind the Internet is to connect databases and users through what has come to be known as the information superhighway. Main arteries carry information between individual networks and their individual users. Each local network that signs on to Internet—such as your university or online service—uses a common language, which is necessary for information from different networks to travel along Internet.

More and more people are using the Internet. The growth of the Internet can be compared with the acceptance of the telephone 75 years ago. Estimates are that by the year 2000, more than 180 million people around the world will log on to Internet. Some observers believe that by the year 2010, more than 80 percent of U.S. homes and businesses will use the Internet in some way.

Students can log onto the Internet in several ways: through their universities that have Internet access; by joining a dial-up service that has Internet access; or by joining a commercial service such as America Online that is a gateway to the Internet. The first alternative, through their educational institutions, is by far the cheapest because there is usually some subscription fee for online services. All services have 800 telephone numbers and interested subscribers can call for rates and services.

The amount of information available through Internet and other large networks is mind-boggling. Students and writers will discover tools that will link them to other networks and enable them to find sources specific to their topics. For example, Internet users can use Gopher to find information sources. World Wide Web allows users to use a system called hypertext to link one document to another. Key words or phrases are the connectors that enable users to find similar or related pieces of information. A writer can combine electronic documents no matter where they are stored on the Internet and avoid accessing unnecessary references in the search for information. Hypermedia follows the same principle of linking or webbing information, but in addition to text, writers can get graphics and sound on their computers.

With the proliferation of available information, however, has come concern about the information superhighway. More and more discussion will ensue on issues surrounding privacy, legal uses, copyright, and ethics. Anyone who uses databases needs to stay current on developments and regulations.

Observation

Observation is an old method of research that still is a key tool in gathering information. At the same time writers note what speakers are saying, they should be noticing how speakers deliver their remarks, how they move their bodies, what they are wearing, and how the crowd reacts to their comments. Such details are part of the reporting process.

Many students and inexperienced writers, however, are reluctant to include too many details. They fear that audiences will doubt their descriptions. They believe that using description borders on being subjective when, in fact, leaving out description may distort an event. For example, a story may reveal a speaker's eloquence and pointed remarks on world peace, but the reporter may not include that only 22 people filled an auditorium that holds 550 people. While the speaker may have been eloquent, the speech title failed to attract a sizable audience.

Seeing Isn't Enough

Many people notice their surroundings or the events happening around them in one dimension. They see. Rarely do people consciously smell, taste, hear, or touch their environment. Even using only sight, most people miss much of what goes on. So do writers. They have not trained themselves to observe events that happen simultaneously. At the state fair, a writer may notice the lines in front of concessions but not see the child wailing for more cotton candy, the youth loaded with three bright green teddy bears, the overflowing garbage at a nearby trash can, and the cigarette hanging from the hawker's lips. The unobservant writer doesn't smell the odor of fried dough, taste the grease in the air near the ferris wheel, hear the ping-ping from the shooting gallery, or feel the slap of heat from the barbecue cookers.

To be skillful observers, writers must hone all their senses. To be complete and successful writers, they must describe scenes to absent audiences. Even when viewers see events on television, they still need the reporter's or news anchor's observations. When television covered the Persian Gulf War, correspondents identified the fiery trails across the night sky as Scud missiles from the Iraqi Army. Without that information, viewers would not have known what they were seeing.

General Observation

Many people exist on autopilot. They drive the same route to work, live in the same house or apartment for years, and work in the same office. They become less and less observant. What about you?

Any person or writer can hone observation skills. Try this experiment: Take a piece of paper. Describe what your roommate or spouse wore to school or work today. Note colors and types of fabric, if possible. What did you eat for breakfast? Can you remember the smell as well as the taste? What about the color or feel? What sounds do you hear in this room? Can you name more than three?

Keep a notebook in your car, backpack, or pocket. Start recording what you see and hear in multidimensional ways. While most people can note different sounds, it is harder to catch and record events happening simultaneously. The oft-told adage is that two people on a street corner would give two different accounts of an accident witnessed by both.

Think of ways to compare what you see with events or items that are common knowledge. When author Barbara Victor met Iraqi leader Saddam Hussein, she noted, "He looked like [singer] Tom Jones in an Yves St. Laurent jumpsuit." She could have said that he looked like a pop singer in a one-piece outfit, but the image would not have been the same.

How Observation Changes the Action

Often you need to take notes unobtrusively, especially when the act of notetaking may change the behavior of an individual you are observing. Did the person across the aisle on the bus sit up straighter when she noticed you writing? Did your friend start picking up his clutter when you started taking notes about the room? Your presence can change the way events unfold.

When reporters cover a meeting, a rally, or a store opening, their presence affects how people behave. The town council members sit up straighter and look busy when the public access television channel is airing the meeting. Rally organizers look efficient and engaged when reporters approach. Store officials beam smiles of success on the first day of business.

The trick to accurate observing is to observe over time. Most people can maintain a facade for some time, but they cannot keep it up forever. You may have to observe for more than a few minutes. Despite the television cameras, the losing team's cheerleaders are hardly as media conscious at the end of a game as they were at the outset. Two hours into a meeting, the mayor may forget the unobtrusive camera and rail against the accusations of an unhappy citizen.

Participant Observation

Social scientists have long used observation by participants as a means of getting information about groups. They join a group as participants to observe individual behavior within a group and the individuals' interactions. Journalists also have adopted the practice, gaining admission and recording the interactions of the group. Such intrusion by journalists affects the way people interact. Over time, however, reporters become accepted, and other members may forget their role.

Because their presence does affect how members relate, some journalists have opted to become members of groups and not to identify themselves as reporters. In the 1890s reporter Nellie Bly pretended to be a mental patient to get a true picture of how the insane were treated at Blackwalls Island, New York's asylum for the mentally ill. Some have joined cults, followed the Hell's Angels, or gotten jobs in nursing homes. One reporter in her mid-20s enrolled in a Philadelphia high school to observe it first hand—and was invited to the senior prom. Before resorting to undercover work, reporters and their editors must determine that a change of identity is the only way to get the story.

In either case, problems can arise when it is time to write. Reporters may feel a kinship to the group and have difficulty setting themselves apart. Journalists who become group members put their impartiality at risk in writing a story. Writers may become too emotional or too attached to sources and not be able to distance themselves. They also run the risk of not knowing completely whether their presence altered the group in any way. They can doublecheck their reactions and observations, however, by interviewing a balanced mix of sources. Reporters may also suffer complaints from group members who may feel betrayed when the article appears.

Nonverbal Communication

While writers get the bulk of their information from sources and from interviewing, they can add details from nonverbal communication. Such cues come from the way people move or act when they say something. A politician may raise his eyebrows at a constituent's question. A child may shift his hands behind his back when leaving the kitchen. A teacher may frown while correcting student essays. Each action implies a thought or behavior to the observer. The politician may be surprised. The child may be guilty of swiping a cookie. The teacher may be unhappy about a good student's low grade.

When recording nonverbal cues, reporters must be careful. The same cue may carry different meanings for different observers. Furrowed eyebrows may indicate puzzlement or anger. Waving hands can mean agitation or enthusiasm. A smile may be sincere or forced. Generally one action alone is not sufficient to indicate how an individual is feeling. The gestures must be catalogued in addition to words and other body movements. A reporter may have to go so far as to ask an individual what a particular posture meant. For example, pacing during an interview may not be a result of nervousness; the interviewee may suffer from restless legs syndrome, but no reporter could tell that simply by observing.

In addition, nonverbal actions may have different meanings across cultures. In some cultures or ethnic groups, individuals do not have eye contact while speaking. An ignorant or inexperienced reporter might be suspicious of such behavior, thereby including a cultural bias. When business leaders from the United States engage in negotiations with Japanese officials, they have to learn etiquette and protocol. For example, the Japanese consider it offensive to write on a business card, while in the United States, executives and others make notations or add home telephone numbers to business cards. The good reporter learns about cultural differences or asks questions to clarify behavior. Such sensivity and awareness is essential to accurate reporting.

Dangers in Observation

In January 1995 John Salvi was charged with murdering two people and injuring five others in shootings at two abortion clinics in Boston. When Salvi was arraigned on weapons charges in conjunction with the shootings, Gary Tuchman of CNN gave a live report and description for audiences who were not in the courtroom. Tuchman described Salvi as wearing a blue blazer, white shirt, white socks, loafers, and nice pants. The description implied that Salvi had dressed conservatively and neatly. A print news account reported that Salvi was wearing "an ill-fitting blazer." The implication here contradicted the neat appearance of Tuchman's report. Which account was right? Audiences who heard and read the two accounts may have noticed the discrepancy and been puzzled. Or maybe it just added to their belief that you can't trust the media to be right.

Tuchman also took his reported observation one step further. He noted to viewers that if they had a stereotype of someone who would be charged with committing murder, Salvi didn't look like that stereotype—that is, Salvi didn't look like someone who would commit murder. Viewers may have wondered: "What does the stereotypical murderer look like? Why didn't Tuchman give us a description of that stereotype?"

Observation plays a major role in writing, but we must be circumspect about the descriptions we use. As was discussed in Chapter 7 on bias, we as writers carry our prejudices and biases with us as we collect information and write. We must be careful. Think about Tuchman's reference to a stereotypical murderer. Can you describe one? Of course not. If murderers were readily identifiable, people who have been killed would have had some warning. But murderers vary in shape, size, age, gender, skin tone, hair color, and clothing preference. They don't all have greasy hair and shifty beady eyes and act furtive or in a suspicious manner.

The Importance of Accuracy

As noted in the account above, Tuchman's observations may have been distorted by his experiences. He may have a stereotypical idea of what a murderer looks like. Writers can bring biases to observation, just as they can to any aspect of reporting. Chapter 7 discusses bias in reporting.

Just as you doublecheck facts, you should be circumspect about your observations. Take emotions into account. If you covered an antiabortion rally, you may have found your emotions surging if you are pro-choice. Despite your role as a journalist, your feelings may not be neutral. Your feelings may influence your description. Be aware.

To ensure accuracy, you should record impressions in your notebook at the scene or as soon as possible afterward. The longer you wait, the fewer details you will remember accurately. Memory fades over time.

Like other kinds of research, observation leads to a more complete message. Description that is simple, clear, and complete also will aid accuracy. Writers should lay out description alongside other facts and allow audiences to judge for themselves. Audiences invariably will apply their own biases to the description and form their own opinions, but the writers' choice of words should not be the deciding factor.

EXERCISES

1. Tom Wicker, *New York Times* syndicated columnist, is coming to campus to give a lecture. Before the lecture, he will have a news conference, and you will attend for the campus newspaper. First, you need to find out more information. Using three biographical sources, answer the following questions. Cite the reference used. One reference should be online.
   a. When and where was Wicker born?
   b. Where did he go to college?
   c. What newspapers did he work for other than the *Times*?
   d. Has he written any books? If so, list the titles.
   e. Has he won any awards? If so, list them.

2. Identify a reporter in your college community or in your hometown by reading bylines and articles in the respective paper. Call the reporter and ask what sources he or she uses in researching stories. Note whether the reporter uses computer databases to retrieve information. Find out how the reporter ensures accuracy in using sources. Share the information with your class.

3. You are the state desk researcher for the local newspaper. The state editor wants to do a story on parents who are charged with killing their children. In making the assignment to a reporter, the editor wants information on parents who are charged with murdering their children. She asks you to do a computer database search of national newspaper and magazine files to find accounts of such crimes. Your task is to prepare a memo to the state editor that lists six references to substantial articles on parents who are charged with killing their children. The references need to be annotated, that is, to contain enough information to enable the reporter to find the articles.

4. Select a computer service, such as America Online. Contact the company and get information about the cost to become a subscriber, how to access it, services, and whether it positions itself as a leader or unique among computer services offering databases and why. Write a synopsis and share it with the class.

5. Attend a campus or town government meeting as an observer along with another student. Use your senses to take notes on what transpires outside the actions of the officials. Write a description of the meeting, using aspects such as the room, the mood, the speakers' attitudes, the officials' attitudes, the tone of the meeting, and how many people attended. Then compare your account with the other student's account. See what each of you chose to include and chose to ignore. Compare the ways you described aspects of the meeting. Then discuss what made your observations different.

REFERENCES

Margaret Jackson, *Selected Resources for Journalists.* Business Administration/Social Sciences Department, Davis Library, University of North Carolina at Chapel Hill, Chapel Hill, NC, 1989.

Lauren Kessler and Duncan McDonald, *Mastering the Message: Media Writing with Substance and Style.* Belmont, CA: Wadsworth, 1992.

Freedom of Information Act, 5 U.S.C. 552, 1966. Amended in 1974, 1986.

Nora Paul, *Computer Assisted Research: A Guide to Tapping Online Information,* 2nd ed. St. Petersburg, Fla.: The Poynter Institute for Media Studies, 1994.

Randy Reddick and Elliot King, *The Online Journalist: Using the Internet and Other Electronic Resources.* Orlando, FL: Harcourt Brace College Publishers, 1995.

Chip Rowe, "A Journalist's Guide to the Internet." *American Journalism Review,* January 1995.

Personal interview with Barbara Semonche, librarian, School of Journalism and Mass Communication, University of North Carolina at Chapel Hill, January 1995.

Speech by Michael Gartner, president, American Society of Newspaper Editors, on national Freedom of Information Day, to the National Press Club, Washington, DC, March 1989.

Bruce D. Itule and Douglas A. Anderson, *News Writing and Reporting for Today's Media,* 3rd ed. New York: McGraw-Hill Inc., 1994.

10

Interviewing, Quotations, and Attribution

"No matter how fine a writer might be, he is crippled if he is not an effective interviewer," noted John Brady in *The Craft of Interviewing.*

Becoming a skilled interviewer takes practice; it isn't something someone does naturally. Most of us interview in a casual way when we are introduced to someone new. We ask questions: "Where are you from? Are you a student? What year are you in school? What is your major?" We get responses that help us learn more about the person.

But if you are going to write about that individual, your questions have to be much more specific. You hardly have enough for a story to know that Mark Monroe is a junior majoring in computer science from Lake Geneva, New York. You need more detailed information, perhaps his career objective and how he sees the role of computers in information retrieval.

So good interviewing is more than just carrying on a casual conversation. It takes skill, and it takes practice. This chapter will start you on the road to becoming a good interviewer. In this chapter you will learn

- How to prepare for an interview,
- How to conduct an interview,

- How to handle off-the-record information,
- How to use quotations in messages, and
- The importance of accuracy, attribution, and punctuation in quotations.

Interviewing as a Challenge

Writers do interviews in different ways. The medium they work for, deadline pressures, the accessibility of interviewees, and people's willingness to talk affect how well a writer can plan and do interviews. Writers face challenges as they work diligently to reach as many sources as possible before a deadline. They become detectives as they figure out just whom they should interview and how. Like anyone else, writers feel nervous and even excited when they have the chance to interview a well-known newsmaker or celebrity. And they feel great satisfaction and accomplishment when an interviewer answers their questions and gives them something extra.

Reporters like Terry Woster of the *Argus Leader* in Sioux Falls, South Dakota, have to be ready for the unexpected when they cover breaking news stories. Woster was the newspaper's state capital correspondent in Pierre, about 225 miles from the newspaper's home office.

Editors called in Woster when South Dakota Governor George Mickelson and seven others died in an airplane crash. The news arrived about 6 p.m. that Monday, and Woster stationed himself at the Capitol to be available to interview state officials who also were looking for news. He and other reporters also checked repeatedly with state highway patrol and sheriff's deputies in Iowa, where the crash occurred, to get information on the crash site. They called Federal Aviation Administration officials, state development leaders, and other officials who might know who was on the airplane. The governor's press secretary eventually confirmed who died.

Five hours after the story broke, Woster filed his story with the main office in Sioux Falls. The news story contained the essential information readers needed to know as well as quotations from state leaders who mourned South Dakota's loss. The story follows. Notice the number of sources in Woster's story and the attribution of information.

Mickelson Killed in Plane Crash

5 Business Leaders, 2 Pilots Also Die at Iowa Farm

BY TERRY WOSTER

Argus Leader Staff

PIERRE—South Dakota Gov. George Mickelson and seven others died Monday when a state airplane crashed and burned in eastern Iowa after developing engine trouble.

Mickelson, 52, was returning to Pierre from Cincinnati, where he and economic development specialists from the state and the city of Sioux Falls had talked with officials of John Morrell & Co., said Janelle Toman, the governor's press secretary.

Former Republican Gov. Bill Janklow mourned the loss late Monday by taking a solitary drive in the country.

"I just wanted to get out and drive around by myself," he said later. "It's a terrible tragedy for the Mickelson family. And we should all remember that there were seven other people on that plane, all special to their families, and each a tremendous loss."

Also killed were:

• Roland Dolly, 37, commissioner of the state Office of Economic Development.

• Ron Reed, 52, Pierre, director of the state Office of Energy Policy.

• Angus Anson, 38, Sioux Falls, general manager, Northern States Power, South Dakota region.

• David Birkeland, 54, Sioux Falls, president and chief executive, First Bank of South Dakota.

• Roger Hainje, 43, Sioux Falls, president, Sioux Falls Development Foundation.

• Ron Becker, 52, Pierre, state's chief pilot.

• David Hansen, 45, Pierre, state pilot.

The crash occurred about 4 p.m. nine miles south of Dubuque, Iowa, officials said. Mickelson's pilot reported engine difficulty and the airplane, a twin-engined Mitsubishi MU2, hit a barn and silo.

Lt. Gov. Walter Dale Miller, 67, a New Underwood rancher who became Mickelson's running mate on the Republican ticket in 1986, will become governor for the remainder of Mickelson's term, through 1994. Miller is to take the oath of office today.

Miller said he'd talk today about plans for a transition. He said he wanted to focus his attention on Mickelson's family Monday night.

"Say a prayer for us," he said as he prepared to leave the Capitol to go to the governor's residence.

The governor's wife, Linda, returned to Pierre on Monday afternoon from a weekend at the family's cabin near Lake Poinsett.

Official confirmation that Mickelson had been killed came several hours after many Cabinet members and other members of the governor's staff gathered in the executive office on the Capitol's second floor.

Chief of Staff Frank Brost took the first call from the Federal Aviation Administration about 5 p.m. The message was that a state-owned airplane had crashed.

When investigators told the governor's staff there were no survivors. Toman said she knew Mickelson had died, because she'd talked with him after he and the rest of the party were airborne from Cincinnati.

Other state officials gathered in the governor's office during the evening.

"It's something so unbelievable you just can't even let it sink in," said Secretary of State Joyce Hazeltine.

Flags at the Capitol were lowered to half-staff about 7:30 p.m.

Woster's interviewing didn't end that night. In subsequent days he wrote stories that included a profile of Lieutenant Governor Walter Dale Miller, who took Mickelson's place; Miller's swearing in; and a memorial service in the Capitol three days after the plane crash. Reporters in Sioux Falls wrote additional follow-up stories. In one story, Woster's brother, Kevin, also a reporter for the *Argus Leader,* covered the motorcade from Pierre to Brookings, South Dakota, where the governor had lived. Kevin Woster drove ahead of the official cars to interview people lining the route. His story focused on South Dakotans' recollections of Mickelson.

Reporters like Woster often don't have much time to plan an interviewing strategy, review sources, and make detailed lists of questions. They have to be resourceful, available, and enterprising. Reporters and writers generally feel much more comfortable approaching an interview when they have had time to prepare.

The Need for Research

The first step, of course, is to know your topic. The second is to do research. Before any interview, you should have a knowledge of your topic and the people you will interview. The general rule is never to go into an interview cold. You will have more success if your source quickly sees that you are prepared. Preparation shows that you are serious about the interview, and it flatters the interviewee.

With deadline pressure, however, some journalists may find that they don't have time to do research before they have to be on site to cover an event. On some occasions you may go into an interview unprepared. Experienced writers or reporters will tell you that such an experience is uncomfortable and often embarrassing. No one wants to walk up to the newest Nobel Prize winner for medicine and ask, "Now just what was your work that caused you to win?" With the advantages of communication today, a reporter can be on her way to an assignment while a researcher combs files for background information. Via remote telephone, the reporter can get data as the researcher finds it and arrive somewhat prepared.

Writers—whether print or broadcast reporters, freelancers, public relations practitioners, or advertising copywriters—look in their own files first for information, then move to the company's or community's library. They may find other articles or broadcasts about their topic, or they may consult research materials such as statistical abstracts. Some who have computers and modems might access the Library of Congress via the Internet or other information database. Specific tips on research can be found in Chapter 9.

Remember that research goes further than printed sources or what is in a computer database, however. In many cases, other people are the best sources of information. When evangelist Billy Graham announced a six-day crusade in Raleigh, North Carolina, a reporter secured an interview with him in Black Mountain, North Carolina. She scoured clippings files and other written materials about Graham and his career. The day before the scheduled interview she and a photographer spent the day in Black Mountain. She interviewed the local golf pro, the pharmacist, and even a local minister who on occasion preached to Graham out in the pews. She secured anecdotes and personal recollections that gave her a more complete picture of Graham the man and the evangelist. The information proved valuable for her stories and also let Graham know that she was well prepared for the interview.

Getting the Interview

Once you have sufficient knowledge, you must determine whom to interview. In a story on a local actor, he would be the primary interviewee. But in many cases, writers must interview experts in certain fields, volunteers, university administrators—whoever is knowledgeable about the subject.

Some names may appear during research, and some may come as referrals from other interviewers.

Setting Up the Interview

When you know whom you want to interview, you need to make an appointment, whether the interview is by telephone or in person. You may have to go through a secretary or a public relations person who maintains the interviewee's schedule, or you may be able to call the interviewee directly.

In setting up the interview, make sure that the source is the best for the topic and has firsthand information. If you are working on a story that requires expert opinion, for example, be sure that the source is the appropriate one. The primary surgeon for a lung transplant is a much better source than a hospital public information officer or a physician who assisted during the operation. People who have never been involved in a child abuse case and are just giving you secondhand or hearsay information are not good sources for a story on that subject. A few filter questions up front can eliminate unnecessary interviews: "I am looking for people who tried to break into the country-western music market. Did you ever sing professionally? Or perhaps prepare a demonstration tape for an agent?"

In setting up the interview, be sure to specify the amount of time you will need. Don't underestimate, or you will lack time to ask all your questions. Some people may be willing to be interviewed on the spot, so be ready with your questions. Others will want to set a specific time at a later date. Ask for more time than you will need.

Select a comfortable place for the interview. The interviewee's terrain is best, as he or she is usually more relaxed in a familiar environment. The reporter also has the opportunity to observe personal items, such as family photographs or a collected memorabilia that can add to the story.

Avoid doing interviews during meals. People have difficulty talking while eating, and a discussion over who should pay for food—source or writer—can be uncomfortable. If the interviewee is from out of town and staying at the local hotel, you may choose to do the interview over coffee—a fairly inexpensive way of meeting and talking.

Dress appropriately for the interview. If you are interviewing the chief executive officer of a Fortune 500 company, wear a suit. If you are meeting a cotton grower in his fields, shuck the high heels. And, if you are meeting with teen-agers at the local hangout, blue jeans are okay.

What to Work Out in Advance

Do not agree to pay for an interview. Only in very rare situations should you consider paying for information. The news organization may agree to pay because the source's information is newsworthy. Any payment should be worked out ahead of time and be consistent with company policy. If you are a freelancer, you should not agree to pay for information; publications may not buy your work if sources were lured by profit.

Before you start on your list, work out arrangements if you plan to use a tape recorder. A tape recorder is advisable if you are planning an interview that is long or one that might contain controversial or important information. You might want a tape as a backup if you suspect the interviewee might question your quotes in the printed article. Some people may feel uncomfortable with a tape recorder present, and they may need reassurance before you show up. One good way to have a source agree to be taped is to stress your need for accuracy in getting quotes right. Few people will argue.

Some interviewees will ask if they can see the article before it is printed or listen to the tape before it is aired. Of course, if you are a public relations practitioner or an ad copy writer, your source—who may be your client—will have final approval. But in the news business, the answer is no. Deadline pressure generally precludes spending the time for a source to review the message. Sources can become editors, wanting to change more than what applies to them.

If a source insists on previewing the piece, check it out with an editor or producer. You may want to find someone else to interview. Be clear if the answer is no. One inexperienced reporter caused herself and her newspaper some unpleasantness because a source thought he would have the right to edit before a story citing him was printed. The reporter didn't flatly say no, and the source misunderstood.

Writing the Questions

Interviewers, no matter how skilled or practiced, should write a list of questions before an interview. The list can be typed and printed or scribbled on an envelope. The questions ensure that all important aspects are covered during the interview. A reporter can review the list before leaving to make sure all points were asked. Questions also serve to keep the interview on track. A minister may divert the interview to a discussion of the writer's religious beliefs. The writer can refer to the list and remind the minister that she is there to interview him. The list can also fill in lags in the conversation.

Covering the Basics

Obviously, when you are planning questions, you want to ask the basics: who, what, when, where, how, and why. But you need to ask other questions to get more information and and to make the message complete. One formula is called GOSS, an acronym for Goals-Obstacles-Solutions-Start, devised by Professor LaRue Gilleland of the University of Nevada. It can be applied to many interviews and is based on the assumption that people have goals, that obstacles loom before goals, and that solutions can be found to obstacles. During the interview, you may discover that you need to "start"— to go back to the beginning of an event or topic to get a more complete understanding.

For example, you may interview a chemist who does research on polymers. Using GOSS, you would ask what are the goals of his research, the obstacles to discovering new uses, and the solutions to overcome the obstacles. "Start" would lead you to ask about the whole field of polymer research and what is happening in this particular lab compared with others.

Ken Metzler, author of *Creative Interviewing,* has suggested two more letters to Gilleland's GOSS: E for evaluation and Y for why. Evaluation suggests a need for an overall assessment of the situation—seeking meaning beyond the facts. To get such information, the writer asks for the interviewee's interpretation. The Y is a reminder not to forget to ask why a situation has occurred.

Think about quantitative questions. How many times has the baseball star struck out? How many ounces of marijuana were in the 20-ton haul, and what is the street value? How many tons of concrete are needed for the runway, and is that equal to filling the high school football stadium to the top row?

When formulating questions, think of the unusual aspects. Don't hesitate to include questions you would like answered. Your audiences might as well. You might even ask friends or colleagues what questions they would include if given the chance.

The Interview Itself

Always be punctual for an interview. Making a source wait is rude and may cost you the interview. If you have trouble, call to let the individual know you will be late.

If you are interviewing a celebrity or high-ranking official, avoid having the air of a fan or worshiper, and avoid appearing nervous or excited. Few people would be calm the first time they interviewed singer Whitney Houston or Senate Majority Leader Robert Dole. Butterflies are to be expected, but you should show respect rather than adulation.

Getting Started

After you introduce yourself, start the interview with some questions that will set a relaxed mood. For example, if you are in the person's home, comment about trophies, collections, or decor. Show you are interested. Don't ask weighty questions right away.

If you are using a tape recorder, put it in an inconspicuous place. A source who is uncomfortable with the tape recorder may spend more time looking at it than at you. Make sure to use a tape that will cover the length of the interview. You don't want to waste time every 15 minutes checking to see whether the tape has run out.

Most states require that you notify people if they are being taped. If you are doing a telephone interview and plan to tape it, you must ask the individual's permission before you turn it on. Rarely if ever will you need to hide a tape recorder in your briefcase or under your clothing.

Avoid starting an interview by asking people what they do. They will know that you haven't done your homework and could be insulted. Try to avoid having to ask routine information about a person. You may need to verify your information, however. A student who interviewed author Barbara Victor discovered in a biographical source that she was born in 1944. A question revealed that Victor actually was born a year later, in 1945.

Asking the Questions

Be straightforward and specific in questioning. Don't beat around the bush. "So, Mr. Rich, you have investments and your construction business. And you have inherited money from your uncle and aunt. And I imagine there are lots of people out there who are wondering how much you are worth." Of course, you can preface a question with a statement, but don't talk around a question—ASK IT. "Mr. Rich, you have investments and inheritance that have many people wondering just how much you are worth."

Maintain control. Don't let the interviewee lead you. Keeping the interview on track may be difficult for a student writer or inexperienced reporter. Someone who is accustomed to being interviewed may have an agenda or may have what seem to be the usual canned responses. A politician, for example, may ignore a question about changes in tax laws and answer instead about his plan for economic development. If the interviewee digresses, wait until there is a suitable pause, then steer the interview back to the subject. Use your list of questions as a reference. If you interrupt the interviewee, you could be cutting off some valuable comments.

Avoid becoming the interviewee. Try to keep yourself out of the interview. Often a person will throw questions at the interviewer. Be polite and firm and remind the interviewee that you are there to do the interview, not to be interviewed.

Watch your body language. Avoid any behavior, like nodding your head, that may subtly indicate you agree with the interviewee. If the interviewee believes you are sympathetic and empathetic, he or she may expect a positive story.

Maintain a professional distance. Don't become the interviewee's friend. In *The Craft of Interviewing,* Brady recounted the story of when Truman Capote interviewed actor Marlon Brando. Brando's friends were incredulous when the published story discussed his mother's alcoholism. Brando responded that Capote shared intimacies of his own life, and Brando felt he had to share some of his secrets. Writers who get too chummy with their sources can create tension when the article is published. The source may believe that the writer betrayed confidences.

Leave all preconceptions and misconceptions at home. You may be a single working journalist with no children, and your interviewee is a stay-at-home mother with five children. Mask any feelings that you envy her domestic life or that her job isn't as fulfilling as yours. Don't be antagonistic if you disagree with a person's philosophy. Some interviewees will open up if they sense that you don't agree with them, however.

Listen to the interviewee. Be aware of inconsistencies. Be willing to divert the conversation from the prescribed list of questions if you hear a tidbit that should be developed through another line of questioning. If you don't understand a response, ask for clarification. Remember: If you aren't clear about information, you'll never convey it clearly to audiences.

The Tough Questions

Save all embarrassing and controversial questions for the end of the interview, such as a person's gambling debts or reports that a director is manic depressive. Of course, if a suitable occasion to ask such a question occurs during the interview, ask it. Be aware that you run the risk of having the interview terminated if you ask a particularly sensitive question. When asking these questions, be straightforward. If you act embarrassed, you will transmit that feeling and possibly not get a response.

Many times writers must interview people who have suffered trauma or witnessed a traumatic event. Such events vary. An individual may have endured years of repeated physical abuse, survived a plane crash, been a hostage in a domestic dispute, or been wounded. A person may have witnessed a friend's drowning, seen a fiery truck crash, or found a house full of diseased and starving animals.

Writers must understand that people who have suffered trauma or an atrocity recover from those events in different ways and at different times, depending upon the particular trauma and their personalities. Judith Lewis Herman notes in her book *Trauma and Recovery* that part of the healing process is remembering and telling the event. People seeking quotes and information may find individuals who are quite willing to talk and others who refuse to be interviewed. Herman writes:

> *People who have survived atrocities often tell their stories in a highly emotional, contradictory, and fragmented manner which undermines their credibility. . . . It is difficult for an observer to remain clearheaded and calm, to see more than a few fragments of the picture at one time, to retain all the pieces, and to fit them together. It is even more difficult to find a language that conveys fully and persuasively what one has seen. Those who attempt to describe the atrocities that they have witnessed also risk their own credibility.*

Reporters must be aware of the psychological state of people who have just experienced a tragedy or atrocity. They should ask the questions but understand when they don't get complete or even accurate responses. Interviewing more than one source may be required to get a full picture of what actually happened. Reporters may have to come back later for follow-up interviews well after a traumatic event occurs.

Just as it is difficult to approach victims and witnesses, it is hard to interview victims' families. Again, reporters must try to ask the questions, but they must respect a person's right not to answer. The media's behavior drew criticism after the space shuttle Challenger blew up. Many observers felt the media were too aggressive, particularly the electronic media, as they asked family members "How do you feel?" In some instances, reporters might find that a family member is willing to talk and is helped by remembering the individual. Again, reporters must use judgment and good taste in what they include in their writing and how far they should go in trying to get information.

The fact that the person doesn't answer a tough question is often noteworthy in a story. A former foreign service diplomat who settles in a small town is arrested for shoplifting. When he refuses to answer reporters' questions after his trial, report it. His silence supports statements that he is close-mouthed about his current life. But don't fail to ask a question in the expectation that a person might not answer it. You may be surprised and get a response.

Off-the-Record Information

In the middle of an interview, a public official says, "The following information needs to be off the record." Stop the official. Don't let him talk any more. Off-the-record means you cannot use the information. As a writer you don't want information you cannot use. Politely refuse the information. Then you can proceed to clarify what the official means. People have different definitions of what off-the-record means: Don't use the information at all; use it but don't attribute it to me; use it to ask questions of others, but I never said it.

As an interviewer you must remember that many people who have information want to share it but may not want to take responsibility for making it public. They will let you as the writer do it anonymously, or let you, the writer, find someone else to confirm it and become the public source. Be careful. Audiences do not necessarily believe information that is attributed to "a source close to the president" or "a high-level State Department official."

Refusing to accept the information from a source may just get it for you. People who have juicy information usually feel important and want to show they know something you don't. Think about it. Has a friend told you some gossip about someone else and sworn you to secrecy? Within 24 hours had you shared it with someone else, despite your promise? If you refuse off-the-record information that you can't use, the source may open up.

Think about the Consequences

A final warning: Make sure you and the source are clear on how the information can be used before you accept it. If you agree to use the information but not the individual's name, you must comply. If you agree the tidbit is confidential, you must not publish it. You may want that person as a source again. If you act unethically and violate the agreement, you can write that person off your source list, and you may attract unflattering attention to yourself and your employer.

Consider the problems the *New York Times* encountered with off-the-record information in January 1995. A *Times* reporter, Marian Burros, was one of five reporters invited to lunch at the White House with First Lady Hillary Clinton. Mrs. Clinton set up the luncheon to discuss her image problems with media representatives. The First Lady's comments during the two-and-a-half hour luncheon moved from on-the-record to off-the-record. A *Times* article on the luncheon included Mrs. Clinton saying that she was politically "naive and dumb" in her health care proposals in 1994. The White House, and even other reporters present at the lunch, claimed those particular comments were among the off-the-record statements. The *Times* defended its reporter.

Confusion would have been avoided if the entire conversation had been either on or off the record, rather than jumping around. The publication of off-the-record comments, such as Mrs. Clinton's, whether in good faith or in error, creates problems between sources and reporters. Sources may be more skeptical and guarded if they have to fear that comments shared in confidence will be attributed to them. Reporters may not have access to necessary background or off-the-record information because sources don't trust the media.

The Clinton snafu occurred on the heels of another much-publicized reporter-source incident. Most people felt that Kathleen Gingrich's comments were private when she confided to CBS anchorwoman Connie Chung the name her son, House Speaker Newt Gingrich, had used in describing First Lady Hillary Clinton. Just before Mrs. Gingrich shared the word, Ms. Chung had assured her that the confidence would be just between the two of them. Television cameras, on hand to tape the interview, kept rolling while Mrs. Gingrich confessed. The segment was aired, Mrs. Gingrich felt betrayed, and Ms. Chung and her ethics—as well as those of CBS—were blasted by citizens, politicians, and the press.

Notetaking Tips

Most people talk faster than an interviewer can write. If you have trouble keeping up, politely stop the source and ask for a moment to catch up on notes. You could preface it by saying, "I want to make sure I record this correctly, so I need a moment to complete your last comment." Few sources would respond: "I don't care if you get it right. I want to keep talking."

Be sure when you are writing comments that you get them completely rather than in bits and pieces that may not fit together when you write the article. Complete notes help you avoid taking quotations out of context or misinterpreting quotations later.

If you have a quote that is complete, put it within quotation marks in your notebook. Then you will know you have the speaker's exact words when you review your notes and are ready to write.

You may find it handy to flag your notes as you take them. Put a word or two in the margin to indicate where certain information occurs. For example, you may have a wide-ranging interview with the incoming Republican speaker of the state legislature. "Welfare," "tax cuts," "power," and "education" would remind you where each topic was discussed.

At the end of the interview, take a few moments to review notes and questions to ensure you have asked all your questions. Most sources won't mind waiting while you double-check. If a quote isn't clear, ask the source to repeat it. "You said during the interview, Mr. Speaker, that changing the rules will help the House pass legislation faster. Could you clarify the parliamentary procedure a little more?" You also might want to ask if you can telephone if any clarification is needed when you are producing the story.

After the Interview

Take time after you leave the interview to review your notes. Fill in any blanks or whatever might appear confusing later. Note your feelings, the qualities of the interviewee, any additional description, and other details while they are fresh in your mind. You may wish to transcribe your notes immediately to retain important details or impressions. If you store your notes on your computer hard drive, you can call them up easily when it is time to create the piece.

After the interview, you may want to write the person a thank-you note.

Selecting and Using Quotations

You have pages of notes from your interview. How do you determine which quotations to use for your message? The same rules for using quotations from interviews applies to selecting quotations from speeches, presentations, or even published works. You want to select quotations that are vivid, show opinion, reflect the speaker's personality, support the speaker's thesis, and unify a piece of writing.

When to Use Quotations

In organizing material, writers have to decide whether to quote an individual, then whether to use that information in an indirect or direct quote.

Direct quotes give the exact words of the speaker. In most cases, writers will clean up grammar, and they may eliminate profanity. But the quotation marks signify to readers "here's exactly what was said." Direct quotes are used for colorful statements, opinion, and emotions. Direct quotes can convey an individual's personality and manner of speaking. One rule to follow is to use a direct quote if it is better than any paraphrase.

Direct quotes can be either complete quotes or partial quotes. Here is a complete direct quote:

"We are not selective about whom we arrest," said police chief Martin Bray.

Or

"The federal government spent millions of dollars to enact the 1986 Truth in Mileage Act, and now it has pulled $600,000 in funding to enforce it," said Charles Bradley, president of the National Odometer and Title Fraud Enforcement Association in Nashville, Tenn.

A partial direct quote would be written as

Company President William Olsen said he would not discuss the reasoning behind the 3 percent pay increase for employees, noting only that "we have to consider many factors in our operating costs and employees' salaries and benefits are part of those factors."

Or even shorter, as in

The coach said the player was "furious at the lack of compassion" exhibited by the fans when he made the error in the third inning.

Or

The senator vowed "to use every last little bit" of his influence to block the bill increasing military spending.

In mixing indirect and direct quotes, be careful not to switch person, for example, switching from third person ("the senator") to the first person ("my influence") as in the following sentence, a flawed rewrite of the one above:

The senator vowed to "use every last little bit of my influence" to block the bill increasing military spending.

A grammatical sentence would use the words "his influence," but then the quote would be inaccurate. In such cases, rewrite, quoting only the phrase "to use every last little bit" as in the first example above.

As a note, most writers avoid using what are called orphan quotes, that is, quotation marks used for emphasis on a single word. For example, The special envoy said the cease-fire represented a "monumental" effort. Why use quotations? "Monumental" is hardly an inflammatory phrase or an unusual adjective.

To Paraphrase or Not

Indirect quotes are used to summarize or paraphrase what individuals say, particularly if they have rambled about an issue or topic. They do not use a speaker's exact words and are not set off with quotation marks. Writers use indirect quotes to keep quotes relevant and precise.

Many writers find indirect quotes particularly valuable when speakers have digressed from the main topic or when they inject jokes or anecdotal material that cannot be used.

Here is an excerpt from a speech by Vice President Dan Quayle to the National Press Club on Freedom of Information Day during his tenure. As with many political speeches, a speaker's comments can be shortened into one indirect quote.

> *I'm particularly pleased to be here on SDX Freedom of Information Day. As I told the national religious broadcasters convention in my first major address as vice president, I come from a First Amendment family, and I'm convinced that a strong, vigorous, and skeptical press is vital to the health and well-being of American democracy, even though some might say that it hasn't always contributed to the health of my own political career. But just as I am convinced that freedom of the press is crucial, I think that all of us recognize that a powerful press poses certain risks as well.*

Translates to

> *Quayle said a strong, vigorous, and skeptical press is vital to the health and well-being of American democracy, but a powerful press poses certain risks.*

Indirect quotes are valuable in providing a source's information. They are effective in balancing direct quotes within copy.

Correcting Speakers' Grammar and Other Slips

Reporters who covered a high-level state official quickly learned that the man was not a good speaker. He had a vernacular accent for that region of the state, used malapropisms much as television character Archie Bunker did on "All in the Family," and stated goals that seemed out of reach. How to quote him?

Early in the official's tenure, most newspaper and print journalists chose to paraphrase his remarks so they could clean up the grammar errors and correct the malapropisms. Even in some of the direct quotes, the official sounded well schooled. But a few print journalists soon discovered that cleaning up the official's language wasn't good practice. Audiences who also watched local television broadcasts saw and heard the official as he really was. The image they read in the newspaper didn't match.

Journalists are faced continually with deciding how to use quotations. If a speaker uses improper subject–verb agreement, should the writer correct it in a direct quote? How far should writers go in cleaning up quotes? In the case of the state official, print journalists figured out they had to be true to the quotes or else paraphrase. They couldn't dramatically clean up the quotes, put them in direct quotations, and tell audiences "Here's exactly what the man said." He didn't.

The *Associated Press Stylebook* advises writers:

> *Never alter quotations even to correct minor grammatical errors or word usage. Casual minor tongue slips may be removed by using ellipses but even that should be done with extreme caution. If there is a question about a quote, either don't use it or ask the speaker to clarify.*

Are Profanities and Obscenities Acceptable?

The *Associated Press Stylebook* also advises writers not to use profanity, obscenities, or vulgarities unless they are part of direct quotations and there is a compelling reason for them. Writers are cautioned to warn editors of writing that contains such language. The language should be confined to a single paragraph so that it can be easily deleted. Writers should not modify profanity such as changing damn to darn. Editors may change the word to d— to indicate that profanity was used by the speaker but no compelling reason exists to spell it out in the story.

Writers need to check with their publications and news organizations to determine their particular rules on profanity, obscenities, and vulgarities. Some specialized publications and television shows include such language. Audiences who subscribe to or buy such publications or who view programs are familiar with such language and either don't find it offensive or overlook it.

Some General Rules about Quotations

- Never make up a quote. Quotes must be accurate.

- Don't take a question that is answered "yes" or "no" and turn it into a direct quote. For example, if an interviewer asks a high school basketball coach if he felt many students bet on the outcome of games, and the coach says, "No," the quotation in the newspaper should not read: Coach Lyman Jones said, "I don't think many students bet on the outcome of our basketball games."

All you can really say is this: When asked whether he thought many students bet on the outcomes of games, Coach Lyman Jones replied, "No."

• Watch out for redundancies when setting up quotations. Use the direct quotes to expand.

Avoid: She said she was surprised at being chosen the School's outstanding senior. "I was so surprised when they called my name," Melissa said.

Rather: Melissa said she was surprised when the principal called her name. "I couldn't move or react," she added. "I felt glued to my chair in shock."

• Set up situations before using the quotation so that readers will have a context for quotes, as in the following:

ATLANTA (AP)—Georgia Tech forward Martice Moore said he is transferring to Colorado, just two years after he was the Atlantic Coast Conference rookie of the year.

Moore will have to sit out next season, after which he will have two years of eligibility remaining.

He chose Colorado because of his friendship with assistant coach Ricardo Patton, who recruited him out of Oak Hill (Va.) Academy three years ago. Moore, 6-foot-8, played at Atlanta's North Fulton High before transferring to Oak Hill for his senior season.

"I didn't feel like this was the place to make the most of my talent," Moore said Tuesday. "I think I tended to get caught up with my friends. None of them are bad friends, but I was putting them before basketball and my school work. I kind of feel like I wasted last season."

• Use "according to" only with printed or factual information. Do not use it as an attribution with a person.

Avoid: The state's prison system is 3,456 inmates above the legally allowed level, according to the secretary of correction.

Rather: The state's prison system is 3,456 inmates above the legally allowed level, said the secretary of correction. According to prison documents, the level has been too high for the past seven years.

• Use attribution in the middle of a sentence only if it occurs at a natural break. Otherwise, put it at the beginning or the end so that you don't interrupt the flow of the person's statement.

Avoid: "We can always," he said, "commission a new statue for the college commons."

Rather: "We can always commission a new statue for the college commons," he said.

Acceptable: "The marine sciences lab is vital to the state's economy," he said, "and we must persuade the legislature to allocate more funds this year."

• Always use attribution for statements that use "hope," "feel," or "believes." You as a writer are not inside another person's head; you know how he or she feels, thinks, believes because you were told.

• *Write:* The district attorney said he feels the verdict fell short of what he expected the jury to do. He said he believes the community will be angered that Ammons was not found guilty of first-degree murder.

More on Attribution

Quotes, whether direct or indirect, must be attributed completely and adequately. Readers or listeners must know who is talking, who is making each statement. They need to know the proper sources of information. The general rule is that attribution should go at the beginning of each new quotation or at the end of the first sentence, whether the quotation is one sentence or more than one sentence.

If the quotation goes on for several paragraphs, attribution usually is placed at least once in every paragraph, and most writers follow the rule of attribution somewhere in the first sentence. Some writers will omit attribution in a middle paragraph if they have several short paragraphs of quotations by the same speaker. The key is to ensure that readers know who is talking.

If paragraphs contain strong statements of opinion, however, the writer must use attribution for every sentence.

For many writers, particularly news writers, "said" is the attribution word of choice. "Said" carries no underlying connotation as to a speaker's emphasis or meaning; it is neutral. "Added" and "told" are also fairly neutral. Attribution words that contain subtle meanings are "emphasized," "stressed," "declared," "demanded," "ordered," "stated," "criticized," and "contended." Writers avoid many of these words.

Do not use words such as "smiled," "laughed," "grimaced," "chuckled," and so on as attribution words. They are descriptive words that tell how a person said something. Rather than writing "'Hello,' he smiled," use "he said with a smile." Prefer phrases such as "she said, and frowned," "he said, and grimaced," and "she said, then laughed."

When using attribution that includes a person's title, don't place the title between person's name and the attribution verb.

> *Avoid:* The University will accept 3,475 freshmen for the 1998 class, Polly Wilson, director of undergraduate admissions, said.

> *Rather:* The University will accept 3,475 freshmen for the 1998 class, said Polly Wilson, director of undergraduate admissions.

Punctuating Quotes

In Chapter 8, "Testing Your Grammar," you will find general punctuation rules. Here are the basic rules for punctuating quotations.

• Attribution at the end of a quote—whether direct or indirect—must be set off with punctuation. In most cases, the punctuation will be a comma.

> *Fifteen barrels of sardines will be delivered Wednesday, he said.*

> *"Fifteen stinking, dripping barrels of sardines will be delivered Wednesday," he said.*

> *"Will you deliver the barrels of sardines before noon?" he asked.*

• Attribution at the beginning of an indirect quote is not set off with punctuation.

> *He said 15 barrels of sardines will be delivered Wednesday.*

• Attribution at the beginning of a direct quote requires punctuation. If the quote is only one sentence long, use a comma. If the quote is two or more sentences long, use a colon.

Correct: Johnson said, "We have spent three days examining the department's books, and we have found no evidence of impropriety."

Correct: Johnson said: "We have spent three days examining the department's books, and we have found no evidence of impropriety. We will recommend that no further action be taken."

• Quotations within a direct quote are set off with single quotation marks.

"He said, 'Go ahead and throw it away, just like you have done every game,' and he walked out and slammed the door," Smithers said.

• Commas and periods go inside quotation marks in direct quotes.

"Fifteen stinking, dripping barrels of sardines will be delivered Wednesday," he said.

Matthews said, "This race should be the test of every man's and every woman's physical and mental stamina."

• When placing the attribution at the end of the first sentence in a direct quote, the attribution is closed with a period.

Wrong: "The new gymnasium is fantastic and humungous," said basketball player Brad Jones, "We're proud to play there. We really feel important playing our games now."

Right: "The new gymnasium is fantastic and humungous," said basketball player Brad Jones. "We're proud to play there. We really feel important playing our games now."

• Question marks go inside or outside quotation marks depending on whether they are part of the quotation.

Mark said, "Are you asking me whether I cheated on the exam?"

One of Dionne Warwick's popular renditions included, "Do you know the way to San Jose?"

• Consider what may be slightly confusing but correct punctuation here:

Sara asked Kate, "Have you ever seen the movie 'Gone With the Wind'?"

Here the writer has a movie title that must be set off with quotation marks within a direct quote plus a question mark that is not part of the title.

• If the attribution breaks up a direct quote, it must be set off with commas and the quotation marks continued.

"Go ahead and throw it away," said Smithers, "just like you have done every game."

• If a speaker is quoted for several continuing paragraphs, the quotation marks are closed only at the final paragraph. Each paragraph must open with quotation marks to indicate the person is still speaking.

Resident John Loftis of Hollowell Road said, "We have been waiting two years for the southeast area to be annexed, and we are getting annoyed that the town council has further delayed a decision.

"I have written and my neighbors have written all the council members to say we want town services and are willing to pay for them.

"We just don't understand what the hold up is," Loftis said. "If a decision doesn't come after the next public hearing, I plan to picket city hall."

Not closing the quotation marks at the end of the first and second paragraphs tells the reader that Loftis hasn't finished talking. The quotation marks at the beginning of graphs two and three reopen the continuous quote from Loftis.

A Parting Shot

Be circumspect in your use of quotations. Remember the *Associated Press Stylebook* rule about correcting quotations. If you are not sure about a quote, follow this rule: When in doubt, leave it out. Don't try to reconstruct it as a direct quote. And be sure you have the gist of the remarks if you convert the comments to an indirect quote.

Many inexperienced writers have a tendency to use mostly indirect, paraphrased quotes because they don't trust their notes or their memories. They should work hard on their notetaking and strive for a mix of direct and indirect quotes in writing.

EXERCISES

1. Interview a friend or classmate about social life on your campus. Take careful notes. Then list five quotes, with correct attribution, that you might use in a finished story about social life at your school. Focus on correct attribution and use of both indirect and direct quotes.

2. Look at the transcript of the speech by Supreme Court Justice Sandra Day O'Connor. Highlight those quotations that you would keep as direct quotes. Explain why. Indicate which quotations could be better paraphrased.

Surviving Cancer

A Private Person's Public Tale

Supreme Court Justice Sandra Day O'Connor addressed the National Coalition for Cancer Survivorship and for the first time publicly talked about her own battle with breast cancer. Following are excerpts from her speech.

I don't have a magic wand to wave. I'm here this morning really to chat very informally with you about this business of being a cancer survivor.

It's been six years since I underwent surgery for breast cancer. The impact of the diagnosis of cancer that I received is one which has not been far from my thoughts at any time during these six years. But ... this is the first time that I have spoken publicly about my experience. And I'm not sure that my experience is any different than anyone else's. In fact, I'm quite sure it isn't. So what I have to say this morning for those of you who are here as survivors or friends or relations of survivors is going to sound hauntingly familiar, I suspect. . . .

We begin with the anxiety of going through the testing, something that's seen in a mammogram or an X-ray or there's some little spot on your back—whatever it is.... And the initial impact for me was one of general disbelief. I felt fine, just fine, but I was told you better go have these tests and find out.

An then...I was told that I had a potentially fatal disease. Now that gets your attention. The Big C. The word cancer, it overwhelms the psyche, just the word. I couldn't believe it. I was unprepared for the enormous emotional jolt that I received from the diagnosis.

I can remember, all of a sudden my face and hands, my whole body tingled, I couldn't believe I was hearing this. It couldn't be true. I'm too busy. I feel fine. You can't be serious!

Well, the next thing was reality sets in.... But I was quite unprepared for the suddenness and the urgency of the rapid treatment decisions to be made. I had planned to go through a couple more rounds of oral argument in court and I said, well maybe in December we can work this out. I was told that was not an option. So I was simply totally lacking in appreciation for the fact that everything had to stop and I had to focus on this and I had to start educating myself about what it was I had and what the treatment options were. This was a very tough time.

I discovered I needed other ears than my own because I was so emotionally involved in this situation that I wasn't sure I was hearing everything.... I brought my husband along [to meet with doctors] because I

thought he could listen with greater objectivity than I could and we both tried to take a few notes so we got everything down. I mean this was a world that was new to us. We didn't know the medical terms, we didn't have any experience with this and I wasn't sure I was even equipped to absorb the information I was hearing....

Added to the stress was that I had to make so many decisions about the course of my treatment. That never occurred to me either. I mean I thought if I got sick, I went to my doctor, the doctor said what ought to be done and that was the end of it. Right? Wrong! With this disease it isn't always that way.... You run into this whole business of what do you do, a lumpectomy, a mastectomy or a radiation approach, do you have chemotherapy, do you not, if you have surgery what kind, how extensive. I just was quite unprepared to...make so many choices.

It helped to have close friends to talk to, people who had gone through the same experience. That meant a lot.... It was amazing how many people would send me a letter or come up to me and say, I've had that too, I've had that, my mother had that, oh my aunt had that. This was good because I then could start to come to grips with the fact that it isn't the end of the line and you are going to have a life that's going to go on....

Now it is clear that the decisions about what to do, what treatments...had to be made promptly. And you just have to sweep in every bit of information you can possibly absorb, just become a real student, like cramming for an exam in college when you let slip all during the semester and you've got to get it all at once.... And then I did what I do at the court. When I'm at the court faced with a case I try to find everything out about that case that I can. I do as much research as I possibly can do and then I make my decision and I don't look back....

Now for me the decision was to have a mastectomy, and the postoperative period was depressing. I felt weak, I felt very emotional, I was hearing things I didn't want to hear, I was in some discomfort. It was really a tough time.... It was so intense that I called that friend of mine at home and I said, could you come down to the hospital by any chance, do you have time, could you come down and see me? And she did. She dropped everything and came down and we shed a tear or two together and we talked everything over and somehow that helped....

I was told you're going to have to have chemotherapy and this is going to take several months....

Somebody suggested that I see a particular hairdresser and it turned out this was one of the kindest, most learned men I have ever met. And he was totally sympathetic and he had lots of women who'd lost their hair and he found a wig or two for me and he just was terrific. And that real-ly did help me.... You do feel lousy and look lousy, so if you can improve that little bit it does help your attitude.

I was tired...and I'm not used to being tired. I had a lot of energy in my life and I couldn't believe that I needed all that sleep. I'm a person that didn't sleep much. Well, I could hardly get up, and in the afternoon I felt like I needed a nap. And this was frightening.

It wasn't just me.... My condition was causing distress to my family.... My husband was affected by it, my children were.... So you feel grateful that I had my work to do....

And it also helped me to resume physical exercise as soon as I could. I'm someone who just loves to have an exercise class...or...to play tennis or golf or ski or do something.... And it was hard because I lost the strength in my arm and it hurt. I was told, well, for at least six weeks you can't do X, Y, and Z. But even long before the six weeks, I went back to my exercise class and there was a lot I couldn't do. But I did a little, I did what I could. My legs were okay so I used those, and I still had a fat stomach so I could work on that. That helped.... Soon...I could chip and putt on the golf course.... And eventually my nice friends were patient and hit a few soft tennis balls to me. So I worked back in.

Now what was the worst? The worst was my public visibility, frankly. There was constant media coverage.

How does she look? When is she going to step down and give the president another vacancy on the court? She looks pale to me, I don't give her six months. This was awful. There were people in the press box with telescopes looking at me in the court room to see just what my condition was. I didn't like that. Press would call my office and say they'd heard all these dire rumors and I better tell them exactly what was what or they were going to publish them all. It was really difficult....

Let me tell you my dream of what I would like to have had in my situation which probably is very much like many of you:

I think it would be helpful to have all those tests done, the biopsies and the X-rays and whatever it is they are going to do, get all that information and then have a consultation with all the experts available at the same time, who've already looked at these things, they've looked at everything and they're all in the same [place] and they are there to help you reach a decision. The surgeon, the ra-

diologist, the oncologist, the plastic surgeon, the nurse, a psychologist and so on—everybody there to help you through the process of what to do. I think that would be terrific.... I thought moving from doctor to doctor with separate appointments and separate approaches and one doctor not hearing what the other said increased the uncertainty and increased the trauma.

[And] we need knowledge. Now how do I deal with the fear of death, where do I find the best and latest research on cancer treatment, what's reliable and what isn't and where is it and what about these state-of-the-art treatments, how do I find that, will my insurance cover the costs, do I need a counselor to help me through this, do my children need help?...

Is there an upside to all of this? Yes, there is. Having this disease made me more aware than ever before of the transitory nature of life here on Earth, of my own life. And it made me value each and every day of life more than ever before....

---

3. Identify a campus leader who has been in the news recently. Select a specific topic related to the leader's expertise. Set up an interview and prepare questions as outlined in the chapter. Take a tape recorder to record the interview. When the interview is over, transcribe the tape and create a question-and-answer format story of the interview.

4. Using your transcribed interview from Exercise 3, write a story that focuses on the campus leader's view. Use a mix of direct and indirect quotes.

5. You are a reporter for the campus newspaper. Your editor has asked you to come up with a story based on money, specific to the campus. Ideas might be the cost of tuition or books, lack of enough financial aid, lack of funds to maintain classrooms, cost of getting settled in a job after graduation, increased student fees. Think of a story that would interest your audience: students. Stick to the campus for interviews. You must use more than one source. If the story relates to campus funding, you will need to talk to an administrator. You would also want to talk with a student who is affected by the service or lack of service. Be sure to have balanced sources. After the interviews, write a story showing both sides of the issue.

6. Many publications reveal how average citizens feel about or react to an event. Editors will select a current topic and assign a reporter to get public reactions. Scan today's daily newspaper and select a current topic, such as an ongoing international conflict, national legislation, a campus issue, or another major event that students and staff would have read or heard about. Interview 10 people. Ask each one the same question. If you have to ask a question that is answered yes or no, you will need a followup "Why?" or your responses will be skimpy. Get each individual's name (check the spelling) and two other identifying labels: year in school, academic major, hometown, age, residence. Your attribution would look like: Jane Smith, a senior chemistry major, or Alex Jones, 19, of Whiteville. Write the story. The first paragraph should have a summary lead, giving the results of your informal poll: Five out of 10 University students interviewed Thursday at the Student Union said they believed the presidency is a tough job that receives little credit, and not one students would want the job. The second paragraph gives the question: The students were asked: "What is your assessment of the job of presidency, and would you want the job?" Then you can proceed with each person's response.

7. You are asked to write a speech for the company's chief executive officer. He is chairman of the state's community college system board, an advisory role. He has been asked to talk to the local Kiwanis Club about the community college system. In your research, whom would you interview? Identify at least two sources. Make a list of questions you would ask each. Compare the list with classmates, and discuss why certain questions were included.

REFERENCES

John Brady, *The Craft of Interviewing.* Cincinnati: Writer's Digest, 1976.

Rene J. Cappon, *The Word: An Associated Press Guide to Good News Writing.* New York: Associated Press, 1991.

Norm Goldstein, ed. *The Associated Press Stylebook and Libel Manual.* New York: Associated Press, 1992.

Judith Lewis Herman, *Trauma and Recovery.* New York: Basic Books, 1992.

Ken Metzler, *Creative Interviewing,* 2nd ed. Englewood Cliffs, NJ: Prentice-Hall, 1989.

11

Electronic Media

WHEN YOU WRITE FOR ELECTRONIC
MEDIA, YOUR COPY WILL LOOK LIKE
THIS: A SCRIPT FORMAT. BUT THE
CONTENT WILL REMAIN ACCURATE,
CONCISE, AND COMPLETE, JUST AS IN
ANY WRITING YOU DO.

Writing for the electronic media—radio and television—requires the basic, good writing skills discussed in earlier chapters. Broadcast messages must be concise, clear, and simple so that audiences can understand the information.

Even though electronic messages are written before they are aired, broadcast writing differs in some respects from writing for print. Audiences tuning in to radio, for example, have to rely on their ears to get the message. Writing must be clear and specific. Writers have only one chance to catch audiences, who can't go back and reread the lead.

In broadcast messages, writers and reporters must look past the written word for audio and visuals that enhance the message. A radio reporter can use an actuality or sound bite, such as a recorded interview or the sounds of traffic. But the actuality must attract audience attention and fit the report. Television reporters must combine writing with audiotapes, videotapes, and even live shots from the scene of an event. The writing must match the visuals and make the report come alive, appealing to the audience's senses.

In this chapter you will learn

- The similarities and differences between print and electronic media writing,
- The essential qualities of electronic media writing,
- How to write a script for radio and for television, and
- One reporter's view on writing for radio and television.

Writing for Print vs. Electronic Media Writing

Similarities exist between good writing for print and electronic media. The media themselves—primarily radio and television—dictate some differences in format and approach for their particular audiences. All reporters, regardless of media, adhere to standards of accuracy, good taste, ethical reporting, and legal requirements. The code for the Radio Television News Directors Association is shown here.

Radio-Television News Directors Association Code of Ethics

The responsibility of radio and television journalists is to gather and report information of importance and interest to the public accurately, honestly and impartially.

The members of the Radio-Television News Directors Association accept these standards and will:

1. Strive to present the source or nature of broadcast news material in a way that is balanced, accurate and fair.
   A. They will evaluate information solely on its merits as news, rejecting sensationalism or misleading emphasis in any form.
   B. They will guard against using audio or video material in a way that deceives the audience.
   C. They will not mislead the public by presenting as spontaneous news any material which is staged or rehearsed.
   D. They will identify people by race, creed, nationality or prior status only when it is relevant.
   E. They will clearly label opinion and commentary.
   F. They will promptly acknowledge and correct errors.

2. Strive to conduct themselves in a manner that protects them from conflicts of interest, real or perceived. They will decline gifts or favors which would influence or appear to influence their judgments.

3. Respect the dignity, privacy and well-being of people with whom they deal.

4. Recognize the need to protect confidential sources. They will promise confidentiality only with the intention of keeping that promise.

5. Respect everyone's right to a fair trial.

6. Broadcast the private transmissions of other broadcasters only with permission.

7. Actively encourage observance of this Code by all journalists, whether members of the Radio-Television News Directors Association or not.

Copyright by Radio-Television News Directors Association. Reproduced here with permission of RTNDA.

Similarities

THE WRITING PROCESS. The skills learned in the writing process discussed in Chapter 1 apply to electronic media. Broadcast reporters start with an idea, do research and interviews, then produce copy that is well written and relevant to their audiences. The writing process stage of outlining is critical for electronic media writers, who must plan a story before they leave the scene of an event. They must have an outline so they can get necessary audiotape, such as a quote from a county commissioner, or videotape, perhaps a shot of fire trucks, that will be needed to produce the final story package. Once in the editing lab, they may not have time to go back and shoot a visual for the 6 p.m. news.

NEWS VALUES. All mass communication writing has to have some news values from among those discussed in Chapter 3: prominence, timeliness, proximity, impact, magnitude, conflict, oddity, and emotional impact. Electronic media writing is no exception. Timeliness is the most critical news element for electronic media. Radio and television, because of their ability to broadcast live, can get information out to audiences as news events occur. Immediacy is the key. For a news clip to last throughout a 24-hour cycle, the event must be compelling. In radio and television, news that happened in the morning may be old in the afternoon, whereas newspapers print yesterday's news today. Conflict is another key news value for electronic journalism. Viewing conflict first hand on television can make an audience remember a story for a lifetime.

CLEAR, CONCISE WRITING. The rules of using short sentences and short words, avoiding jargon and technical language, cutting wordiness, and getting to the point quickly are particularly critical in broadcast writing. Broadcast stories are generally shorter than those in print. While a print news story may use 120 words to tell an event, a broadcast report may have to condense the account to 15 seconds. Newscasters read about 10 words in four seconds; a 15-second broadcast is about 35 words long. Every word counts, therefore, and language must be clear and precise. Few listeners will understand jargon or complicated language.

RESEARCH. Like print reporters, electronic reporters develop sources and do research and interviews. Research can be more difficult. Print reporters can access stories in library files or on computer databases fairly quickly. Electronic media must review tapes to learn what the station may have covered before—a time-consuming process. Most electronic reporters don't accumulate clips and files they can readily consult. Television stations, for example, have file footage, but those archives are not as extensive as are newspaper libraries or morgues.

Electronic media reporters must be generalists and cover a variety of topics, even within a single day. They may attend the governor's news conference in the morning and a fire the same afternoon. Radio reporters rarely have the opportunity to specialize in a particular area or beat, such as medicine, business, or local government. More and more television reporters, however, are carving out special areas, such as consumer and health beats.

Differences

DEADLINES. Electronic media often work under tighter deadlines than print reporters, who may have a 7 p.m. deadline for a morning newspaper whereas a television reporter must be on the air at 5 p.m. The television reporter also may be producing several stories for the evening broadcast, perhaps two news briefs and one that includes a standup, or appearance by the reporter.

WRITING STRUCTURE. Because radio and television reports are shorter than print versions, they must be written to be understood the first time. And they must make it through clutter. Most radio and television audiences are doing other things: driving the car, listening to children's voices, cooking dinner.

Electronic media start a story with a headline to grab listener or viewer attention. Then they give a lead to the story, which generally sets up the context for the story. Next comes explanation. The wrap-up usually focuses on the possible effects. For television, the entire story may run an average 30 seconds; for radio, the report may be only 20 seconds.

In addition to writing the story for television and even radio, the reporter will have to write several advance headlines or teasers that anchors can use to promote an upcoming newscast. In a teaser, reporters give only enough information about a story to make viewers watch it later. For example, a story may need a teaser or lead-in during an afternoon newsbreak, plus another teaser or a lead-in just before the 6 p.m. news. Then a reporter must write a lead-in for anchors before being introduced. Finally, a reporter will give her own lead on the story. All are different and gradually add information but without revealing the entire story.

FORMAT. Because electronic media require audio and visuals, the format for producing or typing stories differs from print format. Electronic and print journalists follow some of the same guidelines, such as double-spaced copy with one-inch margins, but electronic reports must add cues for audio and visual elements. Radio reports are typed across the page, just as print journalism stories are, but notes on what prerecorded elements will be inserted must appear between blocks of copy that will be read aloud.

In television reports, copy fills the right-hand side of the page; cues for audiotape, videotape, and who is speaking appear in the left-hand column. Abbreviations, such as VO for voice over when the announcer or reporter are speaking, are indicated in the left-hand column.

Some broadcast journalists type their copy in all caps, but others prefer upper and lower case. Paragraphs are not split between pages, and each story is typed on a separate page. Specific style rules on how to use abbreviations, numbers, and attribution are explained later in the chapter.

COST. One point to remember is that electronic production—whether for an hour-long documentary or a 20-second news spot—is expensive and requires a team effort. Movies cost millions to produce; budgets for staff and equipment in television newsrooms are costly. For example, print journalists can get by with collecting information in an 89-cent notebook with a 15-cent pencil rather than a television reporter's $800 camcorder and the station's production van that costs tens of thousands of dollars. While print journalists need printing presses, television reporters require editing equipment, studios, and satellite dishes. Radio reporters are on the economical end of electronic media production, requiring less in-house equipment to air their broadcasts.

The Differences in Practice

A radio reporter and a print journalist are rewriting wire service copy for their respective media. How would their leads look, based on the differences between broadcast and print writing? Let's see.

The print journalist writes:

ALBANY, N.Y.—New York Gov. George Pataki may fulfill a campaign promise today and sign legislation to create a death penalty.

The broadcast writer develops this lead:

NEW YORK'S GOVERNOR IS EXPECTED TO SIGN A DEATH PENALTY LAW TODAY.

The broadcast writer does not use a dateline, uses the present tense, avoids a complicated proper name, and establishes a context of death penalty legislation that can be explained later.

Consider two other examples:

A survey reports that working women have similar concerns.

Working women are most concerned about balancing home and job, health insurance, and stress, according to a survey released today.

Which is the broadcast lead? The first one is. It is short and uses attribution at the beginning to establish the source immediately. It also establishes a context for the story to follow.

Electronic Media Writing

Writing for electronic media means writing for the ear, using short sentences, having speech that is more conversational, following a subject-verb-object sentence order, having copy that is clear and understandable, and putting smooth, clear transitions between thoughts. Let's look at producing broadcast copy, following these guidelines.

Broadcast Leads

The lead on a broadcast story is short and gives basic information. As noted earlier, the lead generally establishes a context for the story. Specific information will follow. The lead may be catchy and even entertaining. It draws the audience to stop and listen to the story:

FOUR PEOPLE DIED IN A SHOOTOUT THIS AFTERNOON.

THE MAYOR WILL ANNOUNCE TOMORROW THAT NEW JOBS ARE COMING TO THE AREA.

The context is clear in each example. The first story will be about who died and where. The second lead sets up audiences for a story on economics with information about how many and what kinds of jobs and the name of the company. In both instances, the leads are much shorter than in print.

Broadcast writers who cover continuing or recurring stories try to find leads that will pique audience attention and interest in just a few words.

WHAT'S UP FOR TODAY IN THE O. J. SIMPSON TRIAL?

CHRISTMAS IS COMING EARLY FOR A CARLTON COUPLE.

Broadcast Structure in the Message

Again, the structure of any electronic message must consider the audience's ear. The message must be clear and direct. Sentences are short and are written primarily in subject-verb-object order. Language must be simple. The writer develops the story using the three-part format: context, explanation, and effect. The lead sets out the context or the reason why the story is being written. The lead may focus on one news value or latest information, that is, timeliness. The second part is explanation, whereby listeners or viewers get more information, whether it is background, a historical perspective, or more details of the current situation. Then the writer wraps up with the effect, generally a look to the future or the impact of the event.

Look at this story:

IN ESPANOLA STUDENTS WILL RETURN TO FAIRVIEW ELEMENTARY SCHOOL TOMORROW AFTER ALMOST TWO WEEKS.

THE SCHOOL CLOSED MONDAY OF LAST WEEK AFTER A PLUMBER DOING ROUTINE MAINTENANCE WORK DISCOVERED A GAS LEAK. THE SCHOOL WAS BUILT IN 1966, AND ADMINISTRATORS SAY EXTENSIVE REPAIRS WERE NEEDED.

SCHOOL OFFICIALS PRICED THE REPAIRS AT MORE THAN 20 THOUSAND DOLLARS. THEY SAY THE SYSTEM'S OTHER SCHOOLS WILL BE CHECKED FOR LEAKS NOW, TOO.

The message clearly lets parents in the audience know that children will go back to school, and it gives other general-interest members an update on a story that has been in the news. The writer follows the lead with background on why the school was closed. The next sentence says why the school was closed for so long. Listeners then learn that the repairs were expensive. The impact is an investigation of other schools' plumbing.

As for language, all words are simple. According to the readability formula discussed in Chapter 5, this story is easy for viewers to understand. The most complicated words are "maintenance" and "extensive."

Writing Guidelines

The leads and story used as examples also illustrate basic writing principles for broadcast stories. Because timeliness is crucial to electronic media, writers should use the present tense if possible. Even if they have to shift to past tense later in the story, they find present tense preferable in the lead.

Avoid: A convicted rapist was executed today after months of appeals failed.

Rather: A convicted rapist died today after months of appeals.

Avoid: Sixteen winners were declared in the long-awaited state lottery.

Rather: Sixteen people are winners in the state's long-awaited lottery.

Some other writing rules to follow:

• Avoid strange names or those of little-known people. Describe people in terms of employment or life's work, then name them in the second sentence. Use names only with prominent people.

A ROCKLAND SECOND-GRADE TEACHER IS THE NATION'S
TEACHER OF THE YEAR.
    RONNIE MILLER,....

Or:

ROCKLAND MAYOR JOAN TILLIS IS IN GOOD CONDITION
AFTER BACK SURGERY.

• Avoid tongue-twisters that can cause problems when reports are read on air. Always read copy aloud before it is aired or broadcast. "The clandestine clan committed continual crimes" may look clever on paper, but it may be difficult for an announcer to enunciate.

• Use action verbs. Remember that verbs can paint pictures, an especially important aspect of radio reports. "Race car driver Richard Petty roared to victory" has more life than "Race car driver Richard Petty won."

• Use quotations sparingly. Paraphrased statements are more easily understood. If a quote is particularly good, use it live from the source. Make sure that the writing does not imply the statement is from the reporter or newscaster. Direct quotes using "I" or "we" can cause such confusion. Chamber of commerce president David Fall says, "I have doubts about the town's development practices." Listeners who miss the attribution may infer the reporter is doubtful.

• Put attribution at the beginning of a quotation. Medical experts say the new treatment may cause cancer cells to die. If you must use a direct quote, try "Johnson said in his own words, and I quote, . . ."

• Avoid writing that uses a lot of punctuation. Punctuation—even a question mark—cannot be heard. Listeners may miss the inflection.

• Avoid long introductory clauses with participles, like this one: "While doing a routine maintenance check at the school, a plumber found . . ."

• Avoid separating subjects and verbs, particularly with phrases in apposition. Don't leave verbs at the end of the sentence. Follow subject-verb-object order as much as possible. "Marian Johnson, a director for the Rockland Little Theater, will leave her job in two weeks" becomes "Rockland's Little Theater director will leave her job within two weeks. Marian Johnson . . ."

• Break up lengthy series of modifiers and adjectives. Police described the suspect as a blond, long-haired, blue-eyed, five-foot-two-inch man. Rather write: Police say the suspect has long blond hair and blue eyes. They also say he is about five feet two inches tall.

• Avoid negatives. A listener may miss the negative words "no" and "not" in a broadcast and thereby be misinformed. Use alternatives. Police could find no motive for the shootings can be translated Police say the motive for the shootings is unknown.

• If your report runs long, say more than 30 seconds, look for ways to unify the story. Repetition of key words is one way to help listeners and viewers to follow along.

Style in Copy

In Chapter 5 on editing, we looked at copy editing style for print. Electronic media have style rules for preparing copy.

• If a name is difficult, spell out in parentheses following the name how to pronounce it. Anchors and reporters can stumble in stating people's names. Sound it out. For example, names with "ei" or "ie" can be confusing, such as Janice Weinberger. Write out (WINE BURGER) so the announcer will use a long "i" pronunciation. For Iraqi leader Saddam Hussein, the pronunciation is (WHO SAYN).

• Put titles before names and keep them short. Use Florida Governor Lawton Chiles rather than Lawton Chiles, the governor of Florida. A person who is a university vice chancellor for institutional research services becomes a university administrator. You can use a descriptive title if audiences easily identify a person that way, for example, evangelist Billy Graham or newspaper publisher Katharine Graham.

• Use people's names the way they are commonly referred to. President Clinton is known as Bill Clinton, not William Clinton. Former vice president Dan Quayle was rarely called Daniel T. Quayle.

• Write out numbers between zero and 999. You can combine numerals and words as long as they read clearly. For example, write 10 thousand two hundred and 22 billion.

• Round off numbers. Say more than 10 thousand rather than 10 thousand two hundred and thirty two subscribers.

• Write out dollars and cents, percent, and fractions. Gasoline prices are three to four cents a gallon higher. Three-fourths of town residents say they are pleased with the mayor's performance. About fifty-five percent of what you read, you remember.

• Keep statistics to a minimum. Put them in a format people will understand. If a poll says 67 percent of the state's residents favor the Republican Contract with America, report that two out of three state residents say they favor the Republican Contract with America.

• Write out Roman numerals. Write out Harry Holland the third rather than Harry Holland III, or Queen Elizabeth the second, not Queen Elizabeth II.

• Avoid acronyms. Use the full name, such as Department of Housing and Urban Development, not HUD, and Environmental Protection Agency, not EPA. Some acronyms can be used on second reference, such as FBI after Federal Bureau of Investigation has been the first reference. For local or state law enforcement, it is better just to say police or law officials on subsequent references.

Writing Messages

A major difference between print and electronic media is the format for the final message, as noted earlier. Broadcast media use a script format that indicates the text along with the sound bites or visuals. Time is critical in broadcast writing. Scripts indicate how long the total story runs plus the length of specific segments within the story. Radio reports are typed across the page, much like a print story, with audio cues. See the following example of a radio news script.

12/28/94
MK
CH PLANE CRASH2

QUESTIONABLE ENGINE MAINTENANCE CAUSED THE PLANE CRASH THAT KILLED THREE PEOPLE OUTSIDE CHAPEL HILL IN 1993. THAT'S ACCORDING TO THE NATIONAL TRANSPORTATION SAFETY BOARD, WHICH RECENTLY RELEASED ITS CRASH REPORT. VIRGINIAN GREGORY BERTSCHINGER AND TWO PASSENGERS DIED...WHEN A SINGLE-ENGINE BEECH M-35 WENT DOWN NEAR FINLEY GOLF COURSE, ON DECEMBER 11TH, 1993. THE N-T-S-B'S MICHAEL BENSON SAYS THE ENGINE'S THE CULPRIT.

#910 BENSON :15 Q:...ENGINE CRANKSHAFT INVESTIGATORS FOUND AN UNAUTHORIZED SEALING COMPOUND, AND IMPROPERLY SIZED ENGINE PISTON PINS, WHICH THEY CITE AS EVIDENCE OF AN OVERHAUL. LAB REPORTS INDICATE BERTSCHINGER HAD NO DRUGS, IN HIS SYSTEM. HE AND HIS TRAVELING COMPANIONS

CRASHED SHORTLY AFTER LEAVING CHAPEL HILL ...HEADED FOR MANTEO.
(Reprinted with permission from WCHL radio)

In television reports, the cues on the left-hand side of the page give such information as the title or slug of the story, what newscast it will appear on, the tape number, the length of the story, the name of the anchor, and any graphics to be used. After the story text begins, cues will tell whether the story has a voice-over, that is, a reporter who is not seen reading text to go along with other visuals. Cues also indicate who is speaking, for example, a source who is interviewed for the story, the reporter, or the anchor. The following example shows cues.

Cues	**Explanation**
REALESTATE PG.8	Story slug and page of newscast script.
NEWSCAST=6PM	Tells computer in which newscast to find script.
TAPE#=95-1001	Edited stories are put on numbered tapes for the computer reference system.
ANCHOR=TERESA	Cue for the computer system to connect directly to the teleprompter when the anchor is speaking.
CK=TWO SHOT A7N 6	Tells the director and graphics operator what to put in the Chroma-key. TWO SHOT A7N 6 means the camera operators are to frame both anchors in the shot. The Chroma-key or label is to appear between them and read "Action 7 News Live at Six."
LIVE IN DROPKEY	A computer generated box somewhat like the Chroma-key, but in which a reporter appears as he or she waits to deliver a live report.
TAKE LIVE	Tells the director and technical director to put in the live shot.

ROLLCUE="TO THE OFFER"	Tells the director and the person rolling the tape when to start the videotape to play the story.
RUNS=1:30	Tells the computer how long the package is so it can take the introduction and the tag line and estimate the total run time of the piece.
OUTCUE	Cues the director to return to the anchor desk or to a live shot.

When the story text is typed, all capital letters are used. That helps clarify writing where a lower-case "l" might resemble a capital "I" and create problems for announcers. Capital letters are also easier to read from a distance.

When students study electronic journalism, they learn the codes and copy preparation style early on. The complete radio story may seem to be longer than a story typed for print because cues take up space on the left-hand side of the page. The goal is to make the copy legible for the anchor and the reporter who read from the copy. The following example from KOAT-TV in Albuquerque, New Mexico, shows a story in television script format.

Television News Script

GOVOFFICE PG.3
NEWSCAST=6PM
TAPE #=94–1098
ANCHOR=DICK
CK=JOHNSON

<<(D) GOVERNOR-ELECT GARY JOHNSON IS CONSIDERING RE-PEATING HISTORY BY MOVING THE GOVERNOR'S OFFICE FROM THE STATE CAPITOL TO THE CUR-RENT ATTORNEY GENERAL'S OF-FICE IN THE BATAAN BUILDING.

THAT WAS THE MAIN LEGISLATIVE BUILDING UNTIL THE ROUND-

HOUSE WAS BUILT IN 1966. BUT AS
SABRINA SMITH REPORTS, COST
AND TIMING MAY MAKE THAT
DIFFICULT.

CVTR SOT FULL (******PKG*****)

SUPER=14-Governor's office/
Sante Fe; at:03

SUPER=21-Gary Johnson
Governor-elect; at:15

SUPER=@SSMR-Sante Fe; at:46

RUNS=1:06
OUTCUE="... Action 7 News."

P-GOVOFFICE PG. 3P   UNTIL NOW, IT WAS ASSUMED
GARY JOHNSON WOULD MOVE
INTO THIS OFFICE NOW OCCU-
PIED BY GOVERNOR BRUCE KING
AND HIS STAFF OF 35. BUT JOHN-
SON SAYS TAKING OVER THE AT-
TORNEY GENERAL'S OFFICE
WOULD MAKE HIS ADMINISTRA-
TION MORE EFFICIENT BY PUT-
TING HIM CLOSER TO HIS
FINANCE STAFF.

Radio and Television Careers

Reporting staffs in electronic media are generally small, particularly for radio stations and even in large television markets. Some radio stations have given up having reporters who actually go out and cover events. They rely on wire service copy and some taped telephone interviews to compile their news reports.

Newspaper and even radio reporters are independent compared with television reporters, who always work as part of a team. The team may include a news director, an assignment editor, editors for the story and the visuals, a producer for each newscast, a photographer, a director for technical equipment, a reporter who puts names below visuals, and perhaps a graphics editor.

So dozens of careers exist for students within electronic communication. The key is to get experience while in school and in the first few years after graduation. Real-world experience will help students clarify what type of work interests them most and will help them define their next career moves.

Students may start out as reporters for the local radio station and eventually be promoted to news directors. They may become production assistants for television stations. They may stick with news or move into the station's public affairs department. After years of experience, they may become freelance writers and produce documentaries.

Within the electronic communication field, most professionals have traditionally tended to stay with the medium they started with: radio or television. But more are making the switch from radio to television, and even some print people have moved into electronic fields such as television. One well-known example is Michael Gartner, former president of the American Society of Newspaper Editors. He moved from publisher of the *Courier-Journal* in Louisville, Kentucky, to president of ABC News.

Switching from Radio to Television

Sabrina Smith is a reporter for KOAT-TV in Albuquerque, N.M. She works in the Los Alamos bureau for the ABC affiliate. Smith began her career as a radio reporter, then made the transition from radio to television. She found the transition fairly easy, although she admits that some people in television had doubts about the move. In both jobs, she notes, reporters must write clearly, concisely, and conversationally.

You have to be able to write. In radio, all audiences have is your voice and what they hear. As a reporter, you have to write the story colorfully and to visualize for audiences what they only can hear. If you can do that, you are ahead of the game. In television, good writing is also essential. So many people in television write in a boring way because they rely on visuals. Do this test: To see if the video matches, turn down the volume and just watch the video to see if you know what the story

*is about. As a viewer, you should have some idea. If you can write well and inte-
grate visuals well, then you will do well.*

The biggest difference Smith found in moving from radio to television
was the added element of video. Students who want careers in television
have to know how to shoot videotape. As the reporter in the Los Alamos
bureau, Smith shoots her own videotape, then writes the text.

In television, reporters have to have the pictures that match the words
they are saying. They have to consider what visuals they will need when they
are out in the field and to know what film footage might be available back at
the office. Visuals reinforce the message. If audiences don't get the message,
then the visuals probably didn't match.

*One day I wrote a short story about city services. I went out and shot lots of video
then went back to the office to edit. When I wrote the story, I had two words: fire
protection and road maintenance. But I had no photos of fire trucks and road crews
to put in the story. So I had to go back out and shoot again.*

Television reporters have to do standups. A standup shows the reporter
who is covering the story standing in a location important to the story. A
standup may show the reporter at the beginning of a segment as the anchor
makes a transition from the set to the reporter's package, or it may be the
closing shot. It is the chance for the audience to see the reporter, and audiences should learn something from it. A standup should be specific, not
vague. The standup can be a challenge to the television reporter because it
must fit in with the rest of the story and be coherent.

Wrap Up

Much of the discussion here has focused on electronic media and news. But
student journalists are not limited solely to radio and television news. They
may opt to go into film or into writing scripts for situation comedies or
drama. They may produce documentaries on the plight of endangered animals or women in mass media jobs. They may be public relations professionals who have to produce public service announcements.

Whatever field students choose and whatever job they ultimately hold,
they must be good writers. Experienced electronic media professionals deplore

what they see as a decline in writing skills, in small and large market stations, and stress that clear, accurate, concise copy that addresses audiences is critical. Television is competing now with other information-age technology, and broadcast reporting will have to be compelling to keep audiences tuned in.

EXERCISES

1. Write broadcast leads for the following information:

> Sam Snyder, president of the Rockland Chamber of Commerce, has been elected to the board of directors of the National Chamber of Commerce.
>
> The Federal Reserve Board raised interest rates one-quarter percent, which means consumers will be paying higher rates on their adjustable rate home mortgages and if they are seeking mortgages.
>
> David Parkinson of Waverly County won first place at the county fair yesterday for the largest squash. It weighed 6 and ½ pounds. David is 6 years old.
>
> Competition begins Thursday for the National Collegiate Athletic Association title. The tough competition has been dubbed March madness.

2. Using the formula that a 60-space typed line equals 4 seconds of air time, write a 20-second radio script for the following information:

> A masked man robbed the University dining hall of $3,000 and escaped after locking the dining hall manager in a closet.
>
> Tony Jones, the manager, escaped unharmed. Police are looking for a heavy-set white man about 5-foot-5 and weighing about 175 pounds. He has a round face and broad shoulders. Jones could give no description of the

man's facial features because he had a stocking pulled
over his face.

Jones was preparing the payroll when he heard a
noise in the kitchen. When he went to investigate, he
said the man came charging at him. The man ordered him
to open the safe and put money in a blue sack. Jones
complied, and the robber locked him in a closet before
leaving.

3. Write a 20-second radio script for the following information and indicate an audio you could use to illustrate the spot.

The legal age for minors to buy cigarettes in most
states is 18. Studies show that underage youth or
minors still buy up to 500 million packs of cigarettes
a year, despite the states' laws. About 25 states have
agreed there should be stricter laws on tobacco
products, and even tobacco industry officials claim
their advertising is not geared to teen-agers.

4. Write a 30-second television script for the following information. Type the copy in the right-hand column and indicate what visuals you would use.

A coalition of child-care advocates marched on the
state legislature today. They distributed flyers
encouraging legislators to approve monies during the
current session that would subsidize the cost of day
care for families earning below $16,000 a year. They
claim that day care costs in the state have
skyrocketed, and even working families are finding it
hard to pay for quality day care out of their salaries.
The coalition estimated 15 percent of the state's
population fell below the federal poverty level

```
guidelines last year. The coalition officials said that
last year it had to turn away almost 400 families who
needed financial assistance but funds just weren't
available.
```

5. Watch the local evening news. Do a tally that covers the number of stories, story topics, whether they were local or based on a national event, the length of each, numbers and types of sources used. Write several paragraphs on whether you felt adequately informed about news items from the television account.

6. Based on the information collected in Exercise 5, look at the local or regional newspaper the following day. See how many stories from your evening television newscast were covered in the newspaper. Look at the length of those stories and what new information you learned.

REFERENCES

Seth Finn, *Broadcast Writing as a Liberal Art.* Englewood Cliffs, NJ: Prentice-Hall, 1991.

Floyd McKay, "Writing for Broadcast," Course Packet for Journalism 201, University of Maryland, College Park, MD, Spring 1990.

Interviews with Sabrina Smith, reporter, KOAT-TV, Albuquerque, NM.

J. Clark Weaver, *Broadcast Newswriting as a Process.* New York: Longman, 1984.

Mitchell Stephens, *Broadcast News,* 2nd ed. New York: Holt, Rinehart and Winston, 1986.

12

Public Relations Writing

A student in an introductory writing course told her classmates that she wanted to pursue public relations (PR) as a career. Why? "Because I want to talk to people about the organization I work for," she said.

Her professor quipped, "You won't do much talking; you'll be much too busy writing."

Writing is the single most important skill in public relations, all experts agree. Well-organized prose is at the heart of every successful and effective public relations campaign and event, regardless of who does the talking.

Public relations practitioners must be able to communicate information about their respective organizations to targeted audiences. People will call and talk to an organization only when they know that it exists and what it does. The public relations practitioner must send the news release on company earnings before reporters will call. The mother must read the brochure on a community's child-care offerings before calling for more details. The college student must peruse the flyer about a company's internship program before calling the campus career planning and placement office.

Being a successful public relations practitioner takes more than agility in talking and a ready smile. Public relations practitioners must identify audiences to determine the best methods to communicate with audiences; conduct research; plan and carry out communication strategy; and evaluate plans. Writing is crucial at each stage, but particularly in communicating messages to important publics.

This chapter looks at

*   The importance of good public relations writing,
*   Audiences or publics,
*   Communications tools used by public relations practitioners,
*   The media as a major public, and
*   Methods of reaching audiences.

What Is Public Relations?

Professor James Grunig at the University of Maryland defines public relations as the management of communication between an organization and its publics or audiences: employees, clients, customers, investors, or alumni. Grunig emphasizes the importance of strategy and thinking in approaching those relationships.

Successful public relations builds and maintains good relationships between an organization and its publics via balanced, open communication. Public relations may be as simple as an announcement by the local literacy council about its success rate for the past year. Or it may be a complicated integrated marketing program that incorporates public relations with advertising, investor relations, and market research.

Diverse organizations use public relations: local, state and national non-profit organizations such as the American Heart Association; schools and universities; small companies; multinational corporations; and local, state, and federal government, including the president and the Armed Services. Public relations practitioners share information with the public to help the organization achieve its objectives. The objective of public relations efforts may be to show publics how the company works as a good corporate citizen or as a leader in its field. The objective may be public service, as in a broadcast message to reduce teenage pregnancy or to warn smokers about the risks of heart attacks.

Some people erroneously think of public relations as free publicity, believing that there is no cost. They assume that newspapers and other publications just happen to use an organization's news in a business column. But real public relations—ongoing programs of communication with various publics—is expensive. Organizations must pay salaries and production costs, buy supplies and equipment, and cover additional overhead expenses such as office space and utilities. Most are hidden costs that the public doesn't see or consider.

Public Relations Tools

Public relations practitioners often use the term "public relations tools" or "communications tools" to describe the techniques or methods they use to reach audiences. All require solid writing skills. Among the more common communications tools are these:

• *News releases.* Articles that describe newsworthy events and are sent to media outlets. They are written in a style ready to be used.

• *Feature releases.* More in-depth, less timely articles about organization employees, projects, or services. These generally are targeted to a specific publication.

• *Media kits.* Folders that contain relevant information on the organization or company or a special event. Included are fact sheets, backgrounders, photographs, reprints, biographies, and other material.

• *Direct mail letters.* Letters written to targeted publics, generally to solicit support for a project or event.

• *Brochures.* Booklets or folders that include general information or targeted information about an organization or a special project. These are designed to be easily mailed or distributed at events or in racks.

• *Face-to-face contact.* Speeches or appearances at meetings, conventions, or other programs.

• *Audiovisual presentations.* Slide shows and multimedia shows that supplement information in speeches. Can visually depict an organization or its services.

• *Specialized publications.* Newsletters, annual reports, and magazines produced for internal audiences such as employees or for external audiences such as customers and the general public. In some corporate settings, annual reports are produced by the investor relations department; the public relations practitioner may help with some writing.

- *Video news releases.* Actual film footage with or without sound, especially voiceover, for television stations to have ready-to-use material.

- *Public service announcements (PSAs).* Short announcements, generally sent ready-to-read to radio stations. May be produced in video form for television stations.

- *Image advertising.* Attempts by an organization to improve an audience's perception of it. Often done in conjunction with marketing departments.

How the Tools Are Used

Communications tools are incorporated into plans that serve as guides for public relations activities or campaigns. Corporate communications departments, for example, begin work in the fall on the next year's plan. Staff members consider the company's objectives, such as promoting retail services in the coming year, and develop public relations activities that will support the objective. The goals, specific actions, and target dates are outlined in a document that becomes a guide during the year.

Of course, not all public relations is planned. A reporter may call the corporate communications department about an original story idea, and the public relations practitioner will write a response or arrange for a company executive to reply. Or the practitioner will send the reporter a folder that contains a mix of communications tools, often called collateral materials, such as a news release, a fact sheet, and a brochure. The practitioner will cooperate with the reporter's request for interviews and printed materials.

Public Relations Stages

In the late 1960s Scott Cutlip and Allen Center identified four stages of a public relations campaign: research, planning, communication, and evaluation. Public relations practitioners follow those stages today.

A bank plans to change its checking service in three months. The public relations department is charged with informing the bank's publics of the change. Look at how the public relations practitioner would use each stage.

- *Research.* First, research is essential to enable the bank to state public relations goals, identify relevant publics, describe the service, and identify its strengths and weaknesses. For example, the bank's reputation would be a strength; competition from other banks' services would be a weakness. Research could use focus groups, as discussed in Chapter 2, to determine what the bank's customers would like in a checking account.

- *Planning.* In planning, the practitioner devises a communications plan or strategy. The practitioner determines what communications tools will be used during the next three months and sets deadlines for each one. For example, dates for news releases to trade publications differ from those for statewide media. Magazines usually need copy two months before publication dates; newspapers can print information within 24 hours of receiving it.

- *Communication.* In the communication stage, the practitioner carries out the plan. Information is written and distributed via the communications tools: news releases, brochures, fact sheets, annual reports and other publications, and speeches, just to name a few. While writing is important in developing the plan, good skills are critical in the communication stage.

- *Evaluation.* In evaluation, the practitioner uses qualitative and quantitative ways to evaluate the success of the communications plan and strategy. For example, the bank can use focus groups of customers to determine how well they understand communication about the service. After the news release is distributed, the public relations staff can count the number of newspaper clippings to determine how many times the news release information has appeared in state newspapers.

Public Relations Jobs

Public relations is an exciting profession with varied jobs. As a public relations professional, you could be at the forefront in affecting public opinion about nuclear energy, at the podium conducting a news conference for the State Department, or on the campaign trail for a popular county commissioner who is running for the United States Senate. Practitioners do much more than write news releases and answer the telephone. For example, a power company's public information officer will answer reporters' questions at a news conference about the utility's rate increase. Other public relations people in the same office might write for an employee newsletter or coordinate meetings and special events.

Experienced PR people manage public relations for clients. They oversee company community relations or become presidents of their own public relations agencies. In all of these positions, they write.

If you work for the corporate communications department of a large company, your job description will be specific. You may be the media relations manager for statewide media, coordinating news releases and answering inquiries. Or you may edit all in-house publications from bulletin board announcements to the quarterly company magazine.

In the nonprofit or independent sector, you may do many jobs. Many nonprofit organizations cannot afford to hire large public relations staffs. One person will respond to media inquiries, write news releases, produce a newsletter, design flyers, set up community relations activities, and do whatever else needs to be done.

Public relations is a respectable profession. Some people describe practitioners as hacks or flacks; they believe that practitioners tout the company's best interests and not society's at large. They view public relations as a way to cover up the bad stuff that organizations do and see public relations practitioners as the people who sidestep the truth. They criticize public relations people as trying to control the news and the slant on information.

Some criticism of a few individuals may be justified, just as in any profession. But most people today recognize that public relations practitioners adhere to a code of ethics, usually the code of the Public Relations Society of America shown in the following chart. Practitioners who do not act ethically or who do not tell the truth hurt themselves and their organizations. They need the consistent trust and confidence of their publics if they are to survive. Once an organization loses the public's trust, it may take a major, costly public relations and advertising campaign to win it again. And the investment may not pay off.

Code of Professional Standards for the Practice of Public Relations

Public Relations Society of America

This Code was adopted by the PRSA Assembly in 1988. It replaces a Code of Ethics in force since 1950 and revised in 1954, 1959, 1963, 1977, and 1983. For information on the Code and enforcement procedures, please call the chair of the Board of Ethics through PRSA Headquarters.

Declaration of Principles

Members of the Public Relations Society of America base their professional principles on the fundamental value and dignity of the individual, holding that the free exercise of human rights, especially freedom of speech, freedom of assembly, and freedom of the press, is essential to the practice of public relations.

In serving the interests of clients and employers, we dedicate ourselves to the goals of better communication, understanding, and cooperation among diverse individuals, groups, and institutions of society, and of equal opportunity of employment in the public relations profession.

We pledge:

To conduct ourselves professionally, with truth, accuracy, fairness, and responsibility to the public;

To improve our individual competence and advance the knowledge and proficiency of the profession through continuing research and education;

And to adhere to the articles of the Code of Professional Standards for the Practice of Public Relations as adopted by the the governing Assembly of the Society.

Code of Professional Standards for the Practice of Public Relations

These articles have been adopted by the Public Relations Society of America to promote and maintain high standards of public service and ethical conduct among its members.

1. A member shall conduct his or her professional life in accord with the **public interest.**

2. A member shall exemplify high standards of **honesty and integrity** while carrying out dual obligations to a client or employer and to the democratic process.

3. A member shall **deal fairly** with the public, with past or present clients or employers, and with fellow practitioners, giving due respect to the ideal of free inquiry and to the opinions of others.

4. A member shall adhere to the highest standards of **accuracy and truth,** avoiding extravagant claims or unfair comparisons and giving credit for ideas and words borrowed from others.

5. A member shall not knowingly disseminate **false or misleading information** and shall act promptly to correct erroneous communications for which he or she is responsible.

6. A member shall not engage in any practice which has the purpose of **corrupting** the integrity of channels of communications or the processes of government.

7. A member shall be prepared to **identify publicly** the name of the client or employer on whose behalf any public communication is made.

8. A member shall not use any individual or organization professing to serve or represent an announced cause, or professing to be independent or unbiased, but actually serving another or **undisclosed interest.**

9. A member shall **not guarantee the achievement** of specified results beyond the member's direct control.

10. A member shall **not represent conflicting** or competing interests without the express consent of those concerned, given after a full disclosure of the facts.

11. A member shall not place himself or herself in a position where the member's **personal interest is or may be in conflict** with an obligation to an employer or client, or others, without full disclosure of such interests to all involved.

12. A member shall **not accept fees, commissions, gifts or any other consideration** from anyone except clients or employers for whom services are performed without their express consent, given after full disclosure of the facts.

13. A member shall scrupulously safeguard the **confidences and privacy rights** of present, former, and prospective clients or employers.

14. A member shall not intentionally **damage the professional reputation** or practice of another practitioner.

15. If a member has evidence that another member has been guilty of unethical, illegal, or unfair practices, including those in violation of this Code, the member is obligated to present the information promptly to the proper authorities of the Society for action in accordance with the procedure set forth in Article XII of the Bylaws.

Reprinted with permission of Public Relations Society of America

The Importance of Good Writing

Public relations practitioners must be good writers. In fact, some people would contend that public relations practitioners must be excellent writers because much of their material is sent to critical producers and editors—and to decision makers within their companies. Practitioners must be able to adopt different styles and tones when writing. In the morning they may write a general-interest news release and in the afternoon, a speech in the language of the company president.

Much of public relations writing is grounded in journalistic writing. Many mass communications programs require public relations students to take media writing courses to learn the inverted pyramid and other formats. The courses also teach the fundamentals of grammar, punctuation, and style, and they stress the need for clear, concise, accurate writing that interests and attracts targeted audiences.

Informational vs. Persuasive Writing

Public relations practitioners generally divide writing into two categories: informational and persuasive. The company's objective will determine the tone of the writing.

Informational writing is just what it says: It presents materials in a straightforward, factual manner—just like in journalistic writing. A brochure can be informational, simply listing an organization's history, services, address, and telephone number. A brochure may give specifics about an upcoming program.

Persuasive writing clearly pitches a particular point of view. Some public relations tools are deliberately persuasive. A direct mail letter to university alumni will try to persuade them to donate to endowed professorships. A public service announcement on radio will encourage listeners to donate canned goods to the local food bank.

Persuasive writing follows the tenets of good writing: accuracy, clarity, and conciseness. A brochure can be persuasive and still be informational, using facts and graphics to portray positively the company's position. Figure 12.1 on page 302 shows examples of brochures.

Most public relations writing adheres to journalism standards of fairness and impartiality. Experienced public relations practitioners know that arguments explained factually will have more impact than those that are biased and long-winded.

Considering Audiences or Publics

Just as in any other mass communication field, public relations practitioners must consider their audiences, or—to use the public relations lingo—"publics." The publics are the people who will be reading their news releases or viewing their video news releases. They may be employees, customers, other businesses, town residents, lawmakers, reporters, or officials in local, state, or federal government agencies. Public relations practitioners must identify and know which publics are important to their organization.

FIGURE 12.1 *Examples of Brochures*

Reprinted with permission of the University of North Carolina, General Alumni Association, *left;* the Nuclear Enery Institute, *center;* and the Arts Center in Carrboro/Designer Derrick Ivey, *right.*

Imagine you are the public information director for a university system that is planning a capital campaign to raise funds for new buildings. The university administration has set a goal of $120 million. In planning a public relations campaign, you would have to consider the university's publics: alumni, faculty members, staff members, students, students' parents, potential students, donors, legislature (if the university is public or state supported), the general public, and the media. Out of that list, you might identify five key or important publics.

Practitioners use research such as informal surveys or focus groups as discussed in Chapter 2 to learn about their important publics. Specifically, practitioners need to know how they get information. Then they can decide which media, or communications tools, are most effective in reaching publics. And they can decide the tone and style of the message.

For example, in Chapter 3 we had the example of the Amana Savings and Loan, which plans to open a fitness center in the old YMCA building next to corporate headquarters. The bank's corporate communications department is to make the announcement. The public relations manager decides to notify employees through the company newsletter. The day the newsletter is delivered, the public relations manager will hand-carry a news release to the local newspaper.

For the newsletter, the important public is employees. Its tone and structure are designed to aim information that is directly relevant to them:

```
Amana employees soon will be able to exercise daily at a
new fitness center the company will build next door to the
bank's headquarters on Sycamore Street.

    The bank will renovate the old YMCA building to provide
a convenient way for employees to remain physically fit,
says employee manager Kay Barnes. Employees will have to
get a fitness privilege card but will not be charged to use
the center.

    The estimated cost of the project is $1 million.
```

The release to the local newspaper must take a broader angle and discuss the impact on the community.

Amana Savings and Loan will renovate the old YMCA building on Sycamore Street into a fitness center for employees. The work is expected to be completed within six months.

The project, estimated at $1 million, will rehabilitate prime downtown space that has been empty for a year. The YMCA moved into a larger building last summer.

The center next door to company headquarters will provide a convenient way for employees to remain physically fit, says employee manager Kay Barnes. Employees will have to get a fitness privilege card but will not be charged to use the center.

The Media as a Public

An important public for any public relations practitioner is the media. Practitioners must know the media. They must know the media's audiences, formats, and content. They must convince the media to use the information. Through newspapers, magazines, radio and television stations, specialty publications, and other media, the practitioner reaches other publics.

The Role of Media Lists

Media lists are necessary equipment for public relations. Developing a media list can be time-consuming. A media list should include the name of the reporter, editor, or producer; title; address; telephone number; fax number; and useful information, such as videotape requirements, kinds of stories considered, and deadlines. Information should be updated every three months.

Obviously, media lists provide the addresses for mailing news releases. But many practitioners use their media lists to keep track of their media contacts. Reporters and editors are notorious for moving every few years to different jobs in different locations. Practitioners can also note on the media list when they have called to pitch a story idea, or even personal tidbits such as the reporters' children or favorite hobby. Such knowledge serves as an ice-breaker or a friendly way to wrap up a conversation.

Apart from media lists, most practitioners keep media logs. They note when a reporter called, the media outlet represented, the story or summary of questions, and who responded. The log can be a quantitative way to assess public relations efforts.

The Contents of Media Kits

Many organizations, whether major companies or nonprofit groups, produce materials for media kits. Among the standard pieces are fact sheets, backgrounders, news releases, and reprints of articles about the organization. Each may be subdivided further. A financial institution may have fact sheets on services such as checking accounts, savings accounts, specialty retail programs, student loans, home mortgage or equity plans, or its divisions, such as retail, bank cards, or trust services.

Once the basic pieces are developed, a practitioner can build a media kit depending upon audience need. A reporter new to the financial services beat would get a package with backgrounders, fact sheets, the most recent annual report, the latest news release on company earnings, and any other information the public relations manager believes to be educational. When the bank announces a new retail service, fact sheets on the other services would be included in media kits distributed at a news conference.

The pieces together are called collateral pieces; that is, they fit together with a similar look. The look or image of these pieces represents that of the company. The American Heart Association in 1992 hired a public relations firm to upgrade its image. The AHA wanted its media pieces and other communications tools to have a similar, identifiable look using a single "one heart" logo. Previously the logo had been used randomly on pieces. The redesign gave AHA a more streamlined, consistent look, as shown in the following figure. The flame blows to the right, the type face is modern, and the logo is used on the right side of collateral pieces. The new AHA look offers greater unity, clarity, and visual harmony.

Printed Communications Tools

As discussed earlier, public relations practitioners have many ways they can reach their important audiences. Some are used more often than others. The

FIGURE 12.2   *American Heart Association brochures. The old design is on the left, the new on the right.*

Reprinted with permission from the American Heart Association.

more commonly used ones, and those that require skilled writers, are discussed here.

News Releases

News releases, such as those that follow, provide timely information to media. They may announce a promotion or staff change; a service or product; new information, such as the effects of legislation or the results of a survey; an upcoming event; or community service, such as a new scholarship program. Some news releases, especially those concerning events, are presented in the form of media advisories.

News Release

FOR RELEASE:
5 P.M. EST, TUESDAY
FEBRUARY 28, 1995

CONTACT:
AHA HEALTH & SCIENCE NEWS
(214) 706-1173 OR 706-1396
NR 95-4263 (CIRC/KURNIK)*

AHA journal report:

TPA Most Effective in Evening, While More Heart Attacks Occur in Morning

DALLAS, March 1—The clot-busting drug TPA has a "circadian" pattern of effectiveness, according to a new study. This widely used therapy for heart attacks is most successful in the evening hours—a time when heart attacks are less likely to occur.

Scientists have known for several years that heart attacks happen more commonly in the morning hours from 6 until noon partly due to an increased tendency to form blood clots during that period of time. Circadian rhythms follow the 24-hour cycle of the earth's rotation.

"That made me wonder if the clot-dissolving medications we give to heart attack patients are less effective in the morning and more effective in the evening," says Peter B. Kurnik, M.D., author of the study appearing in today's (March 1) issue of the American Heart Association journal *Circulation*.

Although that's exactly what he found, Kurnik emphasizes that anyone who thinks they might be having a heart attack should not wait until the afternoon to seek treatment.

"No matter what time the heart attack occurs, it's essential that TPA or some other therapy be given as soon as possible," emphasizes Kurnik, associate professor of medicine at the Robert Wood Johnson Medical School and director of the cardiac catherization laboratory at Cooper Hospital, Camden, N.J.

His results were drawn from an analysis of 692 patients who received recombinant TPA within six hours after the onset of chest pain. All the patients underwent catherization within 90 minutes of treatment to assess whether TPA had opened the blocked coronary arteries.

Kurnik found the 90-minute "patency" rate was much higher in heart attack patients who underwent TPA therapy between noon and midnight than in patients treated between midnight and noon. "There is a circadian variation in the ability of TPA to rapidly open coronary arteries, with highest efficacy between noon and midnight," the author concludes.

Reprinted with permission from the American Heart Association.

The Freedom Forum News Release
For immediate release: March 31, 1993

Fifteen High School Students Selected for Freedom Forum Rainbow Institute

BALTIMORE—Fifteen students representing the range of ethnic and racial diversity of the USA have been selected to participate in the second Rainbow Institute at the University of North Carolina (UNC) at Chapel Hill this summer. The Rainbow Institute is funded by a $60,000 grant from The Freedom Forum, the nation's largest foundation dedicated to free press and media issues.

The Freedom Forum, which funded the first Rainbow Institute in 1992, announced the 15 student winners at the American Society of Newspaper Editors (ASNE) annual convention here.

The Rainbow Institute is designed to develop students' interest in journalism as a career through a combination of classroom study, newsroom practice, work with professional mentors and scholarship support. Participants attend seminars on multicultural reporting, newswriting and editing.

The program also emphasizes the importance of diversity in both hiring and news coverage. Participants are sponsored by a newspaper editor who will also provide mentoring when the student returns to his or her hometown after the three weeks in Chapel Hill.

In the last week of the program, students will produce a newspaper to be inserted in UNC's award-winning campus paper, *The Daily Tar Heel*. Upon completion of the Institute, each student will receive a $1,000 scholarship for college work in journalism at the school of his or her choice.

"By exposing these bright, talented students to the newsroom environment, we see benefits for both the students and the newsroom," said Charles L. Overby, president and CEO of The Freedom Forum. "Students learn early on about journalism and the contribution they can make to the field while newsrooms get to see new enthusiastic, diverse talent that can be incorporated into their own newsrooms."

The Institute will be led by co-directors, Chuck Stone, syndicated columnist and a journalism professor at UNC, and Jan Elliott, associate professor of journalism at UNC. The Institute is coordinated by the American Society of Newspaper Editors (ASNE) and the UNC School of Journalism and Mass Communication.

News releases must contain some of the news values discussed in Chapter 3: prominence, timeliness, proximity, impact, and magnitude. They may also include conflict, oddity, or emotional impact. The lead should summarize the relevant information. The rest of the release should be organized in the inverted pyramid style of writing discussed in Chapter 4 and follow Associated Press style, which most news outlets use.

The practitioner's goal in sending a news release is to get publicity. But the practitioner must remember that news releases are uncontrolled; the final story is up to the reporter's and editor's discretion. Reporters may use the release as a basis for an expanded story, or they may use the news release as is and even give the writer a byline. Reporters, editors, and producers need news releases that are complete, accurate, newsworthy, appropriate for their audiences. Few will reject news releases in a ready-to-use format. The less research and rewriting a news organization must do, the more likely the news release will be used.

News releases should contain the public relations contact name, organization, organization address, organization phone number and PR contact's home phone number. The information goes in the upper left-hand corner. If the organization's address is readily visible on letterhead, it can be omitted. Under this information go the date and the headline, setting up the contents of the news release.

Often PR practitioners will include a contact name and telephone number within the text of the news release, usually at the end, to ensure that further information is available to interested publics if the news release is run verbatim.

Fact Sheets

Fact sheets are generally one page long and are designed to be read quickly. Information is given in an outline format that is quickly accessible to reporters and other publics. Information about the organization, a service, a product, or a special activity is highlighted in short segments.

An easy way to develop a fact sheet is to follow the news elements discussed in Chapter 3: who, what, when, where, how and why. A statewide children's forum is planning its annual fundraiser. The fact sheet would be organized:

Who:	The Children's Forum
What:	Annual fundraiser—a black-tie dinner and dance
When:	June 14
Where:	Downtowner Hotel
How:	Ticket prices $75 per individual for the dance and $150 for dinner and dance through the institute offices at 444-1234
Why:	To raise money for administrative and program costs.

Fact sheets should also contain the contact name, organization, and phone numbers for reporters and others who want additional information. When fact sheets are produced or updated, put the date at the bottom of the fact sheet to indicate how current the information is.

Facts sheets are also uncontrolled. Although media personnel have ready access to the information, they can use it any way they wish.

Backgrounders

Backgrounders are not news releases and do not carry news that has immediacy. A backgrounder supplements a news release and gives information a reporter may need about a company or its services. By having the additional information handy, a reporter may not have to call the public relations practitioner. A reporter new to the business beat can learn more about a company before meeting with officials.

Information in a backgrounder does not have to be attributed as it would in a news release. The source is considered to be the company. The information is organized by section, such as introduction, history, specific services, demographics, and other information. The sections enable readers to find specific information quickly.

Like a news release, a backgrounder must be well written and organized clearly and logically. Information must be accurate and should be updated periodically. The backgrounder should be professionally done, with no typos, improper punctuation, or misspelled words. It must also be accurate. Like news releases and fact sheets, a backgrounder is uncontrolled. The practitioner knows that anything in the backgrounder could appear in print or be heard on the airwaves and thus assimilated by the organization's publics.

Brochures

In writing and designing brochures, public relations practitioners are limited only by their talent, creativity, and budget. With the widespread use of desktop publishing, many more organizations, particularly nonprofits, can produce high-quality, good-looking brochures for little cost. The more work that is done in house, the more money saved—and the savings can be used for better paper stock or even for color printing.

In deciding whether to produce a brochure, a public relations practitioner must consider the cost. Brochures can be inexpensive, particularly if a writer is knowledgeable about desktop publishing or knows someone who is. The expense is added for color, photographs, size, paper quality, and other factors.

Questions to determine in writing a brochure are these:

• Is the brochure persuasive or informative? If the brochure's primary role is to persuade, it will be written with emotional language, comparisons, and familiar concepts. If informative, material will be to the point and language straightforward.

• Who is the audience? Whether the audience is specialized or general will determine the level of language used.

• Will the brochure be read and thrown away or saved? Deciding how it will be used will affect the cost and design.

• Will the brochure be a stand-alone piece, such as those in a display rack at a state's welcome station, or a collateral piece in a media kit? A stand-alone brochure must be complete because it cannot rely on information in other pieces that would accompany a collateral piece.

• What is the appropriate format? If the brochure is a self-mailer, it will have to have an address space or fit in envelopes of a certain size. The practitioner and a graphics designer will have to determine the size, the number of folds or pages, and how the brochure will open. Information has to be arranged logically, and decisions have to be made on artwork, such as photographs, and on graphic elements and white space.

Brochure copy should be short. Publics are looking for a quick read. Each panel should stand alone, and copy shouldn't jump from one panel to the next.

Brochures are appealing to PR practitioners because they are controlled messages. The practitioner has the final say-so on copy and design. No one can change the content or wording; the only uncontrolled aspect is placement, for example, whether brochures are left at a doctor's office to be displayed or are given to volunteers to distribute. The concerns are visibility of the brochure rack and whether all brochures are handed out.

Newsletters

Some public relations practitioners debate the effectiveness of newsletters. They contend that they can be time consuming and costly to produce and that few people read them. But newsletters are a primary method used by organizations to communicate with publics, particularly employees and donors. And they are controlled: practitioners determine copy content and page design.

The biggest problem with newsletters is that many are deadly dull. They contain column after column of information. Few headlines break up copy, and few photographs or graphic elements enliven the page. But newsletters can be fun—and even enlightening, informative, and entertaining. They need strong, concise, appealing writing and good design. Design can attract readers, but good writing will keep them.

Short articles, bulleted lists, charts, and graphs can disseminate information quickly. Newsletters also can be produced quickly and rather cheaply with desktop publishing systems. They can be quick-printed or even photocopied and folded in the office.

Newsletters use news style and feature style in writing. Writing for newsletters is not different from writing for other media. Writers have to be clear about purpose, objectives, and audiences. More articles can have a beginning, middle, and end—not just organized in inverted pyramid format. Articles generally will be brief.

As for layout, most newsletters are formatted, like the example in Figure 12.3 on page 314. The president's column, personnel tidbits, safety tips, donor lists, whom to call with problems, and other regular features appear consistently on the same page. Consistency gives readers familiarity, like knowing where the weather map and editorial page are in the local newspaper, and makes them comfortable with the publication. They also can find quickly the facts that most interest them.

Generally the public relations person or someone in employee communications writes the newsletter and sends it out to be printed. Some companies use freelancers to write and lay out their newsletters. The in-house person serves as the editor, assigning and editing stories.

Information for newsletters comes from other newsletters, employees, managers, news events, industry happenings, or seasonal topics. People within the organization or company may be reporters, submitting information from their departments. The only drawback is the editor's dependence on others to generate copy. The editor may find it easier to call and solicit story ideas rather than rely on volunteer reporters. The editor will then write the stories.

Speeches

Many people dread the thought of getting up in front of a crowd and giving a speech. The public relations practitioner who has to write a speech may be relieved that she doesn't have to deliver it, but the task of writing a speech for someone else can be daunting. Speeches are controlled, as they are delivered, but speakers must remember that they may be easy marks afterward for people who may have unflattering questions.

Speeches are not easy to write. They are needed for a variety of reasons: to educate, to state a position or advocate a certain belief, to praise some-

FIGURE 12.3 *An In-House Newsletter*

one's achievement, to entertain, to highlight a special occasion, to establish rapport. Each one requires a special format and writing style. The speech reprint on pages 315–318 was written in a style appropriate for the speech's audience, the National Press Club, and for its speaker, Eugene Roberts of the *New York Times*.

Nothing Succeeds Like Substance

My first newspaper job was the *Goldsboro News-Argus,* which is, for the ill-informed, the leading newspaper in Wayne County, North Carolina. It then had a circulation of 9,000. I wrote its farm column, "Rambling in Rural Wayne." Farmers summoned me to the scene whenever there was a significant farming event.

I wrote, for example about the first farmer of the season to transplant tobacco plants from the seed bed to the field, and about the season's first cotton blossom. I clucked over farmers' wives who made the county's best strawberry preserves and pickled watermelon rind; and they, in turn, clucked over me. I wrote of volatile tobacco prices, of hailstorms and drought. I once wrote about a sweet potato that looked like Gen. Charles de Gaulle.

Because I was linked closely to events that were important to farm families, I—and what I wrote—became memorable to readers in a way that I never was, before or since.

I was reminded vividly of this more than a decade after I left the *News-Argus* and the "Rambling in Rural Wayne" column. It was in 1968 during the Tet offensive, when I was a war correspondent for the *New York Times* in Vietnam.

I heard vague reports of trouble in Hue. I made my way there by truck and helicopter and found that the Marines were surrounded and held only two blocks of the city. The Viet Cong and the North Vietnamese forces held on to the rest. Each day after the Marines were reinforced by fresh units, they retook two or three blocks of the city, only to lose most of it again during the night to enemy troops.

It took about 10 days for the Marines to get 10 blocks or so from their headquarters compound. When they did, they found several American advisors who had been hiding under a house since the night the enemy overran the city. They had little water, even less food, and were hanging on by their nerve ends when the Marines broke through.

The Marines took the survivors to the headquarters compound and, to give them a sense of security, put them in the safest place they could find—a bunker dug deep into the center of the compound. I heard about the survivors and went to interview them.

"My name is Gene Roberts," I said. "I'm with the *New York Times.* I've come to get your story."

Out of the darkness came a voice, and it said: "Hey, did you ever write the 'Rambling in Rural Wayne' column for the *Goldsboro News-Argus?*"

I learned valuable lessons from the *News-Argus* and my tobacco farmer readers. I learned never to underestimate readers. They can laugh with you at the Charles de Gaulle sweet potato stories, but they expect depth when stories arise that are important to them. I learned that if tobacco prices were going up or down there was no limit to their demand for detail. And when the government banned, as it once did, a very productive variety of tobacco seed, no amount of coverage was too great. I could have written the journalistic equivalent of "War and Peace" and the farmers would have read it.

I wish some of today's publishing executives had been out in the tobacco rows with me. They would have learned that formula and slickness cannot substitute for substantive news coverage.

It's interesting to note that when my old boss, John S. Knight, received the National Press Club's Fourth Estate Award 17 years ago, he reflected on the importance of giving readers plenitude of solid news coverage. He reminisced, for example, about how he won the newspaper war in Akron, Ohio, and with the *Beacon Journal* laid the cornerstone of what would become first Knight Newspapers and then Knight-Ridder, Inc. His strategy was simple: print more news than the opposition. "Too many publishers have forgotten that injunction today," Jack Knight told the club in 1976.

He was right then. And 17 years later, far more publishers have forgotten that it was the most substantive newspaper that became dominant in one competitive town after another: in New York, for example, and Phila-

delphia, Boston, Washington, Chicago, Dallas and Miami.

Today, as competition diminishes and disappears, many newspapers seem to be in a race to see which can be the most shortsighted and superficial. We are relying too much—far too much—on weather maps, charts, graphs, briefs, and color.

If we had looked upon these devices as nothing more, or less, than desirable improvements, then our papers would have been all the richer for the additions. But in far too many newspapers, we introduced these devices while slashing newsroom budgets and newsholes. The result, all too often, has been that instead of becoming *additions* to news coverage, the devices have become *substitutes* for news coverage. And this, in a word, is folly.

We, of course, introduced many devices in order to reach out to marginal readers and non-readers. This was good. But when we started cutting back on substance, we put serious, devoted readers at risk by becoming less essential to them. And this was, and is, a very bad tradeoff. I think, quite simply, that we are imperiling newspapers in the name of saving them.

Not only is this trend weakening our hold on to the most loyal readers, it is causing long-term confusion and instability on our staffs, which further threaten our readership. Evidence of this abounds.

Recently, I talked to a newspaper consultant who estimated that he had given advice to more than 100 newsrooms in the past two years. The consultant found a common problem at almost every paper. The mid-level tier of editors seemed traumatized.

The problem? Lack of resources. The mid-level editors didn't think it was possible to perform at an acceptable standard given the resources at their disposal.

You could go to my editors' meeting in the past three or four years and encounter widespread angst. And not meetings of mid-level editors. Top editors.

Reporters are also reeling. Let me tell you just one story. Eighteen months ago, Susumu Shimoyama came here from Japan to study investigative reporting. His plan was to seek out some of the country's best investigative reporters and do a paper on how they practiced their craft. But except at a bare handful of papers, he found it difficult to find reporters who were spending time on projects. Some investigative reporters had been reassigned. Some were leaving journalism. All gave the same reason. Their newspapers had lost interest in in-depth reporting.

"I interviewed quite a number of investigative reporters in this country for this project," Susumu later wrote. "There was one common word with which some of them described themselves in spite of themselves. That was 'dinosaur.'"

Susumu abandoned his original plan. Instead, he did a paper titled,

"The Demise of Investigative Journalism in American Newspapers."

Hopefully, the gap between what Susumu expected to find and what he actually found led him to overstate the problem. I hope and believe that. But I wouldn't bet the farm on it.

But whether or not investigative reporting is threatened with extinction, it is, without question, seriously battered. So are many other forms of substantive reporting, including steady persistent coverage of news beats and subject areas.

Much of the newsroom cutting was done in the name of recession-related downsizing, although some companies say that the downsizing is permanent. But the recession is only part of the problem. The real problem is that we're further along in concentration of newspaper ownership and incorporation.

We're now in the second and third generation of professional corporate managers who are judged and compensated on the profits they generate during their tenure, not on what they do to guarantee the survival of newspapers. It should be noted that even in the worst of the recession, average operating profits, as a percentage of revenue, were in the 14 percent to 15 percent range for publicly held newspapers. Many basic American industries never reach that level of profit even in the best of times. And some newspaper companies reached those levels in recessionary times by mortgaging the future, by stripping away the glue that binds our most loyal readers to our papers.

Just how bleak is the situation? Scary to be sure, but not hopeless if corporations become aware that there is no security in superficiality and here and there, thankfully, are newspapers—a distinct minority—that understand this and are riding out the recession without shortchanging their readers. And there are executives on still other newspapers who are beginning to worry about what they are doing to the future of their papers by focusing on short-term, rather than long-term damage.

Let us hope there is enough understanding to produce a strong counter-movement for substance and continuity. Let us hope that more executives learn what some of us were taught in the streets and fields where the readers are—that you might get a large audience by being a quick, superficial read, but not an intense, dedicated audience.

And journalistic history is, of course, littered with the corpses of large-circulation newspapers that failed to make long-term and lasting reader relationships and, thus, were viewed as dispensable by their readers and consequently, by their advertisers.

Eugene L. Roberts Jr., managing editor of the *New York Times*. He is former executive editor of the *Philadelphia Inquirer,* taught at the University of Maryland College of Journalism, and was an AJR senior editor. He gave this speech at the National Press Club after receiving its Fourth Estate Award. Reprinted by permission of the author.

Primary Considerations

Writing a speech is like other mass communications writing. First the writer must have a subject and a purpose or reason for giving the speech. Then comes the audience. Anyone writing a speech must know the audience; what it already knows about the subject and whether it is likely to favor, oppose, or be undecided about the subject. Knowing the audience will determine the approach to the subject and how to best illustrate it.

A writer must create a speech that fits the speaker's way of talking and delivery. The style, however, must fit the audience's level of understanding and interest. The writer must use speech patterns that are suitable for the audience. For most audiences, the best bet is to use simple, precise language as is discussed in Chapter 5. Simple language will also help the speaker avoid stumbling.

Preparation and research are important. You are asked to write a speech on the benefits of the state's community college system. The speaker is the chief executive officer of your company, who is a member of the state's community college board. An interview with the CEO will give you an idea of his approach and what issues are most important. A phone call to the public relations officer for the local community college will add current numbers and perhaps anecdotes of student successes.

Beginning, Middle, and End

Once you know your audience, are sure of your subject, and have completed research, then you have to put forth ideas in well-organized format. Like a news feature, a speech will have an introduction (that's where all the jokes come), a middle, and an end. The opening and closing phrases of a speech often stay with an audience for years.

The introduction is the attention-getter, just like the lead. The speaker has the chance to establish rapport and to set up what the audience will hear. The introduction can be an anecdote, a question, a statement stressing the importance of the subject, or a striking or structured statement.

The main points will come in the body. Speech writers may help listeners follow the points by listing them: one, two, three. The conclusion reviews and summarizes the points. Sometimes a speaker will make a call to action. Often the most memorable and inspirational quotes come at the end.

Speech Formats

Speech writers generally follow four basic speech structures:

- *Supporting a generalization.* Here the speaker states the generalization, then offers supporting evidence, such as examples and anecdotes. You tell them what you are going to tell them, tell them, and tell them what you told them. For example, the introduction states that heart disease is the largest single killer of women in this country. The body of the speech discusses how many women die each year, the risk factors, and how to lower the risk factors and other causes of death. The end reminds listeners that heart disease is the greatest killer and calls upon women to take steps to reduce their risks.

- *Key words.* A speech is organized around two or three key words that are easy to follow or remember. The key words are part of the introduction, and the speaker repeats and expands each to achieve unity in the speech. The introduction may state that smoking, stress, and fat are contributors to heart disease. The key words are "smoking," "stress," and "fat." The body of the speech would talk about each, and the end would remind people to try to divest their lives of the risk factors.

• *Question and answer (Q & A).* This format leads listeners step by step through the speech by setting up the expectation of an answer. The Q&A also follows a logical format, building on the speaker's theme or topic by using questions to move through the specific points. The format is good for technical topics. A speech in a Q&A format might be written this way:

```
In the next 15 minutes a woman will die of heart disease.
That's almost 100 women every day. So many deaths wouldn't
happen if more women considered the risk factors associated
with heart disease.
```

What is heart disease? Answer.

What are risk factors? Answer.

Why are women susceptible? Answer.

How can women reduce risk factors? Answer.

How can you get more information? Answer.

• *Problem solving.* Here a speaker states the problem, analyzes it and suggests solutions. In discussing solutions, the speaker offers those that would solve the problem, considers would-be solutions, and nixes those that wouldn't work. At the end of the speech, the speaker restates the problem, then reinforces the viable solution or solutions. The speech would follow this format:

```
Heart disease is the largest single killer of women, but
the risks can be reduced.
     Heart disease occurs when . . .
     Risks can be reduced when . . .
     The best solutions are . . .
     Summarize
```

Additional Tips

After you have completed the speech, read it aloud. Make sure the language is simple, the writing flows, the structure is appropriate, and the audience is addressed. Determine whether visuals are needed. Visuals should supplement what the speaker is saying and not detract from it. The speaker should be comfortable using visuals and should talk to the audience, not the screen. If possible, someone other than the speaker should be responsible for operating the equipment.

As a public relations practitioner, remember that the speech will come back to you for changes and rewriting, perhaps several times. That's okay. One public relations practitioner, recalling a speech she wrote for the company president, said she agonized over style and finally submitted a draft. A few days later it came back, completely revised and retyped. "When I read through the 10 pages, I saw one complete sentence that was my own," she said. "But the note from the CEO said, 'Great work!'"

Public Relations and Advertising

As the public relations director for your town's historical society, you want to let many publics know about plans for the society's annual Christmas tour of homes. To send a controlled message to many audiences, you decide to place an ad in the local newspaper. You would write the copy, and you might also solicit a local company to underwrite the cost and give it credit within the ad copy.

Advertising gives organizations the opportunity to produce a controlled message in both copy and placement. In-house staff or freelancers determine the message, then write and design the ad. The organization buys space in a specific magazine or section of the newspaper, or in air time at a certain hour. The ad is printed or broadcast just as the organization produced it.

Most advertising is produced in advertising or marketing departments within large companies. Public relations practitioners are rarely involved in advertising except when their company produces image advertisements. A nonprofit organization may have just one person who does all public relations and advertising work. Advertising is discussed further in Chapter 13.

Image Advertising

Organizations large and small want a positive image before their audiences. The company that pays for the historical society's ad might win compliments from some townspeople. Organizations generate good feelings when they support recycling or support educational projects such as school science fairs. Even ads for products can create positive images. Think about Michelin tire ads that show a baby sitting in the middle of the tire. The message implies that Michelin is concerned about your family's welfare because "so much is riding on your tires." The combination of emotional appeal and safety information creates a powerful, positive message about Michelin.

Image advertising in a larger organization may be done by the PR practitioner in conjunction with the marketing department. Both may develop the objective of the advertisement. The practitioner may have input on ad copy, while the marketing department may buy the advertising space in selected media.

If you are writing an image ad, consider these rules, some of which repeat the rules of good writing you learned in Chapter 5:

- Recognize the importance of headlines. They need to be catchy and attract readers, just like the lead on a news release.
- Use senses and emotions. Perceptions of institutions rarely are based on logic alone.
- Be familiar with the audience. Use "we" rather than the company name. Use "you" rather "consumers" or "customers."
- Write the way you talk.
- Use simple language.
- Use the active voice and present tense if possible with verbs.
- Vary sentence length, and use some short sentences.
- Use good punctuation and grammar.
- Don't be trite or cute.

Communications Planning

To implement a public relations campaign, practitioners need a plan. Plans are written during the second public relations stage, discussed earlier in the chapter. Plans are critical because they guide practitioners about their publics, communications tools, and timing. Once research is completed, practitioners can set out to match the types of communications tools with audiences.

Making the Match

Matching specific communications tools to audiences is one job of the public relations practitioner. Go back to the example of the university capital campaign and the specific publics. As the public relations director, you would consider which media or tools would reach your targeted groups. You might decide to produce a general information brochure that would go to all publics. But for individual publics, you might start a list like this:

- *Alumni.* Direct mail letters, news releases or news features to alumni publications, public service announcements to major radio and television stations in states where large numbers of alumni live, speeches and presentations to alumni club meetings, news releases and fact sheets to statewide media.

- *Faculty members.* News releases, feature releases, and fact sheets to campus publications; direct mail; speeches and audiovisual presentations.

- *Students.* PSAs to popular radio stations; news releases, feature releases, and fact sheets to student publications; speeches and audiovisual presentations; advertisements in campus media.

If you continued the list, you probably would find that some communications tools serve the same publics. Different publics read newspapers and direct mail letters, watch television, and attend civic meetings. Each public has its own interests and language. The focus of the public relations message will vary depending upon the audience.

For example, the direct mail letters to faculty members and alumni would carry the same message of the need for donations and would make a pitch for a contribution. But the faculty letter would explain how new buildings would add classrooms, laboratories, and offices—all to the benefit of teaching. The alumni letter would discuss how new buildings would benefit the university's reputation, thereby maintain the strength of their degrees.

Communications Tools: Controlled and Uncontrolled

When considering communications tools, a public relations practitioner must know whether each is controlled or uncontrolled. In a brochure, the practitioner does the writing and coordinates printing, thereby having control over the final message that goes to publics. The writer has no control over the final format of a news release. Once the release is sent, the final message is determined by an editor or news producer.

Public relations practitioners need a balance. Any good communications plan mixes controlled and uncontrolled tools. That way the company is assured that in some cases the message will reach audiences in exactly the way staff want it written and positioned. To achieve balance, a public relations manager might opt for a news release, which would be uncontrolled for the final message and for whether or when it is used; a flyer or brochure, controlled for content and to some extent placement if used as a direct mail piece; and a videotaped public service announcement, controlled for message but not for when it is aired.

Much of the mix may depend on cost. News releases are fairly inexpensive to produce and distribute, despite postal rate increases. Brochures can be produced cheaply or at great cost, depending upon paper quality, color, photographs, and size. Video public service announcements are expensive. A few companies have in-house production capability and will produce PSAs and video news releases for themselves. On occasion they will do PSAs as donated work for nonprofit organizations. A 30-second PSA can cost as much as $20,000 to produce.

Writing a Plan for a Specific Occasion

Writing a plan requires thinking and often experience. Practitioners often begin by brainstorming or listing random ideas for communicating with publics. Then they start refining, based on time constraints, cost of producing materials, and company style. The final plan includes a statement of the issue or problem, campaign objectives, strategies for reaching objectives, and specific actions. Specific actions are assigned deadlines and an individual responsible for carrying out each action.

Think about the earlier example of the bank that is changing its checking service. Your role as the public relations person is to support the paid advertising done by the marketing department. Research says you need to target newcomers to town, existing customers who may switch type of account, and potential customers who may find the account more attractive than what their bank offers. You decide in the planning stage to develop a brochure that can be mailed to newcomers and to customers in their bank statements. You also want to distribute news releases to area media to attract other nonbank customers.

Your plan would consider the time frame. The service will be introduced in three months. Brochure production takes time, so that is first on the to-do list. The news release will be done later. Your written plan looks like this:

Communications Plan for No-Frills Checking Service

Issue: First City Bank will introduce a new checking service in three months. It will offer customers free checking on balances of $100 or more or if they keep $100 in a savings account. The first 200 checks will be free.

Objective: To attract customers to the service by positioning it as a less expensive way to maintain a checking account, particularly for people who don't need lots of attached services, like credit cards.

Strategy: Use communications tools that will reach newcomers, existing customers and nonbank customers.

Actions:

Date	Action	Responsibility
May 1	Develop outline and content for the brochure	PR manager
May 5	Hire a writer and designer	PR manager
May 23	First draft of brochure copy	Freelance writer
May 24	Design for brochure complete	Freelance designer
May 28	Copy/design sent for approvals	PR manager
June 5	Final brochure complete	PR manager
June 7	Brochure to printer	PR staff
June 13	Brochure sent to account services to be stuffed in next check statement cycle	PR staff

June 15	Secure newcomers' names from chamber of commerce	PR staff
June 30	Mail brochure to newcomers	PR staff
July 1	Consider focus of local/statewide news release	PR manager
July 10	Complete draft of local/statewide news release	PR manager
July 20	Approvals returned on local/statewide news release	PR manager
July 25	Mail release to local and statewide media	PR staff
Aug.1	Checking service begins	

Broader Plans

Public relations departments generally follow a communications plan for the fiscal year. They begin work several months ahead of time, collecting objectives and goals from other departments that generate public relations activities. The overall plan would incorporate year-round actions as well as campaigns for specific services such the new checking account.

The year's communications plan can be lengthy. Parts of the plan are defined by internal and external audiences. Internal audiences include employees, stockholders, board members, and anyone who is involved in the organization's operation. External audiences include the general public, customers, the media, lobbyists, and lawmakers. Communications tools to reach each audience are defined and are included in a communications plan, just as in the checking account example.

Crisis Planning

No organization expects or wants a crisis, but plans must be made in the event a crisis occurs. The crisis could be as large as an oil spill or as small as an error in a newsletter. If any event negatively impacts audiences, an organization has a crisis.

A crisis plan can help an organization make lemonade out of lemons, says Joyce Fitzpatrick, senior vice president for Ruder-Finn, a major public relations firms in the United States. A crisis plan helps a company be prepared. Plans should be easily accessible and reviewed periodically.

Fitzpatrick notes that in a crisis plan, organizations should identify a specific spokesperson. If possible, the spokesperson should be someone who has been in a crisis before—and that person may not be the chief executive officer. Organizations should also establish a sequence of who will be informed first. Affected employees should hear about the crisis before they read about it in the media.

When the crisis occurs, Fitzpatrick advises the companies to respond within the first 24 hours. If the crisis is long-running, companies should set up a specific site and time each day for news conferences. The spokesperson should appear, even if there is no new development, and be ready to say when the company has new developments or information to share.

Wrap Up

This chapter is an introduction to the public relations field, its role, practitioners' responsibilities, and some communications tools. Students majoring in public relations will take specific courses on theory, case studies, and public relations writing. In each course, they will learn more about the field and its opportunities. At the core of each course will be the ability to write.

Public relations practitioners must be able to communicate quickly, accurately, and completely to be effective. They also must know their audiences. Public relations practitioners who can combine those two talents will be successful.

EXERCISES

1. You are the public relations officer for the Campus Literacy Program. You want to recruit more volunteers to serve as readers to children in the community.
   a. Identify the audience(s) you are trying to reach as potential volunteers.
   b. Knowing your audience interests and media usage, identify three communications tools you would use to reach each audience.
   c. What information would your audience(s) need to make a decision whether to volunteer? Make a list.
   d. How could you evaluate the success of your communications effort?

2. You are the public relations director for Bicycle World Equipment Co. You are to write a news release for the local newspaper based on the following information:

Bicycle World planning to sponsor bicycle safety clinics in the public schools that are located in Wayne County, the company headquarters. The clinics will be on two consecutive Saturdays from 10 a.m. to noon. Each of the county's six elementary schools will have the clinics. People who want to attend must call 555-3456 to register. The clinic is open to children 6-12 years of age. Each child must have a helmet.

Bicycle World staff members will check each child's bicycle for safe operation and indicate on a check-off list any equipment that needs repair. Children will be advised of good bicycle safety, such as wearing helmets, riding in bike lanes, using proper hand signals. Then each will be allowed to enter an obstacle which will test their riding proficiency. For example, as they ride down a "road," a dog may run out from between two cars. Children's reactions and reaction times will be monitored. After the road test, they will be briefed on what they did well and what they need to improve. At the end of the course, they will receive a certificate of accomplishment.

"We believe bicycle safety is crucial for children," said company President Dennis Lester. "With just a little guidance, children can learn habits and rules that could save their lives. Those of us in the bicycle business want to ensure that children who use our products do so competently and safely. We want them to enjoy bicycling as a sport they can continue into adulthood."

The clinics are free.

Bicycle World is a three-year-old company that produces bike frames, components, bike helmets,

clothing, and road guides to bicycle routes. Company
President Dennis Lester is a master rider and formed
the company to provide quality equipment to bicycle
enthusiasts.

3. From the above information, write a one-page fact sheet based on the bicycle clinics sponsored by Bicycle World Equipment Co. You would be the contact, 555–2345. The company's address is 67 W. Lane Blvd., Your town, Your zip code.

4. Bicycle World Company President Dennis Lester has been asked to speak to the local Girl Scout council about bike safety. The audience is girls 10–12 years of age. Develop an introduction that would attract them to the speech. Then write an outline of the information you would include when the actual speech is written.

5. Choose a nonprofit organization in your community. Contact the director about preparing a media kit for the organization. The kit could provide information about the organization itself or a special event. The kit would include a fact sheet; a backgrounder; a news release on a timely, relevant topic; a news feature about the organization or one of its services. Use existing materials on the organization as part of your research plus interviews with the director, staff members, and any users of the organization's services.

REFERENCES

Thomas Bivins, *Handbook for Public Relations Writing,* 2nd ed. Chicago: NTC Business Books, 1993.

Scott M. Cutlip, Allen H. Center and Glen H. Broom, *Effective Public Relations,* 7th ed. Englewood Cliffs, NJ: Prentice-Hall, 1994.

J. E. Grunig and Todd Hunt, *Managing Public Relations.* Fort Worth, TX: Harcourt Brace Jovanovich College Publishers, 1984.

Doug Newsom and Bob Carrell, *Public Relations Writing: Form and Style,* 3rd ed. Belmont, CA: Wadsworth Publishing, 1991.

Dennis L. Wilcox and Lawrence W. Nolte, *Public Relations Writing and Media Techniques,* 2nd ed. New York: HarperCollins College Publishers, 1995.

13

Advertising

Advertising is probably the first form of media writing that children notice. Some of our earliest memories are of advertising classics, such as the Campbell's Soup Kids singing "Mmm-mmm-good"; cereal elves chanting "Snap, Crackle, Pop, Rice Krispies"; or Mr. Whipple's whine, "Please don't squeeze the Charmin!"

Kids notice and respond to ads, often before they can talk. Toddlers dance for joy at the words "We're into Barbie"; they excitedly point at Ronald McDonald; and they "read" the golden arches as a sign for food even before they know their ABCs.

By combining color, sound, movement, symbols, and language, advertising creates some of the most powerful messages in our world today. Advertising was the first truly multimedia field and is often considered apart from other message forms. But like all media presentations, good advertising depends on good writing.

"Good advertising writers are writers first. They are personal writers—people who bring their own feelings and reactions to the product," observes Professor John Sweeney, former creative director for a major American advertising agency. "Good advertising slogans are some of the most effective communication available today. They have a concise, pithy, sensory quality that other writers would do well to study and adopt."

But clear, direct communication is and always has been required of ad writers, who are usually referred to as copy writers. Although many people think of ad writers as zany creative types—which they may be—copy writers primarily are just that: writers. Advertising copy writers learn to hook their audiences with the first sound or word of an ad. And as Sweeney says, other writers can benefit from studying their techniques.

This chapter will explain

- Advertising goals in the information age,
- What's in an ad,
- The process of writing for advertising,
- Guidelines for effective ad writing, and
- What all writers can learn from advertising.

By reaching these goals, the ad writer fulfills the goal of marketing, which is to sell the product or service.

Advertising in the Information Age

For more than 100 years, advertising worked this way: Advertising agencies wrote attractive ads for client businesses and placed those ads in places where many people would notice them. On occasion, advertisers planned ads for placement where likely customers would be reading or watching. For example, a Gold Medal Flour ad would go in a women's magazine near the recipe pages; an ad for a stock brokerage would be put in the newspaper near the Wall Street report; Ringling Brothers would advertise its circus on splashy billboards and later during prime-time broadcasts. But overall, early advertisers wanted to get the name of the advertiser in front of the public, as prominently and as often as possible.

This scattershot approach to advertising has changed. Because of the overwhelming number of new media and the changing media habits of audiences, advertisers now take each product and funnel product information to the people who are most likely to use it. In today's lean business environment, advertisers use traditional advertising in innovative ways: in a Prodigy online ad for Easter flowers that may be ordered by clicking on a bouquet in the ad, or in bright slogans painted on a stock car that beams sponsorship of a soft drink to all who watch the Daytona 500.

The goals of ad writers, regardless of medium, have remained constant over the years:

- To communicate availability of products to audiences,
- To communicate product benefits to audiences,

- To provide accessible information about products, and
- To communicate main ideas about products in a few words.

What's in an Ad?

Like other media, advertising is a field that is changing daily. But almost all advertisements are made by combining the same four elements:

1. A headline,
2. An illustration, which may be graphic (pictures) or dramatic,
3. Advertising text—from a few words to a few pages—describing the product, and
4. A signature or logo, usually at the close of the ad.

But simply putting these elements together will not create an advertisement. Advertisements that work must carefully select and intertwine these four elements. And all creation and selection is determined by a strategy.

In their book *The New How to Advertise,* advertising executives Kenneth Roman and Jane Maas list the elements of good advertising strategy.

A good ad will show solutions to a problem. If your problem is needing a heavy-duty vehicle, the advertiser's solution is Dodge Trucks. An advertiser posing the problem of scarce entertainment may propose—advertise, that is—a regional soccer team as a solution.

Effective ads aim for target audiences. Savvy advertisers identify potential groups of customers and learn about the habits of those groups. They gain a portrait of their targeted audience. The advertiser selling trucks will talk with and survey people who, for example, live on farms or do construction work to find out what types of media they consume and what they value in a vehicle.

Memorable ads focus on one key consumer benefit. Advertisers must tell consumers the single most compelling reason that a product is needed. A well-known ad for insecticide reads: "Raid kills bugs dead." Our truck advertiser sells a single benefit: "Dodge Trucks are ram tough."

Good advertising supports its claims with facts and background information. The Dodge dealer will cite the safety and longevity of its trucks and may interview a few satisfied owners.

Every good ad projects the tone, manner, and personality of the product. Through art, photos, and language, the mood of the product is conveyed. Viewers experience the product. For example, the tough truck is pictured hauling a load on a rocky wilderness road, while the language "ram tough" simulates swearing. The overall feel, rugged and strong, is designed to appeal to the target group.

Is Advertising Propaganda?

Some people think of advertising as propaganda—as distorted information designed to lead, or mislead, its audience. Propaganda is manipulative, and so is advertising, some people say.

Unlike most other forms of published writing, advertising is one-sided by its very nature; no one wants to spend his or her advertising budget extolling the benefits of the other guy's product. But the absence of other products from ads does not have to mean that an ad is unfairly biased if the information presented is accurate in and of itself.

"An advertisement is a known one-sided form, like a resumé," explains Professor John Sweeney. "It is not a sinister hiding of information; rather, it is a presentation of your best information."

Advertising writing has work to do; it substitutes for personal, face-to-face contact in the sales process. Like professional salespeople, advertisers deal with factual information and must never forget that they have a public responsibility. Once an advertiser loses public confidence in the accuracy of its claims, that confidence may not be recovered.

Presenting your best to the public, Sweeney explains, is a core value of advertising culture. A one-sided presentation need not be an unfair presentation, and understanding that aspect is part of being an effective professional, Sweeney says. He encourages advertisers to set ethical limits for themselves, adding, "We don't want billboards in the Grand Canyon."

Ethics in Advertising

Advertising that is less than ethical is not advertising; it is propaganda or huckstering or manipulation. Professional advertising writing is an accepted form of argument—a fair argument—and it abides by an ethical code. The Advertising Principles of American Business provide basic guidelines for advertisers that include truth, substantiation, taste, and decency. The code, shown here, demonstrates an overall concern with fairness and with public trust that most advertisers take seriously.

The Advertising Principles of American Business*

Truth
Advertising shall tell the truth, and shall reveal significant facts, the omission of which would mislead the public.

Substantiation
Advertising claims shall be substantiated by evidence in possession of the advertiser and advertising agency, prior to making such claims.

Comparisons
Advertising shall refrain from making false, misleading, or unsubstantiated statements or claims about a competitor or his products or services.

Bait Advertising
Advertising shall not offer products or services for sale unless such offer constitutes a bona fide effort to sell the advertised products or services and is not a device to switch consumers to other goods or services, usually higher priced.

Guarantees and Warranties
Advertising of guarantees and warranties shall be explicit, with suffi-cient information to apprise consumers of their principal terms and limitations or, when space or time restrictions preclude such disclosures, the advertisement should clearly reveal where the full text of the guarantee or warranty can be examined before purchase.

Price Claims
Advertising shall avoid price claims which are false or misleading, or savings claims which do not offer provable savings.

Testimonials
Advertising containing testimonials shall be limited to those of competent witnesses who are reflecting a real and honest opinion or experience.

Taste and Decency
Advertising shall be free of statements, illustrations or implications which are offensive to good taste or public decency.

*Adopted by the American Advertising Federation Board of Directors, March 2, 1984, San Antonio, TX. Reprinted with permission.

Advertisers are subject to many government rules and regulations. The Capital Council of Better Business Bureaus advises that all advertisers stay abreast of regulations through subscription services such as Do's and Don'ts in Advertising or the National Advertising Case Reports. Such subscription services are quite expensive and typically are used by large agencies or companies.

Advertising and Today's Audiences

The environment for advertising has changed tremendously in the past decade. New media and new products compete for audience attention, so that advertisers may no longer assume that mere publicity will lead to success. Today's advertisers must proceed with conscious, sophisticated attention to audiences and audience attitudes. Only through selecting likely audiences and streamlining ads for those groups can advertisers reach information-age consumers.

Before a writer sits down to write an ad, much direction may have been dictated and decided by clients. The writer needs to understand what goes into a marketing strategy, which in turn determines an ad concept.

Targeting Audiences

The process of identifying and communicating with specific audiences is often called targeting. Maybelline may "target" girls 13–15 as a likely audience for messages about a new tinted lip gloss. With the target group in mind, Maybelline's ad writers design messages that will appeal to young teens and place these ads in publications and time slots of which teens are likely consumers. Maybelline, for example, might discuss its new lip gloss with a favorite model in *Seventeen* magazine and between scenes on the show "Beverly Hills 90210."

Targeting is a necessity in an era of budget consciousness. Advertisers no longer can afford to waste funds by advertising to broad audiences that may contain only a few potential customers. To get maximum benefit from advertising dollars, advertisers select target audiences for specific products. Beer, tires, and trucks are advertised in sports sections and broadcasts; toys and sweet cereals are advertised with Saturday morning cartoons; and pain relievers, laxatives, and investments are sold with financial news.

Professional market research is used by major corporations to identify the best possible markets for particular ads. Cluster marketing attempts to impose some order on the new media-and-audience mix, dividing Americans into 40 or more subgroups, and predicting specific media behaviors, products, and services that each group is likely to use. Michael Weiss describes in his book *The Clustering of America* the nation's 40 neighborhood types. One cluster commonly used by advertisers is the "Blue Blood Estates" group. It reads the *New York Times* and watches David Letterman; smart advertisers will place ads for upscale products here. Educated viewers know that such products already are advertised in appropriate places; David Letterman's sponsors include many luxury cars such as Infiniti and Lexus, while ads for furs and jewelry abound in the *Times*.

Tom Burrell, chairman of Burrell Advertising in Chicago, recognizes the need for all communicators to address specific audiences. He was one of the country's first advertising executives to focus his clients' advertisements on the needs, attitudes, interests, and even behaviors of a single ethnic group, African Americans.

"The future is destined to be more complex, more complicated, more diverse and more segmented for media," Burrell predicts. He believes that the whole idea of mass marketing is dying and that agencies more and more will respond to the needs of specific consumer groups such as women, ethnic populations, seniors, urban dwellers, and rural residents.

Even a small advertiser can learn to select target audiences. What kinds of media do most of your customers or clients enjoy? What other products do they use and seek information about? If they are conscious of investments, you may want to advertise alongside ads for stocks and bonds—even if your product is silver polish.

Placement of Advertisements

Today's advertisers cannot afford to waste ad dollars on airing messages to irrelevant audiences; therefore Huggies, maker of disposable diapers and training pants, does not advertise in large newspapers or in general-interest magazines. Rather, the company advertises in magazines for parents; more specifically, it chooses magazines that appeal to a group that values their product and can afford it. Huggies' ads for its new product, Pull-Ups disposable training pants, appear in *Good Housekeeping* magazine (to reach mothers at home), *Parents* magazine (to reach conscientious parents of both genders working both in and outside the home) and *Working Mother* (to reach mothers with little time but with disposable income).

Once the Pull-Ups ads are placed where concerned parents will find them, writing does the rest. Pull-Ups are described with words that appeal to the audience with the headline "Big Kid confidence begins with Pull-Ups!" Because all loving parents want to raise a big kid with confidence, Huggies' mission is accomplished: Pull-Ups are held in mind as necessary for raising a quality kid.

For years, standard forms of advertising were limited to a few familiar media. Advertisers had access to audiences through television, radio, newspapers, magazines, billboards, and direct mail. Audiences for these forms were large and homogeneous: "middle America" for television, billboards, and general-circulation newspapers and magazines; "teen America" for radio and teen magazines; and "older Americans" for direct mail and specialty magazines.

Today, because the audience has fragmented into many small subpopulations, each subgroup uses only its own fractional mix of available media. At the same time, new media are being developed constantly. Advertisers now may use fax, voice mail, and online services, just to name a few newcomers. Much new advertising combines old and new methods. For example, a newspaper ad about vacations in the Bahamas offers fax brochures to anyone who calls in a fax number. As a next step, the ad offers to make reservations instantly by fax or phone.

The combined forces of new media development and audience fragmentation have created a world of opportunity for advertising communication. An advertiser of office supplies can reach area offices with an updated price list, communicating efficiently to fax numbers in local listings. A new tutoring service can reach pupils through a school's electronic mail system. The possibilities call for new creativity in ad design and in ad writing, which also must be specifically designed for audiences.

Targeting and the Writer

In all advertising, writing is the basis of targeting. An ad that is written in a dense or inappropriate style will be ignored, regardless where it appears. Copy writers, who write the words in advertisements, usually work with art directors to produce the final ad design, complete with graphics, photographs, and text.

Let's consider a copy writer who is directed to write an advertisement to sell a new CD by pop artist Barry White. Research shows that young black women, who are frequent buyers of compact disc recordings and music videos, like romantic music and prefer a select group of magazines and newspapers that cater to their interests. Ads would appear in *Essence, People,* and *Spin* magazines, as well as on the Black Entertainment Network, which shows African American music videos.

In advertising the new Barry White CD, the writer decides to appeal to young romantics. To reach that specific group, she could write ads describing White's voice in the words of *People* magazine: ". . . smooth as satin sheets and soothing as a hot-oil backrub." The art director would arrange for photography to illustrate the words. The final ad would combine both to create the sense of White's smooth and soothing voice. Garnering the small "young romantic" audience could increase sales of White's new CD by 5 to 10 percent, which would mean millions of dollars for the company. Remember: fame is not the goal of advertising; *sale* of the product is.

Copy writers have great pressure to keep advertising lean, direct, and on target so that no advertising words and minutes are wasted on an unlikely customer. This pressure affects the advertising writer at every point. The ad message must be structured as carefully as the placement. If an ad is directed to a specific audience, it needs to appear in the correct medium and to convey concepts immediately that are meaningful to the target group.

Here is effective ad writing pitched to its specific audience:

"I never worried too much about nutrition.

"Then, my doctor told me I was HIV positive.

"Now, I do everything I can to maintain my energy, strength, and quality of life."

The advertisement pictures a handsome, athletic man. The product is Advera, a nutrition supplement. The three written lines from the ad demonstrate how specific today's advertisements can be. For the most part, ads today strive not for mass communication but for complete communication with a particular group. The copy writer and art director work as a team, combining language and graphics in a powerful way to produce effective advertisements.

Advertising Writing: The Process

In reaching their audiences, ad writers go through the same process that other writers use: information gathering, thinking, listing, drafting, rewriting, sharing, and polishing. Following is an explanation of how each stage works in advertising.

Stage 1: Information Gathering

Ad writers write nothing until they have gathered information. They spend the time to do careful research in two major areas: research on the product and research on consumers.

First, advertising writers must do extensive product research. Say your product is TrimWalk, an in-home exerciser. The first research task is to use the product. See how it works and identify how you feel. Write down key words that describe your feelings: rejuvenated, energized, relaxed, pleasantly tired.

Second, talk with your client, the TrimWalk company, and read its information about the product, such as brochures and news articles. Search for all possible benefits of the product.

Third, talk with a variety of people about the TrimWalk. Among those who use the product, ask people how they like it, whether they would recommend it, and how it makes them feel. Ask nonusers if they would be interested, and why or why not. Strive for a mix of men and women with different backgrounds and different ages.

Sometimes, when there is strong competition from another company, you will want to do research on competing products. For example, to advertise effectively for Toyota, you might want to compare it with Honda, Toyota's biggest competitor. Take caution: Any comparison requires thorough research so that claims will be accurate and authentic. Most people who have driven a Honda would have to agree, for example, that a Honda has a smooth ride. A good advertising writer, rather than focusing on comfort, needs to make other arguments—those having to do with aesthetics or economy—but only after careful information gathering.

Stage 2: Thinking

The thinking stage begins with looking over notes, recalling sensory impressions, and summarizing who is in your audience and what will interest them.

Ponder all your information and develop an advertising strategy. You may want to state this strategy as a formal goal or objective, for example: Our goal is to sell more TrimWalks to older Americans.

With the objective stated, you may need to return to Stage 1 and add research on older American's needs and lifestyles and on their use of the media.

After further research, you decide that ads emphasizing health, vigor, and youthfulness will be created and that these ads will be placed in several magazines with large circulations among older Americans. Once these "thinking" decisions are made, you know the purpose and the audience of your message. You prepare to write by making lists.

Stage 3: Listing

In this stage, you make simple lists. First, list the important selling points—that is, facts that will entice the audience, older Americans, to consider TrimWalk. Your list of selling points might look like this:

1. TrimWalk is in your home, convenient for workouts at any time or in any weather.
2. TrimWalk is private; no one watches you exercise.
3. TrimWalk can be positioned so that you can watch television or listen to music while working out.
4. TrimWalk is safety inspected to guard against injury.
5. Regular use of TrimWalk leads to weight loss.
6. Regular use of TrimWalk leads to improved circulation.
7. Regular use of TrimWalk leads to improved skin and muscle tone.

All of these points need to be included somewhere in your ad. But before you begin to write, you must list which selling points are most compelling for your audience, and use those at the beginning to hook the reader. But to know the compelling selling points, you must also know your audience. Make another list, one of audience characteristics and goals. In preparation for the TrimWalk ad, the audience list could look like this:

1. Ages 60 and up, men and women.
2. Want high quality of life.
3. Concerned about physical problems.
4. Concerned about looking healthy and vigorous.
5. Concerned about weight control rather than weight loss.

Remember that your goal is to increase TrimWalk use by older Americans. You decide to focus on point 7 on your list of selling points, improved skin and muscle tone, because it will satisfy a primary goal of older Americans—looking healthy and vigorous, point 4 in the audience list.

You may need to make other lists to prepare you for the task of writing. For the TrimWalk ad, you might want to list some statistics on sales and satisfaction among older Americans, or some secondary health benefits. Such lists help you focus on the selling points that match with your audience, while at the same time clearing out clutter from competing information. Many facts surround any product, but good ads will feature only a few. With your information, your lists, and your goal defined, you are finally ready to write.

Stage 4: Drafting—As You Would Tell It

It is important to recall that this stage is called drafting rather than writing. Drafting is the stage of writing in which thoughts on a subject are recorded. For ad writing, as for most forms of media writing, a good idea is to "talk" the information—to tell it in the same words you would use in talking with a friend.

Few of us, when talking, use extended introductions to topics. So it is with ads—they get straight to the point. What would you say to an older friend about TrimWalk?

"Want to look as fit as you feel? Try taking a walk—in your sitting room."

These first words, what you would say first about a product, should form the core of advertising writing. Like a lead, the opening salvo in an ad also sets the tone and establishes the format for the remainder of the message. In this case, the writer would continue with information on how TrimWalk enhances skin and muscle tone, how it helps even the most fit seniors feel even better, and how convenient it is to exercise regularly at home.

A helpful structure for first-time copy writers is to open with a headline. Good examples are all around. The headline for a Rogaine ad states: "John's losing his hair. His mission: get it back." An ad for Pepto-Bismol stomach remedy shows two pink pills and achieves success with a two-word headline: "Utterly Tasteless."

Good headlines grab attention while at the same time communicating some important information. Always remember that a headline needs to reach the audience you want to reach; otherwise, the ad fails. An effective headline grabs the reader and focuses attention on intriguing information.

Some guidelines for writing successful ad headlines are as follows:

- Address the public directly and personally, as if in conversation.
- Refer to a specific problem or goal. The examples just given deal with the problems of hair loss and chalky taste.
- Offer a benefit. Rogaine offers hair; Pepto-Bismol tables offer a taste-free remedy. These notable benefits would be lost later in the copy, so they are communicated in the headline.
- Offer something new. Hair replacement and easy-to-take stomach remedies are novel concepts.
- Feature believable information. Rash claims will be ignored.
- Finally, good headlines are simple, simple, simple. No ad headline should be long or complex.

Once the headline is written, the writer composes two to three short paragraphs of supporting copy, that is, copy that backs up claims in the headline with concrete information. For example, give details on the regimen involved in Rogaine treatments or in a dose of Pepto-Bismol. Copy writers write less copy for everyday purchases and more for bigger purchases. The bigger the purchase, the longer the copy. An ad for a luxury condominium at a resort may run for several pages. One for orange juice would be short.

After drafting the copy, the writer may close with a slogan or symbol for the product—both if there is room. These three elements—the headline, the copy, and the slogan—provide good working materials for designers, and they also follow an advertising format that the public knows. People look for these elements in an ad and the best advertisements provide them.

A draft of an ad is written quickly and reflects key points in the lists made in Stage 3. Never write a draft as if it were final. The loose words and organization of the draft will be fine-tuned—and perhaps entirely rewritten—several times before the final copy is produced. It helps to remember that what you draft is a work in progress; when you and the people you work with realize that drafts are raw rather than finished products, the words will flow more easily.

Stage 5: Rewriting

Yes, rewriting, even though you feel as if you've just finished a noble effort. Even the cleverest ad writers must edit their own work before they pass it on.

As we noted in Chapter 6, the first step in rewriting is to let the draft copy of the ad rest. It may rest on a desk or in a drawer; what's important is that the writer parts from it at least ten or fifteen minutes. Ideally, a draft is put away overnight or for several hours. But when time is limited, leave the copy in a safe place and take a walk. Try to clear your head; perhaps you can get a snack or chat with a friend. Then return to the copy and check it over, answering the following checklist of questions:

- Does the ad, from the opening sentence, work to achieve its goal?
- Does the ad appeal to its intended audience? Will audience members see the benefits of your product after reading only the first few words of the ad?
- Is the language simple, varied, and conversational?
- Is the grammar correct? Are spellings standard?
- Are sentences and paragraphs short so that readers will have easy access to information?
- Have you stayed within space limitations?

Once you have edited your original work, eliminating any problems you detect, you have a revised draft and are ready for the next stage of writing.

Stage 6: Sharing

In advertising, it's especially important to share the revised draft with an outside reader. An ideal outside reader is a member of the intended audience for the ad, but almost anyone will do—a friend, co-worker, or family member. Often people who are unfamiliar with your topic will make the best outside readers.

Let your outside reader look over the revised draft and talk with him or her about it. Ask several questions:

- Can you tell me what's so special about a TrimWalk?
- How does the ad leave you feeling about a TrimWalk?
- Would you notice this ad? Would you read it? Why or why not?
- What would you suggest to improve this ad?
- Do you see any possible errors or inaccuracies in the ad?

Most outside readers, after telling you what a good job you have done in almost any case, will offer helpful information. With their review in mind, along with any other insights you've gained from talking about the revised draft with an outsider, you may create your final masterpiece.

Stage 7: Polishing

If your sharing resulted in a major rewrite of the ad, you may need to repeat Stages 5 and 6, rewriting and sharing. But if you need to make only minor revisions, you are ready to polish your writing so that you can present a final draft to your account executive or the client.

Polishing is a fine-tuning process, in which extra words are eliminated and white space is added by keeping words, sentences, and paragraphs as short as possible. All spellings, especially proper names, and all facts, especially statistics, are checked and rechecked. A computerized spell-check process is applied, and after one last read-through, the final draft is printed. This draft is usually typed and double-spaced, like other media copy. In most cases, designers will select type and add art or photographs.

In some settings, the copy writer also is responsible for desktop publishing and producing a finished advertisement, camera-ready for printing. Writers who face these responsibilities may want to take a course in graphic design or desktop publishing. Writers charged with complete ad design must also remember that writing is the first and most important step in producing ads that reach audiences.

Tips for Ad Copy That Sells

Advertising Professor Jim Plumb, who has 30 years of experience in all aspects of advertising, gives the following tips to copy writers:

1. *Touch on selling points.* Focus on concrete reasons for purchase. An abstract reason to buy a Subaru wagon is safety, but a concrete selling point is that buying a Subaru keeps the driver from shoveling snow or paying a tow truck.

2. *Sell the benefits.* Find and list the benefits of your product that are important to your audience. Build your ad writing around these benefits. List them in the ad if you can, but be sure to mention them in some way. Don't forget to look for intangible benefits. Sometimes the most powerful benefits are intangibles, such as the mood that a perfume creates, or a feeling

of belonging that comes from a health club. Again, the viewer or reader should experience the product.

3. *Identify the single greatest benefit of your product and feature it in the headline.* Research should identify the quality of your product that is most meaningful to your intended audience. Then create a headline or slogan that will convey this benefit to your audience. With "Mmmmm, good!" Campbell's is selling the benefit of good taste. With "Just Do It," Nike sells discipline, an intangible benefit, as its star quality. A slogan in ads for the *Washington Post* reads, "If you don't get it, you don't get it." That is, if you don't take the *Post* regularly, you'll be left out socially. By communicating benefits in a few words, ad writing has the power to modify attitudes and behaviors. The same technique, among others used by copy writers, can work in all forms of writing.

All Writers Can Learn from Advertising

Many advertising students argue that there is no connection between news writing and advertising writing. Likewise, news writing students argue that their work has nothing to do with advertising technique. But Professors Katherine McAdams and John Sweeney studied prize-winning ads and news stories and found that the two have much in common.

"Award-winning news competes for the reader's attention, as does ad copy; both kinds of writing require techniques that catch and reward readers with concise, informative, pleasurable reading," McAdams and Sweeney concluded. They list five factors that they found in both groups of award-winning writing:

1. *Audience.* Both news writing and ad writing aim messages at specific audiences and demonstrate a clear knowledge of audience interests and concerns.

2. *Distillation.* News articles and advertisements both must distill large amounts of information into very limited space, resulting in careful, early placement of key information.

3. *Freshness.* Excellent news writing is involving and rewarding for the reader. The same is true of advertising. The means to success in both fields lies in presenting information with interest and liveliness.

4. *Substance.* Both kinds of writing depend on substantive writing that presents facts. Information—especially new or surprising information—is top priority in both advertising and news.

5. *Easy access.* Unless facts are presented with the reader's ease in mind, the information may not be read. That's why both news writing and advertising writing emphasize short words, short paragraphs, and simple sentences.

These factors apply to all successful writing in the information age. Readers steer clear of murky writing; they want fresh, concise, catchy writing. Advertisers know this, and it shows in their writing. In producing good writing for any medium, today's writers must be concerned with reaching audiences.

Because of competition among products and brands, ad writers were first to identify and target audiences. Today, as all media become conscious of competition, we can learn from their techniques how to satisfy the public hunger for new and relevant information.

EXERCISES

1. Imagine that you have been asked to create an ad that describes the benefits of dining in your campus cafeteria. The ad will appear in your campus newspaper. The audience is undergraduate students.
   a. Begin by doing product research: Visit the cafeteria for a meal, and take note of important information and impressions. List the facts and impressions you gathered in your research visit. Be prepared to discuss the items on your list.
   b. Supplement your product research with audience research. List at least five questions about cafeteria dining that you could use in brief interviews with students. Discuss your questions with your professor and classmates, then use your best questions in interviews with six or more students.
   c. Consider what you learned from your efforts in product and audience research. Divide a blank sheet of paper in half. On one side, list the major benefits that you could write about for your advertising copy. On the other side, list prominent characteristics of your audience.

Turn the page over and write at least three possible headlines for your ad. Each headline should feature at least one cafeteria benefit and appeal to at least one audience characteristic.

2. Invite an advertising professional from your campus or community to visit your class. Ask this person to talk briefly about advertising in today's competitive media environment. You may also want to ask your speaker to look over any headlines or advertising copy the class has written and to select some of examples of good writing.

3. Imagine that you have been asked to write a headline and three paragraphs of advertising copy about the car that you drive most often. Your audience is your fellow students; the ad will appear in a student publication. Begin by taking a research drive and listing the benefits of your automobile; then develop the copy.

4. Find a poorly written advertisement in a newspaper or magazine. Clip the ad, then get out a fresh piece of paper. Rewrite the ad, improving the writing and targeting. Do any research that is needed.

REFERENCES

Katherine McAdams and John Sweeney, "Copy Writing and Newswriting Need Similar Skills." *Journalism Educator,* Winter 1987.

David Ogilvy, *Ogilvy on Advertising.* New York: Crown Publishers, 1983.

Kenneth Roman and Jane Maas, *The New How to Advertise.* New York: St. Martin's Press, 1992.

James Plumb, "Writing Advertising Copy." Lecture, University of Maryland College of Journalism, College Park, MD, 1990.

John Sweeney, "Principles of Advertising." Lecture series, University of North Carolina at Chapel Hill, Chapel Hill, NC, 1986.

John Sweeney, personal interview. University of North Carolina, Chapel Hill, NC, 1995.

APPENDIX A

Libel and Privacy

Writers can unknowingly or carelessly hurt or damage an individual's reputation. Even if a slip is unintentional, if the falsity or libel is in print or is aired, the writer can be sued. So can the newspaper, the television station, the church administration, or the nonprofit group.

Libel can occur in any writing: a news article, a news release, a public service announcement, annual reports, corporate financial statements, a television talk show, or a church bulletin. If a news release is mailed but not published, the writer could still be sued for libel because dissemination of the falsity occurred. While oral defamation is known as slander, a radio or television station that broadcasts slander or libelous statements can be sued under the state's libel laws.

Most libel results when people write about topics they don't really understand. Inexperienced reporters, student writers, and occasional writers are most at risk. Good data collection and good writing techniques can prevent many libel problems, however. Mass communication professors advise their students to be absolutely accurate and scrupulously fair in what they write.

The legal system will protect writers who do a good job of investigating and who use many sources. And the protection often will extend even if they write something that is false and defamatory.

A huge body of law exists on libel. Thousands of libel cases have been filed. Although most writers don't need to be lawyers, they do need to know the basics of libel law. A writer may be the only member of a nonprofit organization's communication staff; she needs to know when she might get into trouble. Libel laws differ from state to state. For example, the statute of limitations, or time within which a person can file a libel suit, varies; it is usually from one to two years. Writers should be familiar with the libel laws in their states or in the states in which the material will be published.

Elements of Libel

In being aware of libel, writers don't have to be afraid to write negative information. If they know the essential elements of libel, they won't be chilled into self-censorship.

An individual—or the person written about—has to prove six essential elements to win a libel case:

- *Defamation.* The individual has to show that the information was defamatory or bad.
- *Identification.* The story clearly identified the individual by name, in a recognizable photo, or through specific description.
- *Publication.* The memo was circulated, the story printed, the news release received, the report aired.
- *Falsity.* The information published was not true. Sometimes the burden of proof of falsity falls on the media, which attempts to prove the information was true.
- *Harm or injury.* The individual has to show harm to his or her reputation or emotional well-being. Proof of monetary loss can increase the amount of money the media have to pay if they lose.
- *Fault.* The individual has to prove that the newspaper, radio station, or whoever was at fault in presenting the libel.

To win a case, the plaintiff has to prove all six elements. All individuals have to prove the first five elements. On the sixth item, court decisions have set different criteria for private citizens and public figures.

Ordinary folks have to prove negligence to win a libel suit. They must show that the writer failed to follow professional standards and acted unreasonably in carrying out his or her research and in writing.

Celebrities or people in power or politics have to go further in establishing fault. They must prove that the writer knew that the information was false or showed reckless disregard as to whether the information was true or false. That is called actual malice. That element came about through the 1964 *New York Times* v. Sullivan case, in which the United States Supreme Court ruled that a public official cannot recover damages for a defamatory falsehood relating to his or her official conduct unless he or she proves that the statement was made with actual malice.

Let's say you are writing a story about your town's mayor. During interviews, an unreliable source tells you that the mayor leaves town twice a year to meet his childhood sweetheart—not his wife—at a mountain cabin. If you were to write that bit of information without further investigation, you would be setting yourself up for a libel suit. It would be reckless disregard for whether the information was true.

People are defamed, perhaps falsely, every day. Just think about the hundreds of police reports naming people who have been arrested. They can prove many of the elements above, such as publication, identification, and defamation. But would they win a libel suit? Rarely.

A Writer's Defenses in a Libel Suit

Within the legal system are defenses writers can use to protect themselves against a libel suit even if the person they wrote about can prove the elements above. The major defenses are these:

• *Truth.* The writer can prove the information was true through reliable witnesses and documentary evidence.

• *Fair reporting or reporter's privilege.* Writers are protected when they report fairly and accurately material from official government proceedings or documents. That is one reason why news media rely so heavily on government meetings and sessions. A witness can accuse someone in court of committing murder, and you as a reporter can print the accusation. You are protected if the charges were made during a court session. Your reporting must be accurate, fair and balanced, substantially complete, and not motivated by malice.

• *Wire service defense.* Some states have adopted what is known as the wire service defense. Newspapers and other media organizations are protected if they get a story from the wire services, such as the Associated Press, and reprint it. It would be impossible for writers to verify every fact that appeared in a wire service story. Wire service clients have to trust that the information sent to them is true.

• *Opinion defense.* The opinion defense protects two kinds of statements. Writers are protected if they are critiquing a performance or service as long as they give a general assessment that is incapable of being proved true or false. For example, a restaurant critic could write that the restaurant food is not good. He could not say that the chef stole the high-quality meats for his family, leaving lesser meats for the restaurant dishes—unless that were true, of course.

The opinion defense also protects what is known as hyperbole: wild exaggeration that no one would believe to be true. For example, a writer may state that the university's chancellor was dressed in 1960s-style clothes and got up on stage to dance at a Dead Heads concert. If the story were printed, reasonable people would not believe it was true. If the chancellor sued, the courts would likely rule that no one would believe such an outrageous story, so the chancellor's reputation had not been damaged.

As a footnote, writers should know that they can't libel the government—state, local, or federal. A writer can say that the federal government or some part of it is an overgrown, bumbling bureaucratic mess without fear of being sued. But he can't use the same words to describe the head of a particular agency without getting into trouble.

How to Avoid Libel Suits

Writers do not want to be sued for libel even if they win. Libel suits are costly, time-consuming, and emotionally draining. They can go on for years. People do win libel cases against media. For example, CapCities Communications lost a $11.5 million libel suit when one of its New York television stations incorrectly identified a restaurant owner as having ties with organized crime. In 1994, an attorney won a $24 million judgment against the *Philadelphia Inquirer,* which had reported he quashed a homicide investigation because it involved the son of a police officer.

Ninety percent of libel cases filed never make it to court. Some are dropped, and some end up in out-of-court settlements, which cost media actual payouts and attorneys' fees. Libel suits are to be avoided.

Some recommendations:

- Don't write lies and publish them.
- Use credible, reliable, multiple sources.
- Recognize the importance of fairness.
- Be accurate.

Also be polite if someone complains about inaccuracy. One study showed that most people who sued decided to do so after they were treated rudely when they pointed out the mistake.

Right of Privacy

Just as in libel, writers must be careful not to violate individuals' right to privacy. The doctrine of the right to privacy has evolved to protect individuals and to give them the right to be let alone, particularly from unwarranted publicity. Decisions from lower courts up to the United States Supreme Court have involved individuals' right to privacy.

In some cases, however, if individuals become part of a newsworthy event, they forfeit their right to privacy. The courts have upheld the forfeiture even if the individual became part of the news event involuntarily. For example, a private citizen may be on an airplane that is hijacked and therefore becomes part of the news event.

Media can use the individuals' names or even photographs in reporting the news events and be protected against an invasion of privacy suit. But courts have not upheld later use of a breaking-news photograph to illustrate a completely different story. For example, a story on airport security two years later could not use the photograph of the hijacked passenger as an illustration and the writer be protected against an invasion of privacy claim.

Just as with libel considerations, writers must be careful to use accuracy and be thorough. The *Associated Press Stylebook and Libel Manual* notes that media "may be liable for invasion of privacy if the facts of a story are changed deliberately or recklessly, or 'fictionalized.'" Writers must be aware that privacy laws are not uniform. Writers should know what constitutes invasion of privacy in their states or in the states where articles will be published or stories aired. When the courts get involved, they are balancing the freedom of the press and the right to publish versus the individual's right to privacy.

REFERENCES

Harold Nelson and Dwight L. Teeter Jr., *Law of Mass Communications: Freedom and Control of Print and Broadcast Media*. Westbury, NY: The Foundation Press, 1986.

Interview with Dr. Cathy Packer, Associate Professor in the School of Journalism and Mass Communication at the University of North Carolina at Chapel Hill, October 1994.

Norm Goldstein, ed., *The Associated Press Stylebook and Libel Manual*. New York: The Associated Press, 1992.

APPENDIX B

The Abused Words List

Writers must pay attention to words that sound alike but are spelled differently, and to words that are spelled and pronounced the same but have different meanings. The words can be confusing and can be used incorrectly.

When writers fail to select the correct word, often readers know it, and the writers' credibility suffers. Writers also teach readers incorrect usage when their writing is not specific and accurate.

Many good writers have come up with lists that caution other writers about the tricky words. Becoming familiar with such a list is extremely important in the age of computers, which may overlook incorrect usage in spell check programs.

Professor Thom Lieb of Towson State University has developed what he calls "the abused words list." Writers need to review the list periodically so that red flags of warning are raised when using a word from the list. Writers can refer to the list to insure they use words correctly. Here is Lieb's list, with a few additions from the authors:

abdicate, abrogate: Abdicate means give up formally (an office, throne, authority), or to surrender or repudiate (a right, responsibility). Abrogate means cancel or repeal by authority, annul.

accept, except: Accept means receive. Except means exclude.

adapt, adopt: Adapt means make fit or suitable by changing or adjusting. Adopt means take up and use, vote to accept, select.

adopted, passed, enacted: Resolutions are adopted or approved; bills are passed. Laws are enacted when they go into effect.

adverse, averse: Adverse is poor or bad; averse is opposed to.

advice, advise: Advice is an opinion given. Advise means to give advice.

affect, effect: To affect is to have an effect on; effect is the noun. But effect as a verb means "bring about."

after, following: After means next in time; following means next in order.

aggravate, irritate: Aggravate means make worse; irritate means to incite or provoke.

agnostic, atheist: An agnostic believes it is impossible to know whether there is a God. Atheists believe there is no God.

aid, aide: Aides (assistants) give aid (help) to their bosses. Aid can also be a verb, but aide can only be a noun.

alleged, intended: Alleged means so declared before proof; intended means meant, planned, or proposed.

all ready, already: All ready means prepared: The team was all ready for the game. Already means beforehand: The opponents were already there.

allusion, delusion, illusion: Allusion is a hint, indirect reference: He made an allusion to her vanity. Note that to allude to something is not to name the thing specifically. Delusion is a false belief, especially a psychotic one. Illusion is unreal perception, misconception, unreal image perception: He had an illusion he could fly across the sea. And there is also, of course, elude, meaning avoid.

alot: It's A lot, and it's best saved for real estate stories.

alright: It's not; it's all right.

altar, alter: Altar is a table-like platform used in a church service; alter, a verb meaning change.

alternative, alternate: Alternative involves a choice; alternate, a verb or adjective that means in turns.

alumna, alumni, alumnus: An alumnus can be of either sex, but is typically male. An alumna is female; plural is alumnae pronounced with a long e sound. Plural of both sexes or males is alumni.

amateur, novice: Amateur is a nonprofessional; novice is a beginner.

among, between: Among refers to more than two things. Between refers to two.

amount, number: Amount is the quantity of things: The amount of testimony was small. Number refers to individual or separate units in a group: The number of times she testified was too small to make a difference.

anxious, eager: You can only be anxious about something; you can't be anxious to do that thing. Anxious implies fear and anxiety. If you are stimulated and excited at the prospect of doing something, then you are *eager* to do it.

avenge, revenge: Avenge for another, revenge for self.

assume, presume: Assume means take to be fact without a basis for belief; to presume is to regard as true because there is reason to do so and no contrary evidence. Presume also means take upon oneself without permission or authority.

bad, badly: Bad is an adjective, used when you want to describe the subject: He felt bad about the report of campaign irregularities. Badly describes some quality of the verb rather than the subject: She took her defeat badly.

bale, bail: A farmer's hay is baled; water is bailed out of a boat; a prisoner is released on bail. (Bond is cash or property given as a security for an appearance or performance.)

basis: Unnecessary in "weekly basis," "timely basis," and so forth.

bi-, semi-: Bi means two; semi means half. Bimonthly—every two months. Semi-monthly—twice a month. However: Biannual means the same as semiannual—twice a year. Biennial means every two years.

bills, legislation: Legislation is laws enacted by legislative body. A president can send proposed legislation or bills.

bloc, block: Bloc is a group or coalition; block has many meanings, but none is the same as bloc.

blond, blonde: The first is an adjective for all sexes and a noun for male; the second is a noun for females.

breach, breech: The first is a failure to observe terms (e.g., of contract). Breech is the rump, the lower or back part of a thing (breech birth) or part of a gun.

burglary, robbery, theft: Burglary involves breaking into a building to commit theft or another felony. Robbery is taking something from another person through the use of violence or intimidation. Theft is the general term for taking another's property without consent. Larceny is the legal term.

canvas, canvass: First is a cloth; second means to solicit.

capital, capitol: Capital: City that is official seat of government; wealth. Capitol: Capital "C," the building in which Congress meets in Washington, D.C. Lowercase "c," the building in which a state legislature meets.

carat, caret, karat: Carat expresses the weight of precious stones. Caret is a proofreader's mark. Karat is the proportion of pure gold used in an alloy.

careen: Leaning sideways or tossing about like a boat under sail—*not* skidding or veering. For that, try CAREER.

censor, censure: A censor is a person who can censor a publication, cutting out anything offensive, obscene, etc. To censure is to condemn as wrong, or to strongly disapprove.

center around: Something can be centered at, centered in, or centered on, but not around.

chafe, chaff: Chafe means to irritate. Chaff means to ridicule good-naturedly; it also means husks or rubbish.

cite, site, sight: Cite means refer or quote. Site is a location. Sight is a view.

collision: Violent contact between moving bodies. A car cannot collide with a telephone pole or unmoving object.

combine: Must involve putting together at least two things: "Maid o' Silk" combined the spirit of old America in modern dress.

compared to, compared with: When you put one thing in the same class or category without examining it closely, use compared to: The inflation rate can be compared to a hot-air balloon with an endless supply of fuel. When you put things side by side to examine similarities and differences, use compared with: The inflation rate is 8 percent, compared with last year's figure of 10 percent.

compliment, complement: They can be noun or verb. Compliment is praise; complement adds to something to make it complete.

compose, comprise: To compose is to make up; to comprise is to include. Fifty states compose the United States. The United States comprises 50 states.

conclude: Arguments conclude. Speeches close or end.

confidant, confident: Confidant is a close, trusted friend in whom one can confide. Confident is sure of oneself.

connote, denote: Connote means suggest or imply something beyond explicit meaning. Denote means be explicit about the meaning.

conscious, aware: We are conscious of what we feel and aware of what we know.

contact: As a verb, it means the physical touching of things: His toe contacted the football.

continual, continuous: Continual means repeated or intermittent; continuous means unbroken.

cords, chords: Cord is a string or small rope, or anatomical structure such as spinal or vocal cord. Or it may be a ribbed fabric or a unit of wood. Chord is a string of a musical instrument or a combination of tones.

council, counsel, consul: Council is an assembly, usually a legislative body. Counsel is advice, a lawyer. Consul is a person appointed by his government to serve his country's interests abroad.

couple of: Like "a pair," needs the "of." Never "A couple tomatoes."

damage, damages: First means loss or harm. Second is only a legal term meaning money paid or ordered to be paid as compensation for loss or injury.

data: Is plural, as are media, strata, phenomena, criteria, and alumni. When the group or quantity is regarded as a unit, it takes a singular verb: The data is invalid. If the word refers to individual items, use plural verb: The data were collected by a team of 20.

deign: Means to condescend, not to dare or care.

dilemma: An argument necessitating a choice between two equally unfavorable or disagreeable alternatives.

discreet, discrete: First means prudent, circumspect; second is detached or separate.

disinterested, uninterested: Disinterested is impartial; uninterested means lack interest.

disorganize, unorganized: The first is a verb, meaning disrupt the organization of. The second is an adjective, meaning lacking order, system, or unity.

due to: Not a synonym for "because of." It should modify a noun: It was an omission due to oversight. BUT: The name was omitted because of oversight.

egregious (i gre jes): Outstanding for undesirable qualities; remarkably bad.

either: Not synonymous with both. Incorrect: The teams lined up at either end of the field. Correct: The teams lined up at both ends.

enrage, outrage: Enrage is a verb meaning put in a rage. Outrage is a noun, meaning an act of extreme violence or viciousness.

emigrate, immigrate: The first means leave a country; the second, enter.

enormity: Applies preferably to abnormal wickedness, but it is often misused to mean enormous.

ensure, insure: First is guarantee: A good writer takes every possible measure to ensure accuracy. Insure is used in references to insurance. And let's not forget assure: make a person sure of something, or convince.

envelop, envelope: To envelop is to wrap up, obscure, hide. An envelope is the paper product that envelops your letters and bills.

epitaph, epithet: The first is an inscription on a tombstone. The second is a descriptive adjective applied to someone.

farther, further: Farther refers to physical distance, further to degree, time, or quantity.

faze, phase: Faze is embarrass or disturb; phase is an aspect or stage.

feel: Generally, best saved for touching and feeling things. Don't use as a synonym for thinking or believing. It is acceptable when you mean to be convinced emotionally rather than intellectually: "The parents of the kidnapped girl feel certain she is safe."

fewer, less: The general rule is that if you can't count it, use less: fewer students, but less interest.

fiance, fiancee: The man has one "e," the woman, two.

flair, flare: Flair is a conspicuous talent; flare means blaze with sudden, bright light or to burst out in anger. Also a noun meaning flame.

flaunt, flout: To flaunt is to show off; to flout is to mock, scoff, or show disdain for.

flounder, founder: Horses flounder—struggle or thrash about—in the mud. Ships founder or sink.

fortunate, fortuitous: The first means coming by good luck, the second means happening by chance.

fulsome: Fulsome praise is insincere, not copious. It means offensively excessive.

gantlet, gauntlet: A gantlet is a section of railroad tracks over a narrow passage where two lines of track overlap. (two lines using only three rails). A gauntlet is a former military punishment in which an offender had to run between two rows of men with clubs. It is also a long glove.

get: Often used instead of a more precise verb. Get around—evade. Get behind—endorse. AND get does not substitute for become: I become cold rather than get cold.

gibe, jibe: The first is to jeer, taunt, or flout. The second is to shift sails, alter a course, or be in harmony.

gorilla, guerrilla: The first is an ape, the second a soldier or raider.

grant, subsidy: A grant is money given to public companies; subsidy is help to a private enterprise.

hanged, hung: Hang, hung, hung refers to objects; hanged refers to people.

hike: What a Boy Scout takes. Not synonymous for increase.

historic, historical: Historic means famous in history. Historical pertains to history, such as historic sites and historical novels.

holdup, holed up: A man with a gun can commit a holdup by forcibly stopping another person and robbing him or her. If the gunman hides out at the place of the holdup, he is holed up.

hopefully: Full of hope. "The hungry child sat hopefully on the steps of the candy shop."

impact: Means a collision or a violent striking together. Does not mean influence or effect: When the car hit the guardrail, the impact caused the front end to jackknife.

impassable, impassible: The first means that a passage is impossible. The second describes lack of sensitivity to pain or suffering.

imply, infer: The speaker implies; the listener infers.

in, into (also: on, onto): If you're in the lake and feel like jumping, you jump in the lake. If you're in a boat on the lake and you feel like jumping overboard, you jump into the lake.

ironically: The contrary of what is expressed; e.g., calling a stupid plan clever. Irony is a form of sarcasm.

last, latest, past: Last few days, in the past, his latest book.

launch: Send into space, not begin, as in "New Sewer System Launched."

liable: Not a good substitute for likely, unless the event designated is injurious or undesirable. It is likely to be sunny and clear; it is liable to rain.

lie, lay: To lie is to recline; to lay, to place. Confusion results mainly from past and past perfect tenses: lie, lay, lay (or lain); lay, laid, laid.

like, as: Like joins nouns and pronouns: "He blocks like a pro." Use as with verbs: "Winston tastes good as a cigarette should."

likewise: Avoid using as a transition. WRONG: He went home. Likewise, his sister went. CORRECT: He went home. So did his sister.

loath, loathe: The first means unwilling; the second means hate.

mad: Means insane, not angry.

majority, plurality: First is more than half of an amount. Second is more than the next highest number.

masterly, masterful: The first means skillful; the second means domineering.

mean, median, average, mode: Mean and average are generally interchangeable: the sum of the units divided by the number of units. Median is the number in the middle (such as the middle score or income); half lie above, half below. Mode is the most commonly occurring number.

meanwhile: Should be used only when a close relationship exists in subject matter, and intervening time is actually meant.

measles: A child has measles, not the measles; same too with mumps. Treat both as singular.

meld: A card game term, it does not mean blend or combine.

meticulous: Being over-careful, finical, or fussy about trivial details.

moral, morale: Moral refers to ethics; morale to mood or spirits. The moral life is the good life. His morale was lifted by the phone call.

nauseated, nauseous: If you are nauseated, you feel or become sick. Something nauseous is sickening or disgusting.

negotiate: You negotiate a loan or treaty; you climb a hill.

noisy, noisome: Noisy is making or accompanied by noise. Noisome is injurious to health, noxious, or harmful, or foul smelling.

off of: Off suffices: Get off my back.

only: Almost invariably misplaced, altering the meaning of the sentence. Try it in front of each word in this sentence to see how it alters meaning: I hit him in the eye yesterday.

oral, verbal: The use of the mouth is essential to oral communications; verbal means simply "using words."

ordinance, ordnance: An ordinance is a direction or command of an authoritative nature. Ordnance is a cannon or artillery.

pedal, peddle: The first is what you do on a bike, or what you put your feet on. The second means sell.

penultimate: The next to the last. The penultimate month of the year is November. The antepenultimate month is October.

percentage, percentage point: They are not the same. When unemployment falls from 10 percent to 8 percent, it is a drop of 2 percentage points—but 20 percent!

persuade, convince: Persuade means induce someone to believe or do something, plead with, or urge. Convince means bring someone to belief or conviction beyond doubt, satisfy by proof. Grace has tried to persuade her to change her story. Finally, she was convinced that Grace was right.

podium, lectern: First is a footstool or platform; second is what speakers thump.

pointed out: You can point out only what is a fact. Make sure you are accepting a statement as a fact if you have someone "pointing it out."

populous, populated, populace: First means crowded or thickly populated; populated means inhabited; populace means common people of a community.

pore, pour: Pore, as a verb, means read or study carefully. Pour is what you do with a liquid.

portentous: Ominous, portending evil.

precipitate, precipitous: Precipitate means cause to happen before anticipated. Precipitous is steep like a precipice.

presently: Means soon, not now. Not synonymous with currently.

pretense, pretext: Pretense is a false show, a more overt act used to conceal personal feelings: "Her compliments were all pretense." Pretext is something put forward to conceal a truth: "They said he was dismissed for tardiness, but that was just a pretext for incompetence."

principal, principle: The first is the head of a school; also means "main." The second is a rule, truth, etc.

prior to, in advance of: Use "before" instead.

prison, jail: Prison is a maximum-security facility for persons convicted of felonies. Jail is a facility normally used to confine persons awaiting trial or sentencing on misdemeanors or felonies, persons serving sentences for misdemeanors, and persons confined for civil matters, such as failure to pay alimony.

prophecy, prophesy: Prophecy is a noun, meaning a forecast. Prophesy is a verb, meaning foretell, predict, forecast.

prone: If a man is lying prone on the beach, no one can step on his stomach. Prone means lying face down. Supine means lying face up.

prostate, prostrate: Prostate is of or relating to the male body. Prostrate is lying with the face downward in a show of great humility or abject submission.

quell, quench: Uprisings, disorders, riots, and the like are quelled. A fire is quenched.

quintessential: Quintessence is the pure, concentrated essence of anything.

rack, wrack: To rack is to trouble, torment or afflict, or to oppress by unfair demands. Also, you rack your brains and something exasperating is nerve-racking. Wrack is properly used as a noun meaning ruin or destruction.

raise, rear, raze: Raise animals, rear children. To raze is to destroy.

ravage, ravish: To ravage is to destroy or ruin: The tornadoes ravaged the town. To ravish is to fill with joy, carry away forcibly, or rape: The army ravished the Trojan women.

record: You do not set a new record or an all-time record; neither is it a record first. It is simply a record.

refute: Means disprove—almost always implies editorial. Generally, rebut or dispute is better.

regime, regimen, regiment: A regime is a political ruling system. A regimen is a system of diet, etc., for improving health. A regiment is a military unit consisting of two or more battalions.

reign, rein: Reign is royal power, authority, or rule. Rein is a strap of leather used to control a horse.

reluctant, reticent: First is unwilling to act; the second is to speak.

role, roll: Role is a part assumed by an actor, or a function assumed by someone. Roll is a noun and verb meaning more than a dozen different things—but not what role does.

sensual, sensuous: Sensual refers to the gratification of the grosser bodily senses of appetite (sex, food); sensuous suggests a strong appeal of that which is pleasing to the senses. A sensuous person is susceptible to the pleasures of sensation. She was given to sensual excesses. The music playing was sensuous.

set, sit: To set is to place: Set the book here. Sit is what you do when you take a seat.

sewage, sewerage: Sewage is human waste, sometimes called sanitary waste. Sewerage is the system to carry away sewage.

since, because: Since is best used when it denotes a period of time, either continuous or broken. Because gives a reason or cause.

suit, suite: You can have a suit of clothes, cards, or a lawsuit. There are suites of music, rooms, and furniture.

tall, high: A building, tree, or man is tall; a plane, bird, or cloud is high.

temperature, weather: The temperature can move higher or lower, but only the weather can become warmer or cooler.

than, then: Than is a conjunction of comparison. Then is an adverb denoting time.

that, which: That restricts or defines; which is nonrestrictive, adding extra but not necessarily essential information.

their, there, they're: Their is the possessive form of the pronoun "they." There is an adverb denoting place or, when used to begin a sentence, it is called an expletive or a false subject: There are only 20 shopping days left until Christmas. They're is the contraction of they and are.

til, till: Use until.

troop, troupe: The first is a group of persons or animals. The second is an ensemble of actors, dancers, singers, etc.

try and: The correct usage is "try to."

via: By way of, not by means of: via I-79, not via bus.

wasted words: These words add nothing: kind of, little, pretty, rather, really, some, sort of. The most wasted: VERY.

would, could, should: Saying a child COULD remain in an institution until age 18 is different from saying he WOULD remain there—or SHOULD. Be careful with these.

APPENDIX C

Spelling in the Computer Age

Writers, BEWARE: Spelling skills are essential in the computer age.

This warning sounds exaggerated when computers can check spellings of hundreds of words in minutes.

But take heed. The following paragraph passed a spell-check program in less than one second without a hitch:

> They're know miss steaks in this newsletter cause we used special soft wear witch checks yore spelling. It is mower or lass a weigh to verify. How ever it can knot correct arrows in punctuation ore usage, an it will not fined words witch are miss used butt spelled rite. Four example, a paragraph could have mini flaws but wood bee past by the spell checker. And it wont catch the sentence fragment witch you. Their fore, the massage is that proofreading is know eliminated but is berry much reek wired.

While the example is exaggerated, it serves to remind that a spell-checker only "checks." It looks to see that all typed words correspond exactly to real words listed in the computer's dictionary. Here's how it works: Spell-checkers look at each word, then check to see whether they have a match in the dictionaries stored in computer memory. A spell-checker highlights only the words that have no match in the computer's dictionary, stopping the checking process at those words so that they may be manually checked by the writer or editor.

What Spell-Checkers Will (and Won't) Do

Memory-based checking systems are a great invention, virtually eliminating senseless typographical errors such as "scuh" and "typograpical," as well as common spelling problems such as "seperate" for separate and "mispell" for misspell. Unfortunately, however, it is not a perfect invention.

Here's the problem: If the computer merely finds a word in its dictionary, it "checks" that word, assuring the writer that the spelling is correct. Say, for example, the computer encounters this sentence: "Robin was going too the fare." The sentence checks. The words "too" and "fare" exist in the dictionary, so they pass muster. And if Robin happens to be spelled correctly "Robyn," that error will go unchecked because "robin" would be found in the computer's dictionary and sail through. Or perhaps the typo is an actual word, such as "count" instead of "court." The error would slip by as correct, and the writer would have created an immediate audience-stopper and confusion.

Remember that a spell-checker indicates only the words that have no match. So spell-checkers aid writers in only some spelling instances, not all of them. Some of the most challenging spelling tasks, which will be listed in the following section, still are the writer's responsibility.

A Do-It-Yourself List

By now it should be clear that spell-checkers won't do everything. The writer has the hands-on, do-it-yourself responsibility of checking the following problems that spell-checkers don't correct.

HOMONYMS. Writers must distinguish among homonyms or words that sound alike but have different meanings and are spelled differently. Any writer's credibility would drop if his readers saw these sentences:

> *Mrs. Margolis consulted two professional piers before suspending the student.*
> Readers will see Mrs. Margolis conferring in a lakeside setting.
> *Barnes said he didn't want to altar his plans.*
> Will Barnes offer his plan during religious services?
> *All navel movements will be approved by the commanding officer.*
> Whose belly buttons?

Such homonyms as "alter" and "altar" escape highlighting by the spell-checker, which recognizes each as dictionary words. Writers may leave simple errors in their writing because of overconfidence in the ability of spell-checkers. Some words writers should watch:

To, two, too

Their, they're, there

No, know

Not, knot

Aid, aide

It's, its

Whose, who's

More subtle—but no less damaging—are the errors made when writers confuse other commonly occurring homonyms, such as those listed here. Good writers distinguish between or among homonyms.

affect (verb)

effect (noun, meaning result, verb meaning bring about)

altogether (adverb meaning entirely)

all together (adjective meaning in a group)

capitol (building)

capital (city)

compliment (flattering statement)

complement (fills up or completes)

dual (two)

duel (combat between two people)

guerrilla (person who engages in warfare)

gorilla (ape)

legislature (body)

legislator (individual officials)

role (in a play)

roll (list)

allude (refer to)

elude (escape)

altar (in a church)

alter (change)

canvas (cloth)

canvass (poll)

counsel (advise, legal adviser)

council (assembly)

consul (diplomatic officer)

flair (style; panache)

flare (torch)

immigrate (come to a new country)

emigrate (leave one's country)

miner (in a mine)

minor (under age)

naval (of the navy)

navel (belly button)

pore (small opening; to examine closely)

pour (to cause to flow)

pier (water walkway)

peer (social equal)

vein (blood vessel)
vain (conceited)
vane (wind detector)
a lot (colloquial expression substi-
    tuted for "many" or "much")
allot (to distribute)

principal (head, first)
principle (lesson, belief)

stationery (paper)
stationary (permanent)

Note: There is no such word as "alot." A lot is two distinct words.

SIMILAR WORDS WITH DIFFERENT USES. No spell-checker knows the difference between "conscience" and "conscious," "affect" and "effect," "flout" and "flaunt," "loose" and "lose," "lead" and "led," "read" and "red," or "populace" and "populous" unless you do. Some grammar-check programs will highlight such problematic words, but these programs require the writer to make the correct choice. Keeping a good stylebook or grammar guide on your desk is the best way to make distinctions among similar words. Again, the writer or editor must catch the error, even though a spell-checker lives within the computer.

IRREGULAR VERBS. Computer programs leave verb choice to the writer, so irregular verbs, used incorrectly, may appear to be spelling errors. The sentence "We sat the boat in the water" should be "We set the boat in the water," but it would most certainly pass spell-checking. Frequently confused pairs of irregular verbs include the following:

lie (recline)

lay (place)

sit (be seated)

set (put or place)

rise (elevate)

raise (nurture, as crops or plants)

rear (nurture throughout childhood; applies to humans only)

COMPOUND WORDS. Some compound words, such as "speedboat" and "bookkeeper," will pass spell-checkers as two words, even though they are correctly spelled as single words. The reason? The spell-checker recognizes the separate words—speed, boat, book, and keeper—as valid entries, leaving the writer appearing not to know the correct spelling.

PROPER NAMES. As we noted earlier, proper names—unlike most units of language—may be spelled any way an individual desires. The infinite variety of name spellings makes it standard for all names to be checked and doublechecked, regardless of what spell-checking approves. Many names, such as Robin and Lily, are also common nouns listed in computer dictionaries. Often the correct spelling for the proper name is different from that offered by a spell-checker. For example, Robin may be "Robyn" and Lily may spell her name "Lillie." Double-check names in any document.

New-Age Spelling Problems

Overall, spell-checking systems help. They solve problems with words that contain "ie" and with words that have idiosyncratic endings, such as -ence, -ance, -ere, -are, -tion, -sion, and so on. But new technologies still leave writers struggling to select from possible spellings and check words not found in the computer dictionary.

Writers should always edit before and after spell-checking because it actually creates some new, computer-age spelling hazards. Keep in mind these problems:

1. Spell-checkers approve any words found in the dictionary. Errors such as using "too" for "to" and "count" for "court" go undetected by checking systems.

2. Spell-checkers require intelligent choices. When checkers encounter an unfamiliar word, the word is highlighted for editing by the writer. Even if the spell-checker offers suggestions for proper spelling from the computer's memory, it asks the writer to do the thinking and to make the correct choice. So writers still must know how to spell.

3. Spell-checkers inspire confidence that may be unwarranted, allowing for careless or lazy editing. Confident that a document has been checked, writers may leave many unwitting and even embarrassing errors (one professor recalled an instance where the computer approved "dick" in a sentence

that called for the word "disk"). Such errors may be detected when careful, non–machine editing is combined with the computer spell-checking process.

Tiresome as they may seem, both spell-checking and manual, word-by-word editing still are "berry much reek wired," as our earlier example stated. No machine can replace the complex decision-making that an editor provides. In the information age, good writers and editors are even more essential to insure accurate writing.

APPENDIX D

Key to Grammar Quizzes

After years of working with these exercises, the authors recognize that no single answer exists for any exercise item. Each answer we provide is what we consider to be the BEST or PREFERRED answer, rather than the only answer.

Grammar Diagnostic Quiz (pages 202–204):

1. 4. Clauses on either side of a semicolon must be independent.
2. 3. It is the LIST that HAS BEEN TRIMMED.
3. 3. Commas may not separate independent clauses.
4. 2. Commas follow all elements in a complete date.
5. 1. The modifying phrase, in its present location, modifies INSE-CURITY rather than FRESHMEN.
6. 2. Use LIE when no action is taken.
7. 1. Modifying the council with hopefully leaves them filled with hope.
8. 2. Semicolons are used to separate punctuated items in a list.
9. 3. Use neither and nor as a matched pair.
10. 2. Use the pronoun IT to agree with the noun COMPANY, a singular thing.
11. 2. Phrases that rename subjects are nonessential. Comma after COMMISSION.
12. 3. LIVES is the verb that agrees with the subject ONE.
13. 2. Commas follow both elements of a city and state combination that occurs in midsentence.
14. 1. The past tense, USED, is correct usage in this idiom.
15. 2. Including WILL PLAY in this phrase makes for faulty parallelism.
16. Sentence fragment.
17. Comma error. Semicolon or period needed.

18. Coordinate conjunction used where a subordinate, such as BE-CAUSE or THAT is needed.
19. Modifier problem. His muscles are not being a weight lifter.
20. Agreement: ITS SKIN.

1. correct. Your princiPAL is your PAL. PrincipLES are LESSONS.
2. sheriff, with one r. SHE and RIFF called the sheriff.
3. marshal, in all cases except for the proper noun, the name.
4. correct. There is A RAT in sepARATe.
5. correct. StationERy is sold by stationERs.
6. correct. To REpeatedly commend.
7. correct. Note also bookkeeper and withholding.
8. seize. Spell carefully in all cases of I-E. Computer checkers help.

Slammer for Commas, Semicolons, and Colons (pages 208–209):

1.	4	7.	4 and 10
2.	7	8.	1
3.	9 and 10	9.	7
4.	2	10.	10
5.	2, 5 and 6	11.	6 and 7
6.	8	12.	2 and 12

Slammer for Subject–Verb Agreement (pages 212–213):

1.	includes	13.	believes
2.	appear	14.	stir
3.	gives	15.	decides
4.	results	16.	typifies
5.	have	17.	are
6.	do	18.	are
7.	is	19.	is
8.	are	20.	is
9.	exhibits	21.	teach
10.	are	22.	is
11.	constitute	23.	consider
12.	was	24.	disagree

Slammer for Pronouns (pages 214–215):

1. his or her
2. its
3. himself
4. its
5. its
6. is
7. was
8. was
9. their
10. is
11. its
12. it
13. are
14. himself or herself
15. his or her

Slammer for Who/Whom and That/Which (pages 217–218):

1. whom
2. who
3. whom
4. who
5. whose

1. gun, which sale,
2. that
3. car, which plates,
4. Texans, who drawl,
5. gun, which compartment,
6. who
7. gun, which
8. that

Modifier Slammer (pages 218–219):

1. The waiter served ice cream, which started melting immediately, in glass bowls.
2. Correct.
3. On the way to our hotel, we saw a herd of sheep.
4. Correct.
5. The house where Mrs. Rooks was born is one of the oldest in Rockville.
6. Correct.
7. Without yelling, I could not convince the child to stop running into the street.
8. The critic said that after the first act of the play, Brooke's performance improves.

9. While we were watching the ball game, Sue's horse ran away.
10. Correct.
11. The bank approves loans of any size to reliable individuals.
12. After I was wheeled into the operating room, the nurse placed a mask over my face.
13. Correct.
14. Aunt Helen asked us to call on her before we left.

INDEX

.